Affirmative Action and the University

Affirmative Action
and the University
A Philosophical Inquiry

Edited by
Steven M. Cahn

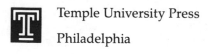

Temple University Press
Philadelphia

Temple University Press, Philadelphia 19122
Copyright © 1993 by Temple University. All rights
reserved
Published 1993
Printed in the United States of America

The paper used in this publication meets the minimum requirements of American National Standard
for Information Sciences—Permanence of Paper for
Printed Library Materials, ANSI Z39.48-1984 ∞

Library of Congress Cataloging-in-Publication Data
Affirmative action and the university : a philosophi-
cal inquiry / edited by Steven M. Cahn.
      p.   cm.
  Includes index.
  ISBN 1-56639-030-3
  1. Discrimination in higher education—United
States. 2. Affirmative action programs—United
States. 3. College teachers—Employment—
United States. 4. Minorities—Education
(Higher)—United States. I. Cahn, Steven M.
LC212.42.A38 1993
370.19′349′0973—dc20   92-18787

To the memory of Charles Frankel

Contents

Affirmative Action and the University

Introduction

In 1965 President Lyndon Johnson issued Executive Order 11246, directing that "all Government contracting agencies . . . take affirmative action to ensure that applicants are employed . . . without regard to their race, creed, color, or national origin." Two years later the order was amended to prohibit discrimination in employment because of sex.

The original order authorized the secretary of labor to "adopt such rules and regulations . . . as he deems necessary and appropriate" pursuant to the order's purposes. In response to this mandate, the Department of Labor required all contractors to develop "an acceptable affirmative action program," including "an analysis of areas within which the contractor is deficient in the utilization of minority groups and women, and further, goals and timetables to which the contractor's good faith efforts must be directed to correct the deficiencies." The term "minority groups" referred to "Blacks, Spanish-surnamed Americans, American Indians, and Orientals." The concept of "under utilization" meant "having fewer minorities or women in a particular job group than would reasonably be expected by their availability." "Goals" were not to be "rigid and inflexible quotas" but "targets reasonably attainable by means of applying every good faith effort to make all aspects of the entire affirmative action program work."

Affirmative action is now an integral part of the appointment process at virtually every college and university in the United States. Announcements of available faculty or administrative positions routinely include statements such as this actual one: "[The University] is an equal opportunity, affirmative action employer which actively seeks and encourages nominations of, and expressions of interest from, minority and female candidates." Every search committee is expected to conduct its activities in accord with federal affirmative action guidelines, and typically compliance is monitored by a school's Office of Affirmative Action.

Each institution regularly updates its affirmative action plan, and progress in achieving goals is systematically reviewed by the Department of Labor. Failure to develop an acceptable plan or substantial deviation from it may result in loss of federal funding.

During the early years of its implementation, affirmative action was the subject of heated debate. Were goals and timetables merely disguised quotas? Were standards being lowered for favored applicants? Were discriminatory practices that judged individuals by irrelevant criteria such as race or sex ever to be ended by programs that differentiated among people on the basis of those same criteria?

Furthermore, assuming affirmative action to be justifiable, was it deserved equally by Blacks, Spanish-surnamed Americans, American Indians, Orientals, and women? Were the bases for the claims in each case the same? Should any other groups have been added to the list? Under what specific circumstances should a group be removed from the list?

As administrators and faculty members put affirmative action into practice, vehement disputes arose regarding a variety of procedural issues. For example, if a search committee failed to find a qualified candidate whose appointment would help fulfill the affirmative action plan, might it be appropriate to leave the position vacant until a more favorable outcome could be achieved? On the other hand, if a department had learned informally of the availability of a suitable candidate, should that appointment be made without any formal announcement or search? In addition, should these institutional policies be publicized.

To some, such questions were of fundamental importance. Others thought them pettifoggery. In either case passions ran high.

But within academia the temper of the times has changed. The torrent of articles for and against affirmative action has become a trickle. Consider, for example, that between 1973 and 1978 the highly regarded journal *Philosophy and Public Affairs*, which concentrates on philosophical discussions of substantive public issues, devoted approximately 10 percent of its pages to the affirmative action controversy. Since that time, however, the magazine has hardly mentioned the matter. Of the hundreds of academic conferences held each year throughout the United States, many continue to focus on the most effective means of achieving the aims of affirmative action, but rarely does one concentrate on examining the aims themselves.

Lest it be supposed that this phenomenon results from consensus having been reached, consider an article I submitted several years ago to *The Chronicle of Higher Education*. The editors agreed to publish it but warned me to expect an intense reaction to its controversial subject. Having previously contributed columns to *The Chronicle* that produced many responses to me and to the newspaper, in this case I foresaw a deluge.

Here is the essay as it appeared:

COLLEGES SHOULD BE EXPLICIT
ABOUT WHO WILL BE CONSIDERED FOR JOBS

A fundamental principle of academic ethics is that the announcement of any available faculty or administrative position should make clear whatever special criteria the institution has established for choosing among applicants. Criteria not specified should not be used.

Today virtually every college or university advertising a position in *The Chronicle* describes itself as an "Equal Opportunity/ Affirmative Action Employer," sometimes adding that it "welcomes and encourages applications from women and minority candidates" (and occasionally "Vietnam-era veterans" or "persons with disabilities"). While such phrases are always supposed to signify that the college or university does not engage in discrimination, sometimes the same words are also intended to convey the important message that the institution strongly prefers, or will give serious consideration only to, members of specific groups.

In fairness to all applicants, departments and schools should be explicit about such matters. If it has been agreed internally that membership in particular groups is to be given strong weight in the decision procedure, the announcement of the position should say so. And in instances in which an institution has decided to fill a position only if a qualified member of a particular group or groups can be found, this information, too, should be stated candidly.

Several university presidents, including those at the University of Wisconsin at Madison and Duke University, recently announced that they had committed their institutions to appointing (within a fixed time) a specific number of faculty members from certain groups. At Memphis State University, the administration's policy is to make available a faculty position for any department that finds a qualified black candidate. At Bucknell University, the Board of Trustees has created five new faculty positions designated specifically for black scholars. Search committees at those institutions are to make choices that will help achieve the stated objectives. Surely, then, job announcements from those schools should inform potential applicants of the special situations, so that people who are, and people who are not, members of the groups in question can decide whether to apply for the positions in light of full information about the conditions governing the searches.

Not everyone agrees about what the most effective and equitable actions are that colleges can take to remedy the pernicious effects of our society's past injustices. But whatever the criteria in effect for a faculty or administrative appointment, the faculty members and administrators who established them certainly consider them within ethical and legal bounds. They should not object, therefore, to stating them publicly, without ambiguity or equivocation. Doing so will help foster institutional goals while sustaining our profession's commitment to truth in advertising. (April 5, 1989)

Did the mail run in favor or opposed? Neither. I received but one piece of correspondence, that from a professor who wrote simply, "I appreciated your column in last week's *Chronicle*, and think I agree with its main argument." As for letters to the editor, not a single one appeared.

Had I found consensus? Hardly, for I was criticizing policies in force at hundreds of colleges and universities. On the basis of available evidence and my conversations with many colleagues around the country, I believe the explanation for the unusual silence surrounding the issue lies not in widespread agreement but in deep-seated, bitter disagreement, too painful to be exposed. Proponents and opponents of affirmative action have tacitly agreed to an uneasy truce in which those on both sides refrain from public debate while still whispering in corners that their adversaries are at best intellectually misguided and at worst morally insensitive.

This situation is injurious to all, for as John Stuart Mill wrote in his classic *On Liberty*: "However unwillingly a person who has a strong opinion may admit the possibility that his opinion may be false, he ought to be moved by the consideration that, however true it may be, if it is not fully, frequently, and fearlessly discussed, it will be held as a dead dogma, not a living truth." Both those who support affirmative action and those who oppose it ought to rethink the bases for their opinions. In doing so they may not discover grounds to modify their views, but at least they will revitalize them.

To encourage such reexamination, I asked three prominent American social philosophers, Leslie P. Francis, Robert L. Simon, and Lawrence C. Becker, who hold divergent views about affirmative action, to write extended essays presenting their most recent thinking on the subject. These constitute Part I. I then sent their work to other distinguished philosophers of all variety of opinions on the subject who had accepted my invitation to comment. Their responses form Part II. No consensus was expected, and none emerged. The result, as planned, was a clash of reasoned judgments.

Mill argued that to avoid intellectual atrophy we need to have our beliefs questioned by those who disagree with us. He even maintained that "if opponents of all-important truths do not exist, it is indispensable to imagine them and supply them with the strongest arguments which the most skillful devil's advocate can conjure up." Those willing to test their ideas on affirmative action against such vigorous and informed challenge are provided herein with that opportunity.

PART I

In Defense of Affirmative Action

1

Leslie Pickering Francis

After more than twenty-five years of affirmative action law in the United States, college and university faculties remain largely white and male. Nearly 90 percent of full-time faculty are white, 4 percent are Asian, 3 percent are African American, 2 percent are Hispanic, and 1 percent are Native American.[1] Just over 25 percent of faculty positions in higher education are held by women. Within these aggregate data are some significant variations by type of institution and by field. There are lower percentages of Hispanics at public Ph.D.-granting institutions, and lower percentages of Asian Americans at public junior colleges. Only 20 percent of the faculty at research universities are women, but nearly 40 percent of the faculty at public junior colleges are women. Fifteen percent of the faculty in engineering programs are Asian Americans, only 3 percent are women, and less than 1 percent are African Americans. Fifteen percent of the faculty in the natural sciences are women, whereas nearly 40 percent of the faculty in education are women.[2]

Within these data, there are also some highly significant recent trends. The situation of women has improved markedly in some fields but much less so in others. In some of the fields of most notable improvement, affirmative action has been taken very seriously; and it is thus likely that some of the improvement may be attributed to the success of the policy.[3] For example, in law the percentage of full-time female faculty has grown from 10.6 percent in 1977 to 21.7 percent in 1987.[4] The recent percentage of new law school appointments who are women has reached 40 percent.[5] In political science, by the mid-1980s over 25 percent of new appointments went to women; even more telling, both the placement success rate of women and the percentage of women placed in Ph.D.-granting institutions began to equal or exceed that of men.[6] Recent trends in some scientific fields stand in sharp contrast. In chemistry, the percentage of women faculty in Ph.D.-granting institutions grew only from 1.5 percent in 1970 to 4.9 percent in 1987; the percentage of women faculty in predominantly undergraduate institutions remained nearly constant at just over 10 percent. There was no significant growth in the number of female assistant professors of chemistry in the 1980s, which does not suggest optimism about whether women can gradually be expected to move up in the ranks. As late as 1986, 55 percent of undergraduate chemistry faculties had no women.[7] These low percentages persisted despite notable growth in the percentages of women receiving Ph.D. degrees in chemistry (from 7.7 percent in 1970 to 21.3 percent in 1987)[8] and postdoctorates in Ph.D.-granting institutions (17 percent in 1986).[9] In mathematics, the recent academic placement rate for women has grown significantly, to around 20 percent, but the growth has been achieved nearly entirely in programs that do not grant Ph.D. degrees and continues to lag in top-ranked Ph.D. programs.[10]

The situation of African Americans, by contrast, has not shown overall improvement. There are important differences by sex: African American women have fared better than men in some disciplines. For example, in law schools the percentage of African American appointments remained steady between 1985 and 1990 at about 6 percent; over half of these appointments went to women.[11] Surely at least part of the explanation for these trends lies in the availability of applicants. The numbers of African American males obtaining Ph.D. degrees fell by 54 percent between 1977 and 1987;[12] the numbers of African American males attending college also fell over the same period, by about 30 percent.[13] By contrast, the numbers of African American women receiving both B.A. and Ph.D. degrees increased slightly during the decade. These trends suggest the need to think differently about the issue of affirmative action for women and for African Americans.

In most universities, affirmative action is a regularized part of the process of recruiting faculty. Recruitment typically begins when a department is alerted to the likelihood of an open position. Department faculty meet to discuss the nature of the position: the field, level, and other characteristics of desired applicants. With administrative approval, a description of the position is formalized. An advertisement is written and its contents cleared with affirmative action officers of the university. The advertisement may contain signals that affirmative action is important to the university administration: "minority and women candidates are especially encouraged to apply," or "the university is an equal opporunity employer." The advertisement will appear in national forums such as *The Chronicle of Higher Education* and in field-specific publications such as *Jobs for Philosophers*. The department also may seek to identify minority and women applicants by writing directly to graduate programs, contacting minorities and women already in the field or advertising in newsletters circulated to these groups. During the process, departments will be urged to keep careful records of applications and efforts to identify affirmative action candidates. They may be forced to explain why affirmative action candidates were rejected. Approval of the department's final choice for the position may depend on whether the university is satisfied with the department's effort toward affirmative action.

The actual process of recruitment and selection is left largely up to individual departments. There may be tension between what the department wants to do and what it perceives as the annoying bureaucratic hurdles of affirmative action. From the outset, the department will need to wait to move on an appointment until the closing date listed in the job advertisment. After applications are received (in great numbers in some fields and in sparser numbers in others), a faculty recruitment committee decides on a shorter list of candidates to interview. Many different factors may influence the selection of interviewees: subjective impressions, reputation of the applicant's graduate program, and familiarity with the applicant's references are surely important. So are personal contacts between faculty in the applicant's graduate program and members of the recruitment committee. A first round of interviews then takes place at large academic conventions: the Labor Day meeting of the American Political Science Association, the Christmas meeting of the Modern Language Association, or the recruitment conference of the Association of American Law Schools. Applicants who cannot get to the conventions, because they or their institutions lack resources, fall out of the process at this point unless their credentials on paper are enormously attractive.[14] As many as twenty or thirty candidates may be interviewed, thirty minutes at a time, in hotel suites or at folding tables in a large room. Some of these interviews will be taken very seriously; others will be pro forma, perhaps driven by the department's need to demonstrate contact with affirmative action candidates. A few candidates will then be invited for a second interview on campus. There they will read papers, teach classes, meet with students, be taken out to dinner, and perhaps be invited to parties. Job interviews on campus are both intellectual and social events; academic professionals are colleagues, not co-workers. The faculty then meet to rank candidates. Their choice is reviewed administratively to ensure compliance with affirmative action guidelines and other university regulations. Finally, if all goes well, an offer is made and accepted. In the overwhelming majority of cases, the successful candidate will still be white and male.

What should we make of the process of academic recruitment and its results? Should the central focus of criticism even be the fairness of the process? One account is that the process is largely fair and that fairness is what matters. Jobs are openly advertised and academic faculty are selected in an unbiased and well-informed way. The disparities in numbers mostly reflect differences in the interests and availability of qualified candidates. The sparsity of African American academics in particular mirrors the sparsity of Ph.D.s, which in turn mirrors the economic depression of American higher education. By opening the recruitment process to public advertisement and scrutiny, affirmative action has largely succeeded in correcting bias and bringing diversity into university faculties. A more critical account is that subtle biases continue to infect the selection process in many departments, for appointments and for other decisions from the selection of graduate students to the awarding of tenure. Affirmative action continues to be important in controlling bias; in some fields, even more aggressive action may be in order. Still other accounts would have us move beyond bias in the selection process to larger disputes about social justice and the role of universities in American society. Some argue that affirmative action is important because higher education is a crucial source of opportunities for members of traditionally disadvantaged groups. Others argue that higher education must train diverse groups of professionals to provide vital services for America's minority communities.

In this essay, I defend a limited form of affirmative action in higher education. Affirmative action has been partially successful in correcting bias, but in many areas the need for corrective strategies continues. Reasons of distributive justice also support change. My claims can be summarized briefly as follows. "Affirmative action" is a broad term, which may require as little as the open advertisement of positions or as much as the imposition of target employment percentages. Despite what is certainly a popular view, affirmative action is not principally justified as compensation for prior injustice. Instead, affirmative action is morally justified as a corrective for discriminatory employment practices. When discrimination is subtle or difficult to eradicate, the morally justified means of correction may include target outcomes. In higher education today, affirmative action including target outcomes remains extremely important as a corrective for biased selection processes. Discussion of whether preferential selection is justified as a separate matter is thus in my view not the most important issue in the current situation of American higher education.[15] I also believe that target outcomes are sometimes justified as redistributive measures, but I shall provide only a partial defense for this claim here.

Affirmative action is a legal policy that has proved highly controversial. Rhetorical charges abound that it requires rigid quotas and gives jobs to unqualified candidates. These charges misunderstand the law of affirmative action as it now stands. To establish a common context for the discussion of affirmative action in higher education, this essay begins with a brief overview of current affirmative action law. It then discusses particular problems in selecting academic faculty that make it difficult to identify discrimination and to design corrective policies. The essay then distinguishes three different kinds of arguments for affirmative action—compensatory, corrective, and redistributive—and argues that the chief reasons that support affirmative action in higher education are corrective and redistributive. Finally, the essay turns to objections to affirmative action, particularly the charges that it is counter-productive, that it deprives some people of what they deserve, and that it upsets legitimate expectations.

Title VII, the Constitution, and Affirmative Action

Title VII of the Civil Rights Act of 1964 prohibits employment discrimination on the grounds of race, color, religion, sex, or national origin.[16] It applies to all colleges and universities, public or private, that have at least fifteen employees.[17] The U.S. Constitution prohibits state action in violation of the equal protection of the laws and applies to all public institutions of higher education. Title VII and the Constitution together determine what is required and permitted with respect to affirmative action in higher education. This section provides an overview of this legal framework.

Title VII does not define illegal discrimination, an absence that has been the subject of litigation ever since. It does specify some employment practices that are not illegal. Some examples of particular relevance to higher education include bona fide seniority systems; job-related tests of ability; or the consideration of religion, sex, or national origin where reasonably necessary for the normal operation of a business.[18] In addition, Title VII explicitly states that it is not prohibited discrimination for a religious institution such as a Catholic college to select employees based on their religious affiliations.[19] Title VII also specifies that preferential treatment is not required simply because of numerical imbalances in a work force.[20]

Title VII has had an intricate and controversial history in the courts.[21] Very early on, courts recognized two different kinds of Title VII lawsuits: suits alleging discriminatory treatment of identified employees and suits challenging the disparate impact of employment practices on groups protected by Title VII.[22] Disparate treatment cases pit the individual plaintiff's charge of intentional bias against the employer's claims that there were legitimate reasons for how the plaintiff was treated. In higher education, disparate treatment cases have been brought largely by disappointed candidates for tenure or promotion. Disparate treatment cases follow a straightforward pattern. First, the employee must raise the inference of discrimination—in legal language, establish a prima facie case—by showing that he or she was qualified for the position at issue but did not receive it. An example would be a disappointed tenure candidate who could bring forth evidence that she met a department's announced criteria. Then, the burden of producing evidence shifts to the employer to assert legitimate reasons for how the plaintiff was treated, for example, that tenure was denied because the candidate's scholarship was deficient in comparison to that of successful tenure candidates. Finally, the plaintiff bears the ultimate burden of persuading the court by a preponderance of the evidence that the employer's asserted reasons were pretextual.[23]

Disparate impact cases in higher education have been brought largely by groups who assert that statistical imbalances among faculty are the result of bias in the selection process. The difficulty in these cases has been to distinguish mere statistical imbalances—which are not prohibited discrimination in themselves—from imbalances that manifest discriminatory practices. This distinction would be at issue when departmental recruitment processes result in a faculty composed largely of white males, for example, in the 55 percent of undergraduate chemistry departments that have no women faculty.

A complex series of disparate impact cases during the 1970s and early 1980s addressed the evidentiary issues involved, distinguishing bias from mere imbalance. To establish a prima facie case of disparate impact, plaintiffs must show significant statistical disparities between the composition of the work force at issue and the composition of the available qualified labor pool and then identify an employment practice as related to these disparities. Thus plaintiffs challenging a chemistry department's appointments process would need to show significant disparities between the composition of department faculty and the postdoctorate or Ph.D. applicant pool, and identify an aspect of the appointments process as related to the disparity. This prima facie case shifts the burden to employers to bring forth evidence of the inadequacy of the statistics or to justify the practices at issue.[24] At this point, allocation of the ultimate burden of persuasion is crucial. Do plaintiffs have to disprove employers' justifications, or is the burden of persuasion on employers? The legal answer to this question remained in dispute through the 1980s. One view was that employers should bear the ultimate burden of justifying challenged employment practices, because it is discriminatory to continue practices that affect groups differently without any good reasons for doing so.[25] Employers contended that this burden would be very difficult for them to meet, especially when judgments about applicants are subjective, as they are in higher education. To avoid the burden of proof, employers argued, they would be driven to adopt rigid numerical quotas. Thus employers concluded that plaintiffs should retain the ultimate burden of showing that the employer could achieve its legitimate purposes without continuing the challenged employment practice.[26]

In a watershed decision in 1989, the U.S. Supreme Court agreed with the employers.[27] The *Wards Cove* decision held that disparate impact plaintiffs cannot rely solely on statistics to establish a prima facie case of discrimination. In addition to the statistical disparities, they must identify a particular practice and link it causally to the statistics. If the employer engages in a number of practices that are alleged to be discriminatory, the plaintiff will need to demonstrate which practice or practices are causally responsible for any discriminatory impact. Thus a challenge to an academic appointments process would need to single out bias in the process and show that it is responsible for the statistical disparities. Only then would the university be required to provide a legitimate justification for the practice. And, just as in disparate treatment cases, the burden of proof would remain with the plaintiff to show that the university's claimed justification was spurious. Thus if a university maintained that its appointments process had been successful in recruiting qualified candidates, the burden would remain on challengers to demonstrate that the method was inadequate or that other methods would do as well.

The *Wards Cove* decision was greeted with the reaction that it overruled twenty-five years of Title VII law. In the fall of 1990, Congress passed a civil rights bill intended to nullify *Wards Cove* by statute. President Bush vetoed the bill, and Congress by one vote failed to override the veto. The president's veto responded to employers' claims that the bill mandated quotas. These claims are disingenuous, however, for the bill did not mandate quotas. The bill would have reestablished the view of some courts before *Wards Cove* that employers should bear the burden of justifying practices that result in statistical imbalances. Certainly, one practical response to this evidentiary burden is to avoid the problem by appointing statistically balanced work forces. But another response is to continue with practices that can be justified despite resulting imbalances. This strategy does put employers on the defensive more often. The result of the president's position and the *Wards Cove* decision, however, is that processes that generate imbalanced results will stay in place unless plaintiffs can disprove any justification for them advanced by employers. Legal challenges to academic appointments processes that yield imbalanced faculties will thus fail unless plaintiffs can isolate specific causes of the imbalance and refute any justifications offered by the university.

In addition to the meaning and proof of discrimination, the selection of available remedies has been a third central area of Title VII controversy. "Affirmative action" is a very broad term. It has gained wide currency since its use in the remedy section of Title VII in 1964: "If the court finds that the respondent has intentionally engaged in or is intentionally engaging in an unlawful employment practice charged in the complaint, the court may enjoin the respondent from engaging in such unlawful employment practice, and order such affirmative action as may be appropriate, which may include, but is not limited to, reinstatement or hiring of employees, with or without back pay . . . , or any other equitable relief as the court deems appropriate." [28]

In Title VII litigation, affirmative action has encompassed a diverse range of remedial orders from courts. It has meant eliminating requirements such as a high school diploma or a minimum score on

an intelligence test, when they are not related to job performance.[29]
It has meant the merger of segregated unions and the elimination of
racially segregated hiring halls.[30] Unions have been required to make
information publicly available about membership opportunities and
the availability of jobs.[31] Membership goals have been imposed upon
unions that have engaged in recalcitrant and extensive discrimination
in admitting members and making referrals for jobs.[32] Hiring and promotion goals have been imposed upon employers with impressive
histories of discrimination.[33] The Supreme Court has held as recently
as 1986 that Title VII permits the use of such goals as a corrective for
persistent and recalcitrant discrimination.[34] It is fair to say, however,
that remedies short of goals are legally preferred whenever they are
reasonably available. In higher education, affirmative action has been
largely voluntary, but has followed many of the court-ordered strategies. Typical forms of affirmative action in faculty recruitment include
public job advertisements, letters urging applications from minorities
and women, and special efforts to identify and interview minority and
women candidates. More aggressive methods include administrative
pressures on departments to appoint minorities and women, special
funding support for affirmative action appointments, and insistence
on filling positions by affirmative action candidates.

In its early years, Title VII was a sword against prejudicial discrimination. As its force has been blunted, voluntary efforts to end
discrimination have assumed increasing importance. In response to
these efforts, white males have sought to use Title VII as a shield
against voluntary affirmative action programs. In 1979, the Supreme
Court's *Weber* decision held that Title VII does not prohibit employers
from adopting voluntary, race-conscious affirmative action plans.[35]
The Supreme Court singled out four factors as crucial to assessing a
voluntary plan under Title VII: that it was designed to break down
patterns of segregation, that it was intended as a benchmark to gauge
progress, that it was temporary, and that it did not unnecessarily tram-
mel the rights of other employees. Title VII thus permits universities
to adopt voluntary affirmative action plans that meet the *Weber* standards. Of the forms of affirmative action frequently used by universities, efforts to locate and interview minority and women candidates
surely meet the *Weber* standards. The more aggressive strategies are
more problematic. Arguably, the *Weber* standards can be met when the
university, responding to discrimination, makes short-term efforts to

increase affirmative action appointments while not entirely foreclosing the ordinary appointments process. Efforts to increase faculty diversity by underwriting new positions such as the proposal made by Lawrence Becker in this volume are almost certainly permissible because they expand rather than foreclose opportunities. On the other hand, the insistence that all appointments be filled by affirmative action candidates would almost surely be impermissible under *Weber* because of the impact on majority candidates. In individual cases, courts will balance the need for the affirmative action to end discrimination against the impact on majority candidates.

Title VII is a statute, enacted under Congress's ability to regulate commerce. Like all statutes, it is limited by the Constitution. The Fifth and Fourteenth Amendments of the Constitution prohibit discriminatory action by the federal and state governments, respectively. Like Title VII, the Constitution was initially used by disadvantaged groups to attack discrimination but more recently has been used to set outside limits to what the federal and state governments may do voluntarily. In 1978, a year before *Weber*, the Supreme Court upheld Allan Bakke's challenge to a minority pool for admissions to the University of California at Davis medical school. In the *Bakke* decision, Justice Powell wrote that the voluntary racial quotas violated equal protection because they were not necessary for the achievement of a compelling state interest. Justice Powell did say, however, that the realization of a diverse student body is a compelling interest and allows a university to pay special attention to race and other background factors in admitting students.[36]

In a series of cases after *Bakke*, the Court worked out the general standard of constitutional equal protection to be applied to governmental affirmative action. In the *Croson* case, decided early in 1989, the Court applied strict scrutiny to affirmative action. Strict scrutiny is a two-part test: the policy must serve a compelling state interest and must be a necessary means to that end. With respect to state interests, the *Croson* Court held that remedying discrimination in society generally is not compelling.[37] Thus under *Croson*, state universities would not be permitted to engage in affirmative action out of general concerns for social justice or the need to remedy the situation of historically disfavored groups. The *Bakke* aim of educational diversity, however, apparently is not rejected as compelling.[38] A government entity's efforts to eradicate its own prior discrimination may also be compelling. With respect to means, *Bakke* suggests that quotas are not necessary means to academic diversity. *Croson* leaves open the possibility that employment goals are permissible when they are necessary to remedy a state agency's own discrimination. State universities, therefore, are probably prohibited by current interpretations of the federal constitution from imposing affirmative action goals on appointments unless they are doing what is absolutely necessary to remedy their own discrimination. They are also probably prohibited from creating new positions on a set-aside basis such as that proposed by Becker. The constitutional standards that apply to state universities are thus more stringent than the Title VII standards that apply to both public and private institutions.[39]

Let me now summarize this discussion with some new terminology, that of process and outcome.[40] Process-based discrimination identifies bias in particular procedures. Outcome-based discrimination identifies bias with results, such as the distribution of groups in job categories. Title VII explicitly refuses to define discrimination in terms of outcomes. Before *Wards Cove*, however, it was interpreted to permit the use of outcome-based data as sufficient evidence for a prima facie case of process-based discrimination. After *Wards Cove*, plaintiffs must show how process-based discrimination has generated disparate outcomes. On the remedy side, process-directed strategies order changes in practices as a means of ending discrimination. Outcome-directed remedies demand a result such as a percentage of new appointments or an overall percentage of employees in the workforce. Under Title VII, process-directed strategies are preferable, but outcome-directed strategies may be mandated to correct stubborn process-based discrimination. Title VII also permits voluntary affirmative action, either process- or outcome-directed, judged in terms of the *Weber* standards. The constitution prohibits state universities from violating equal protection. Voluntary affirmative action is constitutionally permitted to the extent necessary to further compelling state interests. State universities are permitted to consider race as a factor, but not to insist on target outcomes, where the goal is educational diversity. They are also permitted to adopt either process-directed or outcome-directed remedies where necessary to end their own prior discrimination.

Identifying Discrimination in Higher Education

Higher education presents specific and persistent problems for the identification and elimination of process-based employment discrimination. Academic decisions are typically qualitative and multifaceted. Here are some of the ways in which bias might infect the decentralized appointments process described above. From the very beginning, the subject matter field for applicants may be defined in problematic ways: "We can't hire a philosopher of science who is a feminist, because feminist philosophy of science is an oxymoron" (laughter). Despite open advertisements, decisions about whom to interview may be drawn largely from personal contacts, an "old boy" network of white, male friends. "We've tried and tried, but we just can't find any qualified women or minorities" (where "qualified" really means "recommended by people we trust"). Applicants from less well known Ph.D. programs may receive minimal consideration. There may be considerable resentment of university affirmative action requirements. Convention interviews may become a kind of mating ritual. Interviews with preferred candidates may be taken very seriously, carefully scheduled at prime time slots, well attended, and perhaps accompanied by amenities from coffee to expensive dinners. Interviews with unfamiliar faces may be poorly attended and perfunctory. When confronted with the responsibilities of taking women candidates out for a drink or a meal, male faculty may squirm a little (apologetically, if they think of themselves as liberated) or become unexpectedly flirtatious. Arriving for on-campus interviews, preferred candidates may be greeted with the assumption that they are wonderful, that their work is wonderful, and that any little inadequacies will work themselves out in time. Candidates who have not been so blessed may be questioned closely from the beginning and sense quite correctly that the interview is not going well. Minority candidates may be asked repeatedly about their interests in community service. Women may be questioned about teaching rather than research. In these and many other subtle ways, presuppositions slant what happens and what is perceived in the appointments process.

Courts have discussed the difficulties of identifying subtle discrimination in evaluating academic qualifications, largely in the context of promotion and tenure cases. In an unsuccessful suit against Cornell University brought by four women who were denied tenure, the court reviewed the highly decentralized and subjective nature of tenure decisions.[41] Other courts have pointed out the vagueness of tenure criteria, particularly with respect to teaching and service and the balance to be struck among these criteria. For example, a university may insist on service that is relevant to the university's mission but fail to give clear standards of what this means and apparently judge various kinds of community and professional service by different standards.[42] Teaching is most frequently evaluated by student course evaluations, yet data show likely gender bias in these evaluations.[43] Different standards may be applied in judging the rigor of teaching loads for minority and non-minority candidates.[44] Even judgments of research quality and capability may be subject to vague standards and biased assessments. For example, a common charge is that the selection of outside, "peer" reviewers in the retention, promotion, and tenure process is performed in essentially standardless, arbitrary ways, often by means of friendship or "old boy" networks, yet these reviews can be absolutely central to a candidate's fate. Whole fields of research may be downgraded because of improper discrimination against a field of inquiry, as when feminist approaches are viewed as problematic.[45]

In addition to these specific issues of process, larger features of the overall career structure of academic life burden women and minorities in particular. These appear in other professions, but they take specific forms in academic life. For purposes of this essay, I am leaving aside whether these larger structural issues amount to discrimination which ought, morally, to be remedied. Nonetheless, I include them here because they potentially compound and deepen the claim that there is process-based discrimination in academic life. I will highlight three such issues here: the salary and leave packages frequently available to academics; the timing of tenure decisions; and the service obligations often pressed upon minority and women faculty.

The structure of academic salaries and leaves is unique among the professions. University faculty, like schoolteachers, are commonly paid on nine-month contracts and given nine-month teaching assignments. During the remaining three months, they are "free" to earn outside salaries (an unlikely possibility where professional consultancies are infrequent) or to engage in research. But with the heightened research expectations for faculty, this "freedom" has become highly constrained (unlike the analogous freedom of public schoolteachers). Faculty typically use summers for research. Yet this practice intersects differently with men's and women's lives. More women faculty than I care to think about have carefully tried to schedule their babies for the summer months or, failing that, a period of research leave. Whether this is good or bad practice is one thing—the practical result is that children cut into research opportunities for women faculty in a way they may not for male faculty. Moreover, because of the nine-month structure of their jobs, faculty—both men and women—often do not have the other kinds of leave entitlements such as sick leave found outside academic life and often available to nonacademic staff even within universities. The flexibility of academic life, so often viewed as an advantage, is a mixed blessing for parents generally and for women particularly, to the extent that they continue to bear the primary burdens of parenting.

A second problematic background feature of academic life is the pattern of career progression. A typical career pattern for a contemporary academic involves a protracted training period; the median time spent in the completion of a Ph.D. degree is 10.4 years (including nearly seven years of registered study).[46] It may take several years to find a tenure track job, and six or seven years more on the tenure track before a tenure decision is made. Academics thus find it difficult to become securely established before their later childbearing years. Time on the tenure track, even for the fortunate, too often coincides with painful decisions by those in their late thirties about whether to undertake the commitments of becoming a parent or to remain childless. To be sure, these dilemmas also exist in other professions such as law and medicine. However, these professions do not impose such protracted study before receipt of the final professional degree or encounter such difficulty in obtaining a relatively secure job. Moreover, at least in some cases these professions are experimenting with job structures that ease pressures on childbearing years: job sharing or changes in the length of time before promotion or partnership decisions are made. The insistence on a rigid, limited timetable within which tenure decisions must be made may be important in protecting academic freedom and in protecting academics from exploitation generally, but it has difficult and largely undiscussed consequences for parenting faculty, most often women.

A third background difficulty for women and minority faculty is the overall demands of service. Service "opportunities" for faculty are often huge impositions on minorities and women. As universities increasingly strive for diversity on important committees and increasingly attempt to connect with the communities in which they are located, women and minority faculty are pressed into service. The service is important, and there are few of them to do it, so they end up doing it over and over and over again. This pattern is all well and good, because the service gets done. But such service is not research and is not likely to lead to research; and research is often the most important criterion on which tenure decisions have been and continue to be made.

Thus the nature of academic decision making makes it hard to identify and correct discrimination. Decisions about appointments, promotion, and tenure are highly qualitative. Standards may be vague and opportunities for comparison limited. Decisions may be based on both discriminatory and nondiscriminatory reasons, and it may be very hard to separate the two or to determine which predominated or whether the biased reasons changed the outcome. Under current legal standards, allegations of discrimination in academia may be some of the most difficult to establish. When claims of discrimination have been borne out, it has also been difficult to know whether the problematic procedures have been corrected, without insisting on actual success in adding women and minorities to faculties or student bodies—that is, without relying on outcome-directed corrective methods.

JUSTIFICATIONS FOR AFFIRMATIVE ACTION

Many different kinds of justifications have been offered for affirmative action. They have different strengths and weaknesses and are vulnerable to different objections. Compensatory arguments rely on the claim that someone has been wronged and is, therefore, owed compensation. They reply to questions such as "Which groups deserve affirmative action?" Corrective arguments contend that a discriminatory practice should be altered, eliminated, or replaced. They respond to questions such as "Are universities still engaging in discrimination, even in the 1990s? How can any remaining discrimination be brought to an end?" Redistributive arguments claim that affirmative action is justified as a step toward a more distributively just society. They answer questions such as "How can we increase equality of opportunity? What is the role of the university in perpetuating injustices in the larger society?" Affirmative action is commonly defended as compensation owed to victims of past injustices. In what follows, however, I argue that correction and redistribution provide better reasons than compensation for affirmative action in higher education today.

Compensatory Arguments

A compensatory argument begins by identifying someone as the victim of an injury. The injury in turn demands compensation. Someone else perpetrated the injury and ought to pay the compensation to the victim. A convincing compensatory argument thus requires an identification of the victim, an indication of the nature of the injury and why it demands compensation, an account of what compensation is appropriate and why that is the appropriate form of compensation, and an account of who should pay the compensation and why.[47]

Compensatory arguments are most easily defended when an identified individual suffers a particular loss at the hands of another party who was at fault. An example would be a faculty member who could show that she was not given tenure because her department chair was biased against women. Here, the injury demands compensation because it was a wrong; she was treated unjustly. The victim is the sufferer of the loss. The appropriate compensation would make her whole for the loss; and the appropriate compensator is the department chair whose misconduct caused the loss.

Behind these apparently simple claims lie complex theoretical issues about justice and compensation. The claim that it is unjust to make tenure decision based on sex could be defended by arguing that sex is not one of the factors that are normally relevant to tenure decisions. She will be made whole by recouping what she lost by the injustice, a continuing job. In many cases, she can be compensated with exactly what she lost, or its monetary equivalent if she so chooses; but if someone else has assumed the position (such as a unique tenure slot in a particular field), it may not be possible to undo the past exactly, or without resulting costs to others. In addition, the costs to others may not fall on the direct perpetrator of the wrong; the university (which may or may not have been indirectly at fault for inadequately supervising the department chair) may be required to bear the costs of an additional position if she is reinstated, and colleagues (who may or may not have been complicitors in the situation) may have to make adjustments such as altering teaching assignments. This is not to say that reinstatement is unjustified, but that it must be defended as a requirement of compensatory justice that overrides these costs. In this kind of situation, the defense is relatively easy: the injustice was severe, and the costs are limited and diffusely spread. But the argument for reinstatement must be stronger if the costs fall severely on one person—for example, if the reinstatement required firing a junior faculty member who had been appointed as her replacement several years earlier.

More serious problems arise when a compensatory argument is used to justify affirmative action on a larger scale, for example, when a university seeks to increase its percentages of minority and female faculty. Strategies covering an extended group generally affect some who have been identified as victims, but may benefit others as well. They may also exclude others who have been victimized but who are not members of the group covered in the affirmative action order. On a compensatory model, therefore, such affirmative action has been seriously questioned.[48] A reply in terms of the concept of group victimization[49] remains underinclusive if other groups have been victimized in the same ways as the groups claiming compensation. Underinclusivity is not present if the group targeted for affirmative action has suffered a special sort of victimization that demands a response in justice. Arguments that groups such as African Americans have suffered special victimization, however, frequently point not only to the character of the injustice they have suffered, but also to the persistence and scope of the wrongs at issue and their connection to broader problems of social justice. To the extent that these arguments move beyond past wrongs demanding redress, to continuing injustices in need of correction or general problems of distributive justice in society, they are no longer simply compensatory arguments for affirmative action. The ground has been shifted at least in part to corrective or redistributive concerns.

Two further, related issues about group compensation concern what compensation is appropriate and who should bear its burdens. On the analogy to the individual model, compensation should be what will make the group whole for the injuries suffered. But what does this require, particularly when the wrong and its effects continue? One approach is to try to place the group as much as possible in the situation it would have experienced had the injustice not occurred. But this approach may not be clearly or uniquely marked out in situations of long-past, extensive wrongs, such as slavery or the dislocation of Native American peoples. Available forms of compensation may be absurdly inadequate in the face of blighted generations.[50] Crude efforts to turn back the clock—for example, speculating what the employment situation of African Americans in higher education would have been without slavery—are highly conjectural. A more promising approach is to try to understand what justice now requires in light of past or continuing wrongs. Put in this way, however, the compensatory question has once again been transformed into issues of correction and redistribution.

Moreover, the required compensation may impose extensive burdens on those who were not initial perpetrators of the injustices and have not benefited significantly from them. When academic jobs were scarce, concentration on affirmative action appointments virtually foreclosed some white males from academic careers. One response is to argue that these burdens are simply overridden by the enormity of the initial and continuing injustices. But this response fails to confront the enormity and concentration of the burdens themselves. Another possibility is to seek to accommodate these burdens within a general scheme for group redress.[51] Possible strategies here include: modifying the scope or timing of compensation where burdens are severe and concentrated; exploring methods of compensation that expand rather than reallocate opportunities (for example, the training program described in the *Weber* decision or the establishment of a new faculty position centered on affirmative action concerns); or providing alternative opportunities for those who are disadvantaged by affirmative action.[52] To choose among these strategies, it is not enough to refer back to the nature of the wrong suffered. A decision whether to modify redress in light of the burdens imposed on others, to take one example, requires discussion of what it is now just to do in light of all the circumstances. Here again, the compensatory argument runs up against corrective and redistributive issues. Compensation is not the only and perhaps not even the central issue when we move beyond allegations of biased treatment of identified individuals to larger-scale issues about the composition of university faculties. Thus compensation is not the primary argument for affirmative action programs in employment in higher education.

Corrective Arguments

A corrective argument begins by identifying a discriminatory practice. This might be a practice which is intentionally discriminatory. Or, as in the disparate impact cases under Title VII, it arguably might be a practice that yields imbalances without being otherwise justified. Next, an argument must be made that the practice ought to be changed, that it is unjust and the injustice is serious enough to warrant correction. Then, a method of correcting the practice must be selected and defended, principally against concerns that it would be ineffective or unfair. Finally, there must be some means of determining whether the corrective method has succeeded and the injustice has been ended.

The corrective argument's thrust is simple: injustices ought to be eliminated. But as the legal cases reveal, this simple claim glosses over complex questions about what justice requires in unjust situations.[53] Consider as an example a university that leaves appointments decisions largely to departments, which make these decisions principally in the way I described at the outset, resulting in a faculty that is almost entirely white and male. A threshold issue about whether correction is needed here is the identification of the practice at issue: Is it the entire appointments structure, or more narrowly the particular methods used by the separate departments? Then, what is discrimination? Is it limited to intentional or careless bias? Does it extend to the uncritical or routine continuation of practices that have secured few women or minorities? Is this injustice serious enough to warrant attention? Are corrective steps necessary, or is the situation likely to right itself with the recognition of the effects of the practice? What methods of correction are likely to be most effective? Solid answers to these questions are important to the positive case for correction. Other questions arise in response to objections: Will the methods of correction have unintended, counterproductive results? What kinds of burdens does the correction impose on others, and are they fair? At this juncture, I focus on the case for correction, saving the objections for the final section of the essay.

The threshold issue is whether to focus on practices as broadly or narrowly conceived—an entire appointments structure rather than particular elements of that structure. If the focus is particularized, as it was by the Supreme Court in *Wards Cove*, cumulative effects will go unnoticed. It may also be impossible as an evidentiary matter to single out which aspects of a complex practice have principal causal effects on final decisions. To continue with the appointments example, consider how hard it may be to sort out the respective influence of letters of recommendation and interviews. If a candidate is interviewed despite questionable letters of recommendation, these letters may nevertheless influence perceptions of how to conduct the interview and whether the interview was a success. These evidentiary problems are most acute when, as in higher education, appointments decisions are few in number and largely subjective. Insisting on the particularization of *Wards Cove*, therefore, will mean that even some cases of intentional discrimination may go unrecognized when practices are sufficiently complex. Yet if discrimination is a wrong, we should not define the problem in terms of assumptions that militate against its identification. When universities consider voluntary strategies to root out discrimination (rather than whether they are likely to be subjected to a successful lawsuit after *Wards Cove*), they should therefore focus on larger patterns rather than particular appointments decisions.

Once the subject practice has been identified, the next step is to decide what makes a practice discriminatory. Intentional bias in the design or implementation of a practice is unjust because it treats some— or, more likely, many—individuals differently on irrelevant grounds. An example would be a recruitment committee that discounts the credentials of women applicants. The failure to observe and root out unintended, cumulative vestiges of discrimination is also unjust because it treats some on irrelevant grounds and allows these effects to accumulate. One example would be an interview process that assumes that African American applicants are primarily interested in teaching and serving minority students. A second example would be the automatic devaluation of applicants from lesser graduate programs. Yet another example would be the failure to take any steps—even educational ones—to blunt harsh questions from biased faculty members during an interview. To be sure, whether conduct does reveal bias may be controversial; the line between asking difficult questions to test an applicant's abilities under pressure and asking difficult questions with the unarticulated motivation of discomfiting women or minority candidates may be hard to discern even for the questioners themselves. Here numbers and patterns can be telling; when women or minorities are persistently questioned in ways that put them off balance, while white men are not, bias is strongly suggested.[54]

The most controversial kind of situation in which a process is claimed to be discriminatory is the disparate impact case that was typical before *Wards Cove*: a practice results in decisions that yield fewer members of targeted groups than might be expected given the available applicant pool, and the practice is not otherwise preferable to alternatives that might have significantly different results. An example is reliance on contacts with friends for information about which applicants to interview, a version of the old boy network. This practice may have produced good applicants for many years, and may be continued because it is familiar and convenient. But is it discriminatory if it results in an interview pool that is nearly entirely white and male? The answer lies in the arguments that support the familiar practice in comparison to alternatives such as expanding direct contacts with references to include referees for all candidates. Arguments for contacts with friends are familiarity, convenience, and apparent past success. But there are also educational disadvantages: reinforcement of received pedagogy, the marginalization of new perspectives, and the failure to reach out to new populations both within and outside the academy. At the same time, the practice is a significant force in excluding members of target groups. This is the strongest argument to be made for the claim that it is discriminatory: a subtle kind of bias is shown by acquiescence in a practice that is not supported by good reasons, and that operates significantly to exclude members of historically disadvantaged groups.

Employers who argue against this theory of disparate impact generally do not challenge the claim that it is unjust to continue a practice with exclusionary consequences when there are no otherwise good reasons for doing so. Instead, they either argue that there are good reasons for the practice—such as that it yields more qualified applicants— or that they will be forced by the recognition of this kind of injustice into numerical quotas that will result in new injustices.[55] The first point is not disputed by defenders of disparate impact theories. If the employer can show good, employment-related reasons for continuing a practice, it is not discriminatory to do so; but it should be up to the employer to make this showing in light of the very real differences flowing from the contested practice. Construed in this way, disparate impact theory targets process-based discrimination, with outcome data relevant only insofar as they reveal bias in the practice or in the decision not to explore alternatives. The second point made by employers—about the possible injustices introduced by remedies—does not address whether continuing the practice is unjust, but whether given remedial strategies are defensible, a topic to which I shall return in the final section.

In the positive case for correction, the final questions are whether correction is necessary and whether it is likely to be effective. As to need, university departments might argue that they are well intentioned, and that once discrimination is recognized they will voluntarily take steps to ensure that it comes to an end. At the outset, these claims may well be persuasive. But if bias continues, albeit more subtly, good intentions become failure to confront reality, self-deception, or bad faith.

The other troubling question is whether corrective forms of affirmative action are likely to work. The results of less aggressive forms of affirmative action have been mixed. Widely advertised searches that continue to yield interview lists drawn from personal contacts are a familiar part of the academic landscape. Nonetheless, although it often fails, the requirement of open advertising at least brings the issue into the foreground and has resulted in progress at some schools. When less aggressive strategies falter, we might decide to give up and hope that discrimination will gradually diminish over time. This approach leaves injustice to continue and is deeply problematic whenever the injustice is relatively serious. Another approach is to move more aggressively to outcome-directed corrective strategies such as target appointments percentages. The aggressive approach is preferable to doing nothing, because it at least brings the possibility of curtaining persistent injustice. As the data indicate, however, the problems of recruiting male African American faculty may differ significantly from the problems of recruiting women faculty. In order to be successful, affirmative action programs will need to respond to these differences. For example, the American Political Science Association has undertaken several programs to augment the numbers of African American graduate students in political science.[56] Moreover, targets bring problems of their own. In the next section, I shall discuss whether these problems are serious enough to override the case for outcome-directed corrective strategies.

Redistributive Arguments

Redistributive arguments rest on claims that society is in some ways unjust. The injustice is sufficient to warrant taking steps toward a more just situation. Some form of affirmative action would be the most justified step to take under the circumstances. Thus we ought to undertake the affirmative action that would be the most justified step to take. This is not to say that the step would be perfectly just, however. It is only to say that it is the best next step under circumstances of injustice. The progression to a more just situation need not be linear; we may need to take apparent steps backward in order to take more significant steps forward.

For several reasons, the academy has been cast in a central role in attacking more general problems of social justice. Education is a traditional (although by no means the only) way of expanding opportunities for disadvantaged groups. Higher education is a particular source of entry into the professions and upper-income jobs. So the expansion of opportunities for college education has been a standard target for disadvantaged groups. Higher education also trains professionals who will engage in important service activities: nurses and physicians for rural and inner-city areas, lawyers for the poor, or schoolteachers for Native American communities. While the connections are surely imperfect, increasing the percentages of minorities in these fields may contribute to increased delivery of services. It may also provide a pool of professionals who share cultural, ethnic, or racial identities with those in need of services. The issues here are not just whether professionals from disadvantaged communities are likely to return to serve there, but also whether they share the identities that make it more likely that they will be able to deliver services effectively. These arguments from social justice focus principally on the admission of students, but they relate secondarily to the selection of faculty to the extent that faculty diversity is helpful to the development of minority students. The argument that minority and women faculty are important as role models is based partially on the claim that they will encourage students to follow in their footsteps.[57] But it is also based on the claim that they are likely to be more sensitive to the learning styles and values of different kinds of students.[58]

It is beyond the scope of this chapter to provide the full defense of a theory of distributive justice that would be necessary to determine which inequalities warrant major redistributive efforts. If there are social inequalities that should be addressed, however, the academy is a likely place to look for programs that expand opportunities for the disadvantaged. These programs most likely will be outcome directed, insofar as they are aimed at improving opportunities in society more generally. After the *Croson* decision, however, state universities developing redistributive programs will need to meet the test of strict scrutiny. They will not be able to do so with the aim of remedying historical discrimination. Thus their programs either must avoid race as a criterion (substituting disadvantage, for example) or must aim narrowly at educational diversity. A program setting aside graduate fellowships for African American graduate students in order to increase their numbers would likely fail constitutional scrutiny. The imaginative compromise proposed in this volume by Lawrence Becker would also likely fail constitutional scrutiny, if undertaken unilaterally by a state university. Although I shall not develop the argument here, I think that more far-reaching programs are morally justifiable than can pass current constitutional standards, especially in light of the situation of male African Americans in higher education.

OBJECTIONS TO AFFIRMATIVE ACTION

In assessing arguments against affirmative action, it is important to be clear about the justification and form of affirmative action that are the subject of the objection. For example, the objection that affirmative action is unjustified because it benefits nonvictims and leaves other victims unbenefited is directed against the argument that affirmative action compensates those who have been wronged by discrimination.[59] This objection is irrelevant when affirmative action is being defended as a means of correcting currently unjust practices or as a redistributive measure. In the discussion to follow, I focus on the three most powerful objections to process-directed affirmation justified as a corrective for process-based discrimination: that the method chosen will introduce other problematic consequences, that it fails to give people what they deserve, and that it disappoints legitimate expectations.

Problematic Consequences of Affirmative Action

The concern that affirmative action remedies will backfire has been much voiced of late. Thomas Sowell is a major exponent of this view; his empirical claims are that affirmative action generally benefits the privileged among the targeted group and that it becomes a self-perpetuating source of preference.[60] These claims are clearly telling against affirmative action as compensation. If well grounded, they also question the efficacy or fairness of corrective or redistributive methods. Sowell's data are drawn largely from third world countries, in which he reports that preferential politics have been a means for excluded groups to assume a share of the social product. It is unclear how generalizable they are to the United States. When Sowell refers specifically to policies in the United States, he overdescribes what was legally required in the United States even before *Wards Cove*. He presents no examples of the entrenchment of African American privilege in the United States.[61] Thus at this point Sowell does not establish an empirical case against affirmative action in the United States.

Suppose instead that we take Sowell's argument as a hypothesis about what is likely to happen when affirmative action is used frequently to correct process-based discrimination. The supposition would then be that affirmative action becomes a continuing source of entrenched privilege. This supposition works quite differently for process-directed and outcome-directed methods of affirmative action. Affirmative action that corrects a discriminatory practice by replacing it with a nondiscriminatory one does not introduce or entrench privilege. It displaces existing privilege. Open advertising of positions, for example, has displaced privileged access to information about jobs. Sowell's supposition is more plausible against the use of outcome-directed affirmative action. Is the use of outcome targets to correct discriminatory practices likely to entrench privileges uncontrollably? One reply is that targets are self-limiting as well as outcome-forcing. Indeed, proponents of affirmative action point out that because targets are self-limiting, they focus attention on achievement of the target rather than on correction of the underlying injustice. Once the target has been attained, minority or women candidates drop from consideration once again. These concerns underline the importance of connecting targets to the process-based discrimination at issue and of understanding what counts as a successful correction. But it remains an empirical issue whether carefully drawn targets will have worse effects than letting a discriminatory practice continue. The judgments here must be comparative. On the one side is a practice that has been shown to be discriminatory and incorrigible. So, continuing the practice is almost certainly to allow discrimination to continue. On the other side are the risks of targets, which can be minimized if targets are focused on correcting the discriminatory practice. My own view is that the risks of continuing discrimination are greater, although I recognize that the data are inconclusive.[62]

Shelby Steele raises a different concern about the efficacy of affirmative action: that it will lead people to believe that the appointment or admission of any woman or minority candidate is tainted by unjustified favoritism in the evaluation of credentials.[63] Affirmative action, then, will not work as a corrective but instead will entrench unjust stereotypes. Steele favors affirmative action that replaces a discriminatory process with a nondiscriminatory one, despite the recognition that proponents of the old process may be (unjustifiably) suspicious of the results of the new. Steele's concern is the ironic possibility that outcome targets, by generating legitimate doubts about successful candidates, will compromise efforts to correct discriminatory processes. The doubts arise if targets dilute qualifications. Steele points to a real dilemma here. On the one hand, targets may be the only way to attack a process that repeatedly devalues the qualifications of women and minorities. Employment goals may force faculty to act in spite of bias, to see new qualifications as relevant, or to devote renewed scrutiny to candidates. On the other hand, faculty faced with outcome targets may feel forced to "bend" qualifications and react with resentment. In some cases, but not all, these judgments will be correct. There are risks on both sides, and the inquiry must be comparative. The risks of targets can be minimized if they are focused and responsive to issues about qualifications, for example by allowing a department to demonstrate that it could not find suitable candidates. There is also safety in numbers; as percentages of minority and women faculty increase, it will be more difficult to discount the qualifications of particular faculty members, and they will find ready sources of support. Here, however, the difference between the success rates of women and African American males may be especially important. At least in the social sciences and humanities, women have entered departments in significant numbers; African American males have not, and they remain far more vulnerable to the doubting Steele portrays. On the other side, if discriminatory practices are allowed to continue, it will also be difficult to minimize risks. If aggressive steps are not taken to intervene in a recalcitrant discriminatory process, the process is unlikely to change. Participants in the process will continue to discount the qualifications of minority and women applicants.[64] There will be no safety in numbers to counteract this devaluation. Targets are a convenient excuse for devaluation, but any final assessment of Steele's argument must not ignore the extent to which minority and woman candidates are devalued in any event in contexts of persistent discrimination. My own speculation here is that in most circumstances the risks of allowing recalcitrant discrimination to continue are more severe, but the underlying issue is an empirical one, and generalizations may be unwise.

Desert

Other objections to affirmative action focus on what happens to those who lose out when the policy is implemented. By hypothesis, affirmative action does make changes if it is successful. Some affirmative action strategies create identifiable, singular losers: those who without affirmative action would have received the job or the admission at issue. Other strategies create diffuse losers: taxpayers or students who bear the costs of a new faculty position. All of these people are in some sense harmed by affirmative action. As an objection to affirmative action, however, the issue is whether they are harmed or wronged in such a way as to override the argument for affirmative action. One basis for saying that they are is that they are denied their just deserts.

Allan Bakke is often cited as a clear example of a deserving, singular loser resulting from affirmative action.[65] Described somewhat abstractly, Bakke had these characteristics. He worked hard, earned good grades and test scores, and on these measures fell above the minority set-aside pool. There have been many apparent Bakke-like figures applying for academic jobs within the past twenty years: white males who have worked hard and done well in Ph.D. programs, but who claim to have lost out on job opportunities that have been awarded to affirmative action candidates. It is difficult to know what really happened in many of these cases. Are any of them genuine Bakke-type losers? Or are they disappointed applicants looking for ways to salvage pride? Or did departments try to disappoint them gently by telling them with less than complete candor that they really were the preferred candidate but affirmative action got in the way? In the discussion that follows, I will consider only the possible desert claims of the genuine Bakke-type losers.

claim to have lost out on job opportunities that have been awarded to affirmative action candidates. It is difficult to know what really happened in many of these cases. Are any of them genuine Bakke-type losers? Or are they disappointed applicants looking for ways to salvage pride? Or did departments try to disappoint them gently by telling them with less than complete candor that they really were the preferred candidate but affirmative action got in the way? In the discussion that follows, I will consider only the possible desert claims of the genuine Bakke-type losers.

There are several different ways in which to understand these desert claims. One approach to understanding why traditional measures are thought to be bases for desert[66] is in terms of what they reveal about the individual. Grades and letters of recommendation, it may be argued, have been earned; they reveal effort on the part of the individual who achieved them. In fact, however, performance on these measures is at best partially earned. Grades are influenced by many factors beyond effort, principally background opportunities and ability. Letters of recommendation may be influenced by the quality of work, but also by background similarities between the letter writer and the applicant. (It is not easy for women or African Americans to find mentors.) Moreover, effort alone is not sufficient to explain why traditional indicators should matter uniquely in university decisions. Applicants put effort into many different enterprises: teaching during graduate school, community service, raising children, or supporting a family. A higher percentage of female than male graduate students, for example, is self-supporting, and this gap has been growing.[67] If pure effort alone is what matters, these factors too should be given weight in decisions about academic appointments. Effort may be part of an account of what can be a desert basis in academic decision making, but more is needed.

A more promising approach to understanding why traditional measures are thought to be the basis for desert is to look at what they are being used as selection criteria *for:* academic jobs in the discussion here. George Sher's recent study of desert is the most comprehensive discussion of this issue.[68] Sher explores several ways in which we might make connections based on desert between selection criteria and the underlying enterprise. Sher's basic view is that desert claims have an expressive function: they convey information about the merit of the person pronounced deserving. To deviate from publicly known conventions specifying performance criteria is to be untruthful. Where there are no public, conventionally understood criteria, however, Sher recognizes that this argument from truthfulness ceases to apply. Sher believes that the argument from desert for academic appointments does go beyond the argument from truthfulness.[69] Sher does not make clear whether he reaches this conclusion because he believes that there are no publicly known conventions governing criteria for academic appointments, and so the argument from truthfulness ceases to apply, or because he thinks that additional desert considerations support the traditional academic standards. Because affirmative action challenges the traditional standards, it seems unwise to premise an argument from desert on public acceptance of these standards. So I follow Sher in exploring other arguments for whether traditional measures are desert bases for academic appointments.

Sher argues for the traditional criteria by drawing internal connections between the criteria and the purposes of the positions at issue. His example is student admissions. Because the purpose of being a student is to learn, Sher reasons, universities have reason to admit those students who are best able to learn. But are such students owed admission? Sher contends that they are, because by concentrating on people's abilities to perform, we treat them as persons who matter. We affirm their ability "to make a difference in the world" and their "involvement in the wider life of the community."[70] But Sher's argument here rests on controversial assumptions. Are traditional measures the best ways to gauge abilities to learn? What kinds of learning matter in a university? Is traditional scholarship even the central purpose of a contemporary university? This point emerges even more forcefully when Sher's argument is applied to academic appointments rather than student admissions. What are the purposes for which faculty are selected? Suppose we say that faculty should be capable of enhancing learning at the highest level. Does this mean a focus on research, teaching, or both? Does it mean research in fields as traditionally defined, or in newer fields such as feminist theory, critical legal studies, or international political economy? Does it mean graduate teaching, undergraduate teaching, or teaching nontraditional students? Different abilities are relevant to these different purposes. Race or sex may be closely linked with these abilities; forcing departments to take race or sex into account may be the only means we have to open up consideration of these abilities. Recognizing the value choices involved, and making them in one way or another, does not discount candidates as those whose abilities matter in the world. Rather, it recognizes that different abilities may matter for different purposes, even within the university, and that candidates with these different abilities may be similarly deserving.

Thus Sher does not convincingly show that affirmative action fails to give traditionally qualified applicants what they deserve. Effort is not determinative of the case for traditional selection criteria. Traditional criteria may be poor measures of skills or may be based on controversial views about the purposes of a university. Applicants deserve to be judged exclusively by traditional measures only if they are the sole criteria that are relevant. But other criteria may be relevant if we view the university as multifaceted or if we think that corrective measures are sometimes justified.

Expectations

In my judgment, desert is not the best explanation for the moral sympathy that many people feel for traditionally qualified applicants such as Allan Bakke who lose out under affirmative action programs. A better explanation is the belief that these applicants lose out on what they had good reason to expect, what they had counted on. The rules of the game have been changed on them. Their legitimate expectations have been disappointed. In the late 1960s, for example, when many white males entered graduate school, academic appointments were made in the traditional way. Graduate students knew how these decisions were made and positioned themselves accordingly. But by the mid-1970s, the process of finding academic jobs had changed radically. Not all severe disappointments are morally problematic, however. A full understanding of why disappointments have moral significance requires a moral theory of legitimate expectations—of when expectations have moral force in their own right and how much moral force they have. Does it matter morally that many would-be academics did not get jobs because universities ceased to expand in the ways that had been predicted? Are disappointments morally significant in a different way if they can be traced to affirmative action? I can describe only briefly some features of expectations that are relevant to whether they matter morally and show how they might relate to disappointments under affirmative action.

A limited view about expectations is that they matter morally when they are based on moral or legal rights. This view will not be very helpful to disappointed applicants such as Allan Bakke. Whether they have legitimate expectations based in law will rest on how we understand and craft the law.[71] As described above, affirmative action remains legally permissible in some circumstances today. We could widen the range of permissible affirmative action, prospectively if necessary to respect currently entrenched legal rights.

With respect to moral rights, I have already argued that desert claims do not establish rights of traditionally qualified applicants to be judged by the traditional criteria. Another possibility is that traditionally qualified applicants have rights based on promises made by academic institutions about how decisions will be made. Academic institutions do publish accounts of how they make their admissions decisions, for example, in official catalogues. But they do not promise that these criteria will remain unchanged. They also advertise descriptions of available jobs. There is an argument to be made from expectations that job descriptions should not be advertised in a misleading way. For example, candidates should not be encouraged to believe that affirmative action is irrelevant when it will be a significant factor in an appointment decision. But a single job advertisement cannot be construed as binding the institution for the future. The expectations of traditionally qualified applicants, therefore, cannot be said to be legitimate because they are based on promises by the academy to continue announced traditional standards.

Nonetheless, there are other features of the expectations of traditionally qualified applicants that might seem to give them some moral force. Their expectations are reasonable, insofar as they are founded on well-known practices that seem likely to continue. They are indirectly encouraged by the institutions, which publish announcements year after year in the effort to lure applicants for academic positions. Expectations are also encouraged by the ways universities continue to structure their graduate programs, in terms of traditional fields of inquiry and informal mentoring arrangements. Applicants have invested a great deal in the pursuit of these expectations. To the extent that expectations matter morally when they are reasonable, encouraged, and central to the lives of those who have them, the expectations of traditionally qualified applicants fit this model.

In the final analysis, this argument from expectations seems to me to account for the moral sympathy many feel for those who lose out under affirmative action. Ironically, while most of the attention has focused on admissions decisions, the moral argument from expectations seems to me to be somewhat stronger in the case of academic appointments. Disappointed seekers of academic jobs probably have a great deal more at stake than disappointed students. To the extent that students are mobile and there are many different programs, a rejection by one program is most likely to mean the need to attend a different, perhaps slightly less prestigious program. But at least in years when there are very few academic jobs, the loss of a job may well mean the loss of a chance to enjoy one's chosen profession, and this after many years of preparation. On the other hand, to the extent that traditional criteria have been more clearly articulated for admissions decisions than for appointments, arguably the former expectations are more reasonable.

As just described, the argument from expectations rests not on legal or moral rights, but on the ways in which affirmative action may disrupt peoples' lives. I think these concerns are important, but not morally important enough to override the need to correct persistent injustices in how decisions are made. They are concerns based in sympathy rather than in justice. On the other hand, the moral pull of expectations may provide us with reason to design affirmative action programs very carefully and to accommodate them to minimizing the disappointment of expectations where possible. For example, it is preferable to use process-directed rather than outcome-directed methods wherever possible to end discrimination. It is also preferable where possible to utilize means that spread costs diffusely rather than imposing significant disappointments on particular individuals—for example, to add new academic positions rather than to reserve an already-shrunken set of academic opportunities for a particular group. Although this comment is speculative, these accommodationist strategies may also be less likely to cause people to resent and discount those who are successful under affirmative action programs.

CONCLUSION

My principal aim in this essay has been to argue that affirmative action is justified as a corrective for discriminatory processes. I have sought to establish this claim for both process-directed and outcome-directed affirmative action when necessary to correct continuing discrimination. Affirmative action has been successful in bringing many more women into faculty positions in some fields but has been less successful in others. The situation of African Americans in higher education remains precarious. There is thus need for continued scrutiny of decision-making processes at all levels in higher education, from selecting students to making tenure decisions. There is, in short, a great deal of continued scope for affirmative action as a corrective policy, without reaching the issue of whether affirmative action can be defended as a form of preferential selection. I have also suggested lines along which affirmative action might be justified as a redistributive policy. My overall strategy has been to understand what kinds of affirmative action are being defended, and on what grounds. I have also tried to show that the most telling argument against affirmative action understood as a corrective—that it is likely to disappoint reasonable, encouraged, and important expectations—at best suggests accommodationist strategies. If I am right, the current legal retrenchment against affirmative action is profoundly disturbing. *Wards Cove* makes it nearly impossible for plaintiffs to identify and prove some kinds of process-based discrimination when there is a moral argument for correction. *Croson* makes it very difficult for state universities to defend any kind of redistributive affirmative action. The legal insistence on the careful design of affirmative action programs, by contrast, is more reasonable. The criteria set forth by the Court in the *Weber* decision—that affirmative action programs should be designed to break down discriminatory practices, should be a benchmark for gauging progress in ending discrimination, should have an understood stopping point as discrimination is brought to an end, and should not unnecessarily disadvantage others—are reasonable guidelines for both correcting discrimination and accommodating the expectations of others. Lawrence Becker's proposal, set forth later in this volume, is a thoughtful suggestion about how these guidelines can be met.

NOTES

1. National Center for Education Statistics, *Survey Report: Faculty in Higher Education Institutions, 1988* (Washington, D.C.: United States Department of Education, Office of Educational Research and Improvement, 1990), p. 5.

2. Ibid., p. 6.

3. This hypothesis must remain speculative. Disciplines vary widely in the extent to which they track gender and minority status of new appointments. For example, the American Philosophical Association does not track the sex or race of new appointments in philosophy.

4. Betty M. Vetter, ed., *Professional Women and Minorities: A Manpower Data Resource Service*, 8th ed. (Washington, D.C.: Commission on Professionals in Science and Technology, 1989), p. 83.

5. For the past five years, the actual percentages of new appointments in law teaching who were women were as follows: 1985–86, 38 percent (data may include some part-time appointments); 1986–87, 34 percent; 1987–88, 33 percent; 1988–89, 35 percent; 1989–90, 43 percent. Data source: Association of American Law Schools.

6. Sheilah Mann, "Finding Jobs: Placement of Political Scientists, 1988," *PS: Political Science and Politics* 23 (1990): 495–99.

7. Vetter, *Professional Women and Minorities*, p. 142.

8. Ibid., p. 133.

9. Ibid., p. 126.

10. According to data supplied by the American Mathematical Society and the Mathematical Association of America, the exact percentages of women were as follows: 1986–87, total academic placement 17.7 percent, Group I placement 7.1 percent, undergraduate placement 21.8 percent; 1987–88, total academic 12.3 percent, Group I 12.3 percent, undergraduate 19.5 percent; 1988–89, total academic 22.4 percent, Group I 9 percent, undergraduate 28.2 percent; 1989–90, total academic 19.3 percent, Group I 11.9 percent, undergraduate 21.4 percent. Group I institutions include the thirty-nine top-ranked Ph.D. programs in mathematics. In 1989–90, 22 percent of the mathematics doctorates awarded in the United States went to women.

11. Data supplied by the Association of American Law Schools.

12. Denise K. Magner, "Decline in Doctorates Earned by Black and White Men Persists, Study Finds; Foreign Students and U.S. Women Fill Gaps," *Chronicle of Higher Education*, March 1, 1989, p. A11, col. 2.

13. American Council on Education, *Minorities in Higher Education, 8th Annual Status Report* (Washington, D.C.: American Council on Education, 1989), p. 10.

14. For a challenge to the practice of interviewing at conventions, see Constance B. Bouchard, "Opinion: The System of Using Scholarly Meetings to Interview Candidates for Faculty Jobs Is Fundamentally Unfair," *Chronicle of Higher Education*, July 25, 1990, p. B1, col. 2.

15. In his contribution to this volume, Robert Simon takes preferential treatment to be the central issue. We disagree on this point, I suspect in part because I would view as justified correctives many policies that he would classify as preferential. For example, I would regard as corrective the decision to force a department to take race or sex into account because unexplained, persistently disappointing failures to appoint women or minorities suggest hidden bias in the appointments process. Part of what I shall argue is that the need for correction explains why some groups—women or African Americans, for example—are appropriate targets for affirmative action, while other groups—Asian Americans, under most circumstances—are not.

16. 42 U.S.C. § 2000e-2(a).

17. 42 U.S.C. § 2000e(b).

18. 42 U.S.C. § 2000e-2(e), (h).

19. 42 U.S.C. § 2000e-2(e)(2).

20. 42 U.S.C. § 2000e-2 (j). It is important to understand that Title VII does not require, and never has required, statistically balanced work forces. Until quite recently statistical disparities that are unusual in comparison to the relevant hiring pool have been taken to raise a rebuttable inference of discrimination, but that is quite different from equating discrimination with the statistical disparities themselves. Thomas Sowell's recent criticism of pref-

erential politics repeatedly blurs this distinction. Thomas Sowell, *Preferential Policies* (New York: William Morrow & Co., 1990), especially ch. 5.

21. Probably the best summaries of Title VII law are Barbara Schlei and Paul Grossman, *Employment Discrimination Law*, 2d ed. (Washington, D.C.: Bureau of National Affairs, 1983) and idem, *Employment Discrimination Law, Five Year Cumulative Supplement* (Washington, D.C.: Bureau of National Affairs, 1989).

22. *Griggs v. Duke Power Co.*, 401 U.S. 424 (1971).

23. For example, see *Texas Department of Community Affairs v. Burdine*, 450 U.S. 248 (1981); *Kunda v. Muhlenberg College*, 621 F.2d 532, 541 (3d Cir. 1980). An additional complication is posed when the employer has "mixed motives" for the decision—for example, when in a highly subjective professional context both biased and legitimate reasons played a role in employer decision making. (An academic example would be a tenure decision influenced partially by sexual stereotyping and partially by judgments about the research competence of the candidate.) In such contexts, the employee still bears the burden of proving that discrimination played a role in the decision making; the employer may then avoid liability by taking the additional step of proving by a preponderance of the evidence that it would have made the same decision even if it had not taken the discriminatory reason into account. *Price Waterhouse v. Hopkins*, 490 U.S. —, 104 L.Ed. 268 (1989). Because of the highly subjective nature of decisions regarding academic appointments and promotions, however, courts often give great deference to universities' judgments about professional qualifications. For example, see *Brown v. Trustees of Boston University*, 891 F.2d 335, 346 (1st Cir. 1990); *Zahorik v. Cornell University*, 729 F.2d 85, 92 (2d Cir. 1984).

24. For example, see *Hazelwood School District v. United States*, 433 U.S. 299 (1977). Although the disparate impact theory originally was developed for analyzing objective employment criteria such as standardized tests or high school diplomas, it has been extended to subjective processes such as promotion by supervisors or academic appointments decisions. *Watson v. Fort Worth Bank and Trust*, 487 U.S. 977 (1988).

25. *Watson v. Fort Worth Bank and Trust* at 1002 (Blackmun, J., concurring in part and concurring in the judgment).

26. Ibid. at 997.

27. *Wards Cove Packing Co. v. Atonio*, 109 S.Ct. 2115 (1989). The employers in this case, salmon canneries open only during the summer, had variable hiring needs. They maintained two classifications of employees, unskilled cannery jobs on the line and skilled noncannery jobs of a wide variety. The two classes of employees lived and ate separately, enjoyed noticeably different living amenities, and confronted markedly different wage scales. The plaintiffs, nonwhites in cannery jobs, alleged that many of the company's employment processes were discriminatory: nepotism, rehire preferences, the failure

to post noncannery jobs, the lack of objective hiring criteria, the maintenance of separate hiring channels, the practice of not promoting from within, and segregated living facilities. The statistical disparities within the work force were clear: most cannery jobs were filled by nonwhites, and most noncannery jobs were filled by whites. The minority employees claimed that the employer's means of contacting and hiring employees had given rise to the disparities.

28. 42 U.S.C.A. § 2000e-5(g) (1981). The phrase may have originated in President Kennedy's executive order directing equal opportunity for government contracts (Executive Order no. 10,925, 26 Fed. Reg. 1977, March 6, 1961). Although there had been earlier efforts to encourage nondiscrimination in government contracts, this order was the first to contain any enforcement mechanisms. United States Equal Employment Opportunity Commission, *Legislative History of Titles VII and IX of the Civil Rights Act of 1964* (Washington, D.C.: Government Printing Office, 1968), pp. 3–4.

29. For example, see *Griggs v. Duke Power Co.*, 401 U.S. 424 (1971). *Griggs* was the seminal case developing the "disparate impact" theory of Title VII violations.

30. For example, see *Bailey v. Ryan Stevedoring Co.*, 613 F.2d 588 (5th Cir. 1980), cert. denied, 450 U.S. 964 (1981).

31. For example, see *United States v. Sheet Metal Workers*, Local 36, 416 F.2d 123 (8th Cir. 1969).

32. See *Local 28, Sheet Metal Workers' International Association v. EEOC*, 478 U.S. 421 (1986).

33. For example, see *Thompson v. Sawyer*, 678 F.2d 257 (D.C. Cir. 1982), later proceeding sub nom. *Thompson v. Kennickell*, 797 F.2d 1015 (D.C. Cir. 1986), cert. denied, 480 U.S. 905 (1987).

34. *Local 28, Sheet Metal Workers' International Association v. EEOC*, 478 U.S. 421 (1986).

35. *United Steelworkers of America v. Weber*, 443 U.S. 193 (1979). Weber's employer, Kaiser Aluminum, had traditionally filled craft positions from segregated union training programs. Against this background, in cooperation with the union, Kaiser established a new training program that would include at least 50 percent blacks while otherwise basing admission on seniority. The Court has reaffirmed the *Weber* decision as recently as 1987. *Johnson v. Transportation Agency*, 107 S.Ct. 1442 (1987).

36. *Regents of the University of California v. Bakke*, 438 U.S. 265 (1978).

37. *City of Richmond v. J. A. Croson Co.*, 57 U.S.L.W. 4132 (1989). Richmond, Virginia, had sought to defend its set-aside program for minority contractors on the grounds of widespread statistical disparities between the numbers of minority contractors and the percentages of minorities in society as a whole. Only specific findings of its own discrimination or of discrimination in the

construction industry in Richmond would suffice to justify affirmative action methods directed specifically to correct the identified discrimination.

38. Ibid. at 4139.

39. Because *Croson* left open the possibility that Congress has wider constitutional latitude than state governments in identifying and eradicating discrimination, the *Croson* standards should not automatically be read into Title VII.

40. For the distinction between process- and outcome-based social policies, see, for example, David L. Kirp, Mark G. Yudof, and Marlene Strong Franks, *Gender Justice* (Chicago: University of Chicago Press, 1986), p. 11.

41. *Zahorik v. Cornell University*, 729 F.2d 85 (2d Cir. 1984).

42. For an example of disagreement about standards for service, see *Roebuck v. Drexel University*, 852 F.2d 715 (3d Cir. 1988). Drexel's tenure regulations required consideration of the candidate's "record of performance in . . . University, collegial, and departmental service, and community service relevant to the mission of the institution." Roebuck contended that his extensive service in the black community of West Philadelphia warranted an "excellent" rating for service. His department chair rated his service as "satisfactory," because he questioned whether the service to the black community was relevant to the mission of Drexel.

43. For example, see D. Kierstead, P. D'Agostin, and H. Dill, "Sex Role Stereotyping of College Professors: Bias in Students' Ratings of Instructors," *Journal of Educational Psychology* 80 (1988): 342–44. Typical forms of bias include competence grades for women faculty that correlate with stereotypes about gender-appropriate behavior; ratings based on the expectation that women faculty be nurturant; and negative correlations for women faculty, but not for male faculty, between the perceived difficulty of grading and overall rating of teaching effectiveness.

44. For example, see *Bennun v. Rutgers*, 737 F.Supp. 1393 (D.N.J. 1990).

45. For example, see *Brown v. Trustees of Boston University*, 891 F.2d 337 (1st Cir. 1990).

46. These figures are somewhat shorter for Ph.D.s in the sciences (engineering, 5.8 years of registered study; physical sciences, 6.0 years; life sciences, 6.5 years), longer for Ph.D.s in the social sciences (7.2 years of registered study), and longest in the humanities (8.4 years of registered study). But even in the sciences the periods of registered study are longer than in law (3 years) or medicine (4 years). Theodore Ziolkowski, "The Ph.D. Squid," *American Scholar* 59 (1990): 177–95.

47. These four features of a compensatory argument—identified victim, wrong, compensation, and compensator—are also singled out in Alan Goldman's extensive discussion of compensatory arguments for preferential policies. However, Goldman limits the paradigm case of deserved compensation

to rights violations and restoration of victims to the positions they would have held without the violations. Alan H. Goldman, *Discrimination and Reverse Discrimination* (Princeton: Princeton University Press, 1979), p. 67. I do not wish to limit the general statement of the compensatory argument to a particular political theory about when compensation is owed.

48. Alan Goldman, *Justice and Reverse Discrimination* (Princeton: Princeton University Press, 1979), p. 76.

49. For example, see Owen Fiss, "Groups and the Equal Protection Clause," *Philosophy and Public Affairs* 5 (1976): 107–77.

50. This point is made by Shelby Steele, *The Content of Our Character: A New Vision of Race in America* (New York: St. Martin's Press, 1990), p. 119: "It is impossible to repay blacks living today for the historic suffering of the race. If all blacks were given a million dollars tomorrow morning it would not amount to a dime on the dollar of three centuries of oppression, nor would it obviate the residues of that oppression that we still carry today."

51. See, for example, Owen Fiss, "Foreword: The Forms of Justice," *Harvard Law Review* 93 (1979): 1–58.

52. Given the decentralization of academic appointments, universities are unlikely to be able to arrange alternative positions for candidates who lose out to an affirmative action program. Probably some "retraining" did occur, as disappointed Ph.D.s fled to law schools. Little was done, however, to explore underwriting some of these retraining costs to offset the burdens of affirmative action.

53. Rawls allocates issues about justice under conditions of partial injustice to "partial compliance theory." See John Rawls, *A Theory of Justice* (Cambridge: Harvard University Press, 1971), p. 246.

54. For a discussion of affirmative action as a corrective, that includes evidence of continuing discrimination in the mid-1970s, see Tom L. Beauchamp, "The Justification of Reverse Discrimination," in W. T. Blackstone and Robert Heslep, eds., *Social Justice and Preferential Treatment* (Athens: University of Georgia Press, 1976).

55. Brief for the American Society for Personnel Administration as Amicus Curiae Supporting Petitioners, *Wards Cove Packing Co. v. Atonio,* 109 S.Ct. 2115 (1989) (no. 87-1387).

56. Mann, "Finding Jobs," p. 498.

57. See, for example, Alan H. Goldman, "Diversity within University Faculties," in Steven M. Cahn, ed., *Morality, Responsibility, and the University: Studies in Academic Ethics* (Philadelphia: Temple University Press, 1990).

58. See, for example, Mary Field Belenky, Blythe McVicker Clinchy, Nancy Rule Goldberger, and Jill Mattuck Tarule, *Women's Ways of Knowing: The Development of Self, Voice, and Mind* (New York: Basic Books, 1986); Carol Gilligan, *In a Different Voice: Psychological Theory and Women's Development* (Cambridge: Harvard University Press, 1982).

59. See, e.g., Sidney Hook, *Philosophy and Public Policy*, p. 139 (Carbondale and Edwardsville: Southern Illinois University Press, 1980).

60. Thomas Sowell, *Preferential Policies* (New York: William Morrow & Co., 1990).

61. Could he have given any examples? Are there any examples? Perhaps the *Croson* situation comes close. When it adopted the set-aside program for minority subcontractors, the Richmond city council was controlled by an African American majority. But the program did not pass strict scrutiny in the eyes of the Supreme Court and quite likely would not have passed even less exacting scrutiny. *City of Richmond v. J. A. Croson Co.*, 57 U.S.L.W. 4142 (1989). In the United States, there are legal checks on the entrenchment of privilege. Even those who argue that the strict scrutiny standard is too strong when applied to affirmative action do not dispute the importance of equal protection review.

62. Sowell may also think that continuing discrimination is less important than any new discrimination that might be introduced by targets. If so, he is resting his objection to targets on other normative grounds that need to be articulated and defended. I explore some of the normative objections to targets in the remainder of this essay.

63. Steele, *The Content of Our Character*, especially pp. 111–25. See also Don Wycliff, "Blacks Debate the Costs of Affirmative Action," *New York Times*, June 10, 1990, p. E3, col. 1.

64. In his contribution to this volume, Robert Simon suggests we can rely on appeals processes to correct unjust stereotyping within an appointments process. But this ignores the very real ways in which appeals processes victimize the complainant, who becomes an identified troublemaker at the least.

65. For a full description of Bakke's situation, see *Regents of the University of California v. Bakke*, 438 U.S. 265 (1978).

66. The term "desert basis," used to refer to the kind of characteristic of an individual that can be the basis for a desert claim, derives from Joel Feinberg's wonderful discussion of the concept of desert. Joel Feinberg, "Justice and Personal Desert," in Feinberg, *Doing and Deserving* (Princeton: Princeton University Press, 1970), pp. 55–94.

67. Vetter, *Professional Women and Minorities*, p. 53.

68. George Sher, *Desert* (Princeton: Princeton University Press, 1987), especially pp. 109–28.

69. Ibid., p. 119.

70. Ibid., p. 121.

71. For an excellent discussion of legitimate expectations as expectations that are legally supported, see Stephen Munzer, *A Theory of Property* (Cambridge: Cambridge University Press, 1990). Part of Munzer's view is that we need a complex account of what rights are entrenched in law in order to understand when expectations based on law are legitimate.

Affirmative Action and the University: Faculty Appointment and Preferential Treatment

2

Robert L. Simon

"Each person to count for one; no one to count for more than one." This formula has long been regarded as expressing the heart of egalitarianism. But while many may agree superficially on the words of the abstract formula, they often disagree vehemently about how it is best to be applied. One such disagreement, a disagreement which cuts to the heart of our society's commitment to equality and social justice, is raised by the cluster of policies commonly grouped together under the heading of "affirmative action."

Affirmative action, in its many forms, is in large part a response to the long, cruel, and shameful history of racial discrimination in the United States and particularly to the plight of black Americans. To many, it is an appropriate response to the injustices of the past. To its supporters, it is morally permissible (and perhaps morally required) to take account of such factors as the race and sex of applicants in order to remedy the effects of past injustice. To its critics, affirmative action raises issues of reverse discrimination against white males. It has been particularly controversial on college and university campuses, whose students and faculty often have strong commitments to egalitarian conceptions of social justice, but where the principle of making faculty appointments according to allegedly meritocratic academic criteria also is widely supported.

The debate over affirmative action, particularly those forms that involve preferential treatment by race and sex, has inspired thoughtful theoretical analysis and sometimes bitter controversy. It is highly unlikely that yet another article on the subject will resolve the issues generated by this debate. In fact, my own attitudes toward preferential treatment are ambivalent. Nevertheless, I still believe that in spite of the major defenses of preferential treatment which have been developed in the last fifteen years, major problems remain. These problems seem to me to be especially acute in an academic context, where preferential appointment of college and university faculty is at issue. In fact, some of the arguments used to justify preferential appointment in an academic context, including arguments from "diversity" and "pluralism," have received relatively little attention in the philosophical literature. While some versions of these arguments may have force, I believe they face serious objections as well.

My goal in this essay, then, is not to offer a solution to the debate over affirmative action. Rather, my major goal here is to point out what I see as major difficulties with preferential appointment of faculty in an academic context. The extent, if any, to which these difficulties call for modification, or even abandonment, of different forms of affirmative action, can then be the subject of further inquiry both in the concluding section of this paper and by other contributors to the collection. Throughout this chapter, but particularly in the concluding section, I will suggest possible areas of compromise between advocates and critics of preferential treatment, point out standards that might be used in adjudicating their disputes, and, in conclusion, consider briefly what can be said in favor of "neutral" policies that do not involve preference by race, sex, or ethnicity.

AFFIRMATIVE ACTION, PREFERENCE, AND FACULTY APPOINTMENT

"Affirmative action" is a name that has been applied to a cluster of policies, generated in part by Title VII of the Civil Rights Act of 1964 and especially by a series of executive orders issued by President Lyndon Johnson. Since the label "affirmative action" has been applied to very different sorts of policies, it is important to sort out these differences so that we can be sure how it is used in a given context.

In its least controversial sense, affirmative action refers to positive procedural requirements which employers or admissions officers must meet to ensure that their pool of candidates is representative of some larger body, such as the overall pool of qualified personnel in the region. Such requirements might include open advertising of positions as well as attempts to inform members of groups which are underrepresented in the applicant pool of the opportunities available to them. Let us call this the *procedural* form of affirmative action.

Affirmative action policies of a different sort require employers or admissions officers to make numerical projections specifying the number of members of designated groups who would be appointed under a fair, open, and proper selection procedure. These projections are called goals. Although critics have argued that in fact such goals turn into quotas, the professed intent of this form of affirmative action is not to actually prefer members of designated groups to non-members, but to set up a reasonable numerical projection of what results a proper search would produce.[1] Let us call this the *regulatory* form of affirmative action.

Sometimes, however, affirmative action is thought of as a form of preferential selection, in which candidates from designated groups are favored over nonmembers. This is the *preferential* form of affirmative action, which of course is the most controversial form. It will be the topic of discussion in what follows. Preference can be minimal when it is extended only among otherwise equally qualified candidates, weak when a less qualified candidate is preferred over a more qualified one, and strong when preference is extended to the unqualified over the qualified. To the best of my knowledge, strong forms of preferential selection have not been defended in serious theoretical discussions about public policy, although some critics of affirmative action might argue that strong forms of preferential treatment have sometimes been applied in practice.

Although affirmative action policies of various sorts have been in place for well over ten years, the number of blacks entering the professoriate has been disappointing. Over the last ten years, slightly less than 4 percent of the nation's new Ph.D.s were awarded to blacks, and the recipients have been disproportionately concentrated in a very few disciplines, such as education.[2] Women currently receive slightly over 40 percent of the doctorates awarded to U.S. citizens and have received about 37 percent of those awarded over the last ten years.[3] However, women make up somewhat less than one-third of our full-time faculty, are employed relatively infrequently in mathematics and the sciences, and often tend to be concentrated in lower ranks at many institutions, although significant gains by women in academia have taken place in recent years as once younger cohorts move up the promotion ladder. It also is frequently charged, often with merit, that women are underrepresented in the ranks of the tenured senior faculty in some of the most prestigious research universities. Thus, the debate over affirmative action in academia takes place in a context in which blacks and members of some other racial minorities are found in small numbers, and women, while present in far larger numbers, have made their greatest advances only recently and have even more to make. Accordingly, affirmative action has been seen by many women and minorities as an important policy for opening up college and university faculties and creating equal opportunity in academia.

But should affirmative action in such contexts include preferential treatment? Preferential appointment raises special issues when applied within institutions of higher education. These issues come into sharpest focus where the appointment of faculty is of concern. As we will see, preferential selection of faculty raises special issues that go to the very foundations of the academic enterprise itself.

Of course, preferential appointment of college and university faculty by race or sex also raises some of the same issues that it does elsewhere. For example, if a black or female candidate for a faculty position is preferred over an equally or more qualified white male, is that invidious discrimination in reverse?

However, preference by race or sex also raises special concerns where the appointment of faculty is concerned because many would argue that the criteria for making meritocratic distinctions, particularly scholarship and teaching ability, are relatively noncontroversial and often allow clear distinctions to be made in the qualifications of candidates for faculty positions. Thus, it often is argued that the evaluation of candidates for a faculty position at an academic institution of excellence normally can be expected to yield supportable qualitative differences in the way they are ranked.[4] Some proponents of affirmative action would reply that the standards used in the selection of faculty often are applied in a biased or unfair manner. Still others would claim that the standards themselves are often inherently biased in favor of white males.[5] Thus, the debate over affirmative action in academic contexts raises the important issue of the objectivity of standards of merit and the weight they should be given in appointment decisions.

In addition, many would argue that colleges and universities have a special obligation to select a diverse faculty and student body. Although various arguments can be given for and against such a view, arguments that we will explore in detail later, the main point seems to be that intellectual inquiry is best carried out when significantly different perspectives and outlooks are represented. But is ethnic and gender diversity the kind of diversity that ought to be at issue here, and does preferential appointment actually promote it? What kinds of diversity need to be distinguished, and which should be promoted within the academic enterprise?

Finally, unlike the preferential selection of undergraduates or of candidates to many entry-level positions, the preferential selection of academic faculty imposes especially heavy costs on rejected white males. Since rejected white male candidates for academic positions have invested more in highly specialized preparation for their career and are likely to have fewer alternatives than those at earlier stages of career development, the costs of rejection are higher for them. Therefore, if the imposition of the costs of preferential treatment generally raises issues of distributive justice and fairness, it does so with special force at this level of application.

The discussion that follows will concern the preferential appointment of faculty at colleges and universities. However, while attention will mainly be focused on the issues raised by preferential appointment in academia, the general issue of alleged reverse discrimination should not be avoided. In particular, if the charge of reverse discrimination can be defeated, then while important policy issues concerning preferential appointment still will remain, the principal argument for the claim that preferential appointment is seriously unjust will have been undermined. On the other hand, if the charge of reverse discrimination, or something like it, can be sustained, it is at best unclear if preferential treatment is even permissible as a form of social policy.

The debate about alleged reverse discrimination has been going on for well over a decade. As Lawrence Becker points out in his contribution to this volume, it is unlikely that any new intellectual breakthrough capable of yielding a decisive victory to either side will emerge at this late date. Nevertheless, a brief review of some of the main issues of the debate may be useful for at least two reasons. First, it may remind us that there are points of intellectual merit made on different sides of the controversy. Second, and more important, such a review seems to me to suggest a principle of adjudication which may be acceptable to both critics and defenders of preferential treatment, at least in so far as they acknowledge that their opponents have arguments of significance which must be given due weight.

THE REVERSE DISCRIMINATION CONTROVERSY

The argument that preference based on race or sex is a form of invidious or "reverse" discrimination is quite simple. It states that if past discrimination against blacks, women, and other minorities was wrong, present discrimination in their favor must also be wrong. Both forms are wrong because they are based on the irrelevant properties of race, sex, and ethnicity. These properties are irrelevant because they have nothing to do with one's ability to perform a job or with one's qualities as a human being or moral person. Hence, both forms of discrimination are morally parallel; it simply is unjust to base the distribution of benefits and burdens on the irrelevant properties of race, sex, and ethnicity.

However, proponents of preferential treatment reject this argument as unsound. Thus, writers such as Ronald Dworkin and Thomas Nagel argue that present preferential treatment, unlike past invidious discrimination, does not express prejudice or bias toward a group and is not based on the idea that one group of people is inherently less worthy or has less moral standing than another because of race, sex, or ethnicity. Hence, preferential treatment lacks the crucial element of prejudice toward a group that characterizes past invidious discrimination and so is morally in a different category.

Such a view has been most fully developed by Ronald Dworkin. Dworkin points out, first of all, that no one has a *right* to a specific position, whether it be in the first-year class of a law school or an assistant professorship in a college or university. This is because there is no basic moral right to be treated identically with everyone else— no basic right to what Dworkin calls equal (or identical) treatment. However, there is a fundamental right to be treated as an equal, with respect and consideration equal to that shown to others.

Thus, past invidious discrimination is based on the despicable idea that one race or sex is inherently inferior, while present preferential treatment in favor of members of formerly victimized groups has no such basis. The two, then, are fundamentally different. As Thomas Nagel argues, "Racial and sexual discrimination are based on contempt or even loathing for the excluded group, a feeling that certain contacts with them are degrading to members of the dominant group, that they are fit only for subordinate positions or menial work. . . . Affirmative action involves none of this; it is simply a means of increasing the social and economic strength of formerly victimized groups, and does not stigmatize others."[6] Dworkin makes a similar point when he writes that white males disadvantaged by preferential treatment are "being excluded not by prejudice but because of a rational calculation about the socially most beneficial use of limited resources."[7]

On this view, past discrimination against minorities does violate the right to treatment as an equal, since it is based on prejudice against and contempt for the victimized group. It does not treat everyone with equal respect and concern. Since present preferential treatment neither is based upon a prejudicial attitude nor expresses contempt, but is instead designed to remedy the effects of past discrimination, it is in a morally different category.

Thus, proponents of affirmative action such as Nagel and Dworkin conclude that preferential treatment is to be judged simply as good or bad public policy. Since it does not constitute invidious discrimination in reverse, it does not violate the rights of white males and so cannot be ruled out as inherently unjust and unfair.

To what extent is their view acceptable? They do seem to have pointed out a morally significant difference between many forms of past invidious discrimination and the remedial intent of affirmative action policies. For this reason, it may indeed be a misnomer to refer to preferential forms of affirmative action as "reverse discrimination."

However, this by itself is not sufficient to show either that preferential policies avoid committing other sorts of injustice or that such injustice is not similar in some respects to some forms of invidious discrimination. In particular, not every form of invidious discrimination need be based on prejudice against or contempt and loathing for the victimized group. For example, much discrimination against women was based on the paternalistic idea that women needed special protection against some of the rigors of ordinary life. Other forms of sex discrimination were based on statistical generalizations. For example, in *Frontiero v. Richardson*, the Supreme Court refused to accept the argument of the army that because most women did not have male dependents, female soldiers should have the burden of proof (not required of male soldiers) of proving that males claimed as dependents actually were dependents. Here, the rationale for the difference in treatment was not contempt or prejudice but a concern for administrative efficiency. It was simply easier for the army to assume without proof that women were dependents of men, since in most cases such an assumption would have been true. Since women did not generally have adult male dependents, it seemed reasonable to place the burden of proof upon them when they claimed males as dependents. To cite another kind of example, if a large firm refused to hire members of a minority religious group, not because of contempt for or prejudice against those excluded, but to promote greater harmony and efficiency among workers due to their religious unity, its hiring practices surely would be regarded as discriminatory and unfair nevertheless.

Accordingly, it is doubtful if a practice is discriminatory only if it expresses contempt for or prejudice against an excluded group. At the very least, other sorts of exclusionary practices can be morally suspect in ways related to the way in which the core kinds of discrimination are morally suspect. Is preferential treatment based on race, ethnicity, or sex morally suspect in such a way?

Before turning directly to that question, however, it is important to understand the implications of what Dworkin and Nagel regard as the fundamental element of the right to equality. Dworkin, remember, distinguishes the right to equal or identical treatment, which is not morally fundamental, from the right to treatment as an equal, that is, the right to be treated with equal concern and respect, which is fundamental. Preferential treatment does not violate the latter right because it is not based on prejudice or contempt toward those white males disadvantaged by the policy. "An individual's right to be treated as an equal means that his potential loss must be treated as a matter of concern; but that loss may nevertheless be outweighed by gains to the community as a whole."[8]

So understood, the right to treatment as an equal, which Dworkin and perhaps Nagel regard as fundamental, looks suspiciously like the utilitarian requirement that everyone's welfare be counted the same in computing the costs and benefits of social policy. But unmodified utilitarianism is notorious for allowing the claims of individuals to be overridden by the welfare of the group. A host of writers, including John Rawls, Robert Nozick, and Dworkin himself, have objected that standard forms of utilitarianism do not take individual rights seriously enough. Thus, in a famous passage, Rawls writes that "Each person possesses an inviolability founded on justice that even the welfare of society as a whole cannot override."[9]

Accordingly, if the claim that preferential treatment does not violate the individual rights of disadvantaged white males amounts only to the claim that preferential hiring might be justified on utilitarian grounds, it might well be true. However, it will hardly satisfy those who view individual rights as more than mere entitlements to be counted fairly in the utilitarian calculus of consequences. If our most fundamental right is only the right to be counted without prejudice in the computation of the effects of social policy, it follows that individual interests in principle can always be subordinated to a larger social welfare. Our rights acquire an "accordion-like" quality and no longer can serve as bulwarks against either the state or oppressive majorities, since it is the interests of the state, or of the majority, that determine the extent of our rights.[10]

Perhaps, however, the defense of preferential treatment we are considering need not rest on such an attenuated account of individual rights. Nagel, after all, distinguishes preferential treatment from past invidious discrimination against minorities, not by appeal to utilitarian consequences broadly conceived, but to its specific effects in remedying the situation of previously victimized groups. Dworkin himself sometimes suggests that consequences that justify preferential treatment are of a special sort, namely, increases in the overall social justice of the system.

On this revised view, the fundamental right to treatment as an equal, which requires equal concern and respect for all individuals, would be violated by differences in treatment based on race or sex unless such treatment was itself necessary to treat others with equal respect and concern. Preferential treatment does not violate this right, because it equalizes the position of those who previously have been treated unjustly. It restores the equilibrium required by social justice.

However, this claim, which clearly is more attractive than the utilitarian perspective to those who regard rights as trumps against social welfare, can itself be interpreted in two ways. First, preferential treatment may be defended as a form of compensatory justice for individuals. Second, it may be defended, as Nagel puts it, as "a means of increasing the social and economic strength of formerly victimized groups." Let us briefly consider each interpretation in turn.

Although preferential treatment has sometimes been defended in the philosophical literature as a means of compensating individuals for past injustices committed against them, this compensatory defense also has been the subject of sustained and forceful criticism. Perhaps because the criticisms are telling, the idea of compensation for individuals has not played a prominent role in the major legal defenses of racial preference. Moreover, the general objections to preferential treatment as a form of individualistic compensatory justice are reinforced by special difficulties when attempts are made to apply the argument to appointment in higher education.

The major objections to viewing preferential treatment as a form of compensation for individuals are numerous, but among the most important are the following. First, and perhaps most important, little if any attempt is made to apportion the kind of compensation at issue to the degree of injury suffered. Even if we assume that all members of the groups designated to receive preference have been injured, it is possible and even likely that those who perform best academically and receive the most attractive positions have been injured least. In such cases, those most severely injured would be compensated less than those minimally harmed. Second, individuals who are not members of victimized groups may have been victimized by social injustice, yet receive no compensation. Third, those who pay the costs, the white males who would have gotten the positions if not for preferential treatment, are not necessarily guilty of any wrongdoing. Why should they bear the burden of compensation when other white males pay no cost whatsoever?

Of course, various defenses against these objections have been offered. Proponents of the compensatory defense may admit, for example, that the fit between compensation and degree of victimization is not perfect, but argue on the basis of administrative efficiency that it is convenient to allow group membership to function as a stand-in for degree of past injury. And while it is acknowledged that many young white males may not have been responsible for past discrimination against minorities and women, they are held to be innocent beneficiaries of injustice who are merely being asked to give back unearned benefits that arose from unjust social practices.

Critics have not found such replies convincing. Administrative efficiency has not been accepted as a reason for imposing special burdens on women and minorities as a class, and critics of preferential treatment deny that convenience and efficiency are good enough reasons for disadvantaging anyone else because of race and sex. And while many white males may indeed be innocent beneficiaries of injustice, critics question the fairness of imposing large costs of compensation on arbitrarily selected white males while others bear no burden at all. In addition, critics point to the "underinclusiveness" of preferential treatment. Thus, some white males may themselves be victims rather than innocent beneficiaries of injustice, while some members of preferred groups, such as middle and upper class women, may have benefited far more from past discrimination than some disadvantaged white males and yet are not required to make any compensation at all.

Accordingly, it seems extremely difficult to justify preferential treatment as a form of compensation for individual injury. The case for individual compensatory justice is especially difficult to make, I suggest, in the context of appointment for faculty positions in higher education. The principal reason for this is the especially heavy costs imposed on those disadvantaged by the practice. White males who are candidates for faculty positions may have invested five to ten years in acquiring the specialized training needed to be competitive in the academic job market. Moreover, unlike the situation facing applicants to undergraduate institutions, or even candidates for law and medical schools, who often will have many options open to them, even the best academic job candidates in many fields may find it extremely difficult to secure even one desirable position. Loss of a position seems an unfairly high price to impose, especially when the victim may at most have only minimally benefited from injustice and when other similarly situated white males may have no costs imposed upon them at all, because of the different nature of the competition for jobs for which they have applied.

In addition, consider the situation of the beneficiaries of preferential treatment in higher education. They will be either Ph.D.s or Ph.D. candidates, many from the nation's most prestigious graduate institutions. It is far from clear that all such individuals are best conceived of as victims simply because of group membership, when in fact their situation is advantaged compared to that of a large proportion of the general population. Moreover, some may already have been beneficiaries of preference earlier in their academic careers and so already have been (partially) compensated. Although these considerations may not rule out additional compensation, particularly for black scholars, who in my view have had to overcome especially heavy burdens to get where they are, they do suggest that the requirements of compensatory justice have less weight where faculty appointment is concerned than in other contexts.

Accordingly, preferential appointment of faculty by race or sex seems quite difficult to defend as a form of compensatory justice for individuals. What if it is defended instead as a means of strengthening the position of disadvantaged groups? Proponents of such a view might agree that preferential appointment as so conceived does involve minimal injustice or unfairness to white males harmed by the practice but maintain that such losses are outweighed by the greater overall social justice that preferential appointment promotes.

How one assesses this group defense depends on the assessment of a number of crucial underlying issues. Even if one accepts the basic premise that present unjust treatment of some individuals now is defensible if it leads to a greater degree of just treatment in the future, other questions remain. How probable must the future gains be? Surely, it is questionable that the actual losses of some persons can be outweighed by greater future gains for others if the probability of actually attaining those gains is low. What groups should be the beneficiaries of preferential treatment? Clearly, the strongest case can be made on behalf of blacks, but should Asian-Americans and women also be favored? What about black subgroups, such as those of Jamaican descent, who exceed the national average in terms of income and years of education? What about some white ethnic groups? Of what magnitude must the gains in future justice be to sufficiently outweigh the present losses of those disadvantaged by preferential treatment? In the case of appointing college faculty, if one believes that most individuals who are preferred on grounds of race and sex would have obtained equivalent or nearly equivalent positions elsewhere, the gains may seem minimal. On the other hand, if one believes that minorities and women would be virtually absent from the faculties of the top colleges and universities without preferential treatment, the benefits of the practice may seem overwhelming.

Perhaps most important, to what extent is justice a matter of group rather than individual relations? Moreover, even if principles of justice do apply to groups, how does benefiting a relatively few highly trained members of disadvantaged groups actually benefit the group as such?

Sometimes, the group defense is not presented in terms of promoting overall social justice but rather focuses on narrower but especially significant goals. One version has particular relevance to the debate about preferential treatment in higher education because it concerns the impact of this practice directly upon the educational process itself.

According to this educational defense, preferential treatment can be defended on grounds of its educational utility. On this view, preferential treatment leads to a more diverse educational community, which in turn sharpens intellectual debate and enhances the quality of higher education. In fact, proponents of such an argument may well deny that giving special weight to race and sex in the appointment of college faculty members is "preferential" at all, at least if that term implies that factors other than those relevant to job performance were taken into account. For according to the educational defense, race or sex, if not relevant qualifications themselves, may be at least significant indicators of ability to make a special contribution to the educational enterprise.

The educational defense fits quite nicely with the kind of argument made by Dworkin and Nagel. It implies that when white males are disfavored when in competition with minorities and women, no disrespect is shown to them as persons. Rather, when qualifications are understood to encompass overall ability to contribute to the educational process, to which race and sex are relevant, the most qualified candidates arguably were appointed. This argument will be considered in more depth later.

To summarize, proponents of preferential treatment respond to the charge of reverse discrimination in a variety of ways. They may argue that preferential treatment differs from past invidious discrimination in that it treats all concerned with equal respect and concern (i.e., as equals), while past discriminatory practices treated the victims with prejudice and contempt. They also may argue that preferential treatment is a form of compensatory justice, making up for crimes against individuals in the past, or a means for promoting a more just society in the future. Finally, they may argue in the context of higher education that race and sex are factors that ought to be considered in appointment because of their relevance to enhancing the educational experience of all affected.

In my view, these arguments do go some way toward defusing the charge of reverse discrimination. But how far? As we have seen, the first defense rests on the morally quite thin notion of treatment as equal, which guarantees individuals only the right to be counted without prejudice in the calculation of consequences of policy. Not only does this fail to rule out all forms of discrimination, it does not do justice to our intuitive notions of individual rights, which as Dworkin himself acknowledges, should function as protections for individuals against majoritarian or community interests.

Moreover, even if preferential treatment is not properly characterized as reverse discrimination, it can still be regarded as morally suspect. In part, this is because the arbitrary imposition of costs and burdens on a small subclass of white males seems unfair and unjust. In greater part, it is because the disfavoring of someone because of the immutable properties of race or sex, however well intentioned, seems not easily reconcilable with respecting them as persons. For to disfavor someone on such grounds is to eliminate them from consideration on the basis of qualities they did not choose and either cannot or should not be expected to modify, qualities that, unlike our capacities to reason or choose, are irrelevant to our status as moral persons.[11]

Accordingly, while I do not regard preferential treatment as equivalent to past invidious discrimination and so reject the idea that it is reverse discrimination, I also question the claim that it is just another social policy, to be evaluated solely according to whether the benefits it produces outweigh the costs. To borrow the language of the courts, a higher standard of proof seems reasonable to impose.[12] While we may differ over the precise formulation of such a standard, perhaps something like the following will suffice. At the very least, preferential treatment would be justified only if there is strong reason to think it produces benefits of unusually great significance that cannot be obtained through less obtrusive policy options.[13]

Even if this standard of proof seems too demanding to some and not demanding enough to others, it may represent a reasonable compromise between competing positions. It certainly is not so demanding as to make justification of preferential appointment virtually impossible, but it does not propose to treat it as ordinary social policy either. Proponents concede, if only for the sake of compromise, that preferential treatment raises serious moral concerns. Opponents concede that it is not strictly equivalent to reverse discrimination, while continuing to assert that some especially weighty form of justification is required.

In any case, let us see if the kinds of considerations cited above, such as the educational defense and the appeal to future justice, can meet such a standard of proof in the context of faculty appointment in higher education.

PREFERENTIAL TREATMENT AND FACULTY APPOINTMENT

Preference for Whom?

The groups legally designated as minorities for affirmative action purposes are blacks, Hispanics, Asians and Pacific Islanders, women, and Native Americans. If affirmative action is construed as procedural or regulatory, rather than requiring preferential treatment, search committees are required to monitor the percentage of applicants from such groups in their pool, among applicants, among those considered for positions, and among those actually appointed. Disproportional representation of designated groups in the appointment process places the burden of proof on the employer to show that the process was fair and open.

Our concern, however, is whether preferential appointment of members of the designated groups for faculty positions in colleges and universities is justified. What groups, if any, should receive preference in appointments?

One characteristic that may support the inclusion of those groups is that each has been the target of systematic and pervasive discrimination in our society. However, many other groups not normally designated as recipients of affirmative actions, such as Jews, Irish, and other white ethnic groups, have also been the target of unjust discriminatory practices. While historical discrimination against blacks is perhaps unique in America, it is far from clear that all of the designated groups have been more seriously victimized than all groups that have not been included. Accordingly, the principle that groups that have been victimized by systematic pervasive discrimination now receive affirmative action does not support the current application of affirmative action policies. Rather, it seems either underinclusive, in that other groups have claims to inclusion similar in force to those of some designated groups, or overinclusive, in that only groups with the very strongest claims ought to receive preference. Thus, the principle that preference should be granted to members of victimized groups does not seem to provide an adequate justification for the current selection of designated groups for purposes of affirmative action.

Perhaps preference should be given to members of those groups that were both discriminated against in a systematic and pervasive manner and that have not yet overcome the competitive disadvantages arising from such discrimination. On this view, preferential treatment is designed to give a competitive boost to those who have been unfairly handicapped because of past injustice.

While this principle clearly supports extending preferential treatment for black Americans, it arguably would exclude Asians, and perhaps women. Asians far exceed the national norm for income and years of education, and the rationale for extending preference to them as a group is far from clear in any case. Again, it seems clear, based on grades and performance on many standardized tests as well as on the job, that in the absence of discrimination and other forms of unfair treatment, women perform as well or better than men in academic capacities. Thus, since women do not seem to be competitively disadvantaged by past discrimination, at least not to the same extent as some racial minorities, it is at best unclear whether they are encompassed by the principle under consideration.[14] Once again, the selection of designated groups appears arbitrary from the perspective of principle.

Perhaps a third principle of selection might explain why certain groups but not others should receive preference. According to this principle, members of groups that have been discriminated against and that are not well represented on college and university faculties should receive special preference.

Of course, we need to make clear what we mean by "not well represented," a notion that often is interpreted differently by different sides in debates over affirmative action. Perhaps we should understand "not well represented" as meaning something like having lower representation on the faculty than among qualified job applicants.[15] Are blacks underrepresented by this test? Clearly, there are few blacks on college and university faculties, but only a very small portion of Ph.D.s are black. Not only is preferential treatment unable to increase the representation of blacks on college faculties if few blacks enter the graduate programs that lead to academic jobs, the present principle, as we are interpreting it, does not encompass blacks, since they are not underrepresented in the sense specified. But surely any interpretation that implies that black Americans should not be covered by affirmative action misrepresents the intent of its supporters and so should be rejected for that reason alone.

Perhaps a modification of the interpretation we are examining will do the job. According to this principle, a group is not well represented on college and university faculties if the percentage of its members of such faculties is significantly below its representation among the general population, and the disparity is best explained as a consequence of past discrimination.

On this interpretation, blacks as a group clearly seem to be covered by the principle. But are they? A sceptic might point out that the majority of black graduates of undergraduate institutions go on to careers in areas other than academia, such as business or law. On this sceptical view, while the general plight of black Americans is due in significant part to discrimination and racism, the small number of blacks seeking academic positions is best explained by the choices of qualified blacks within the job market.

Proponents of the principle can reply that such "choices" may themselves reflect the influence of past discrimination. For example, higher salaries may make careers in law especially attractive to members of disadvantaged groups. Some blacks may also believe they can be of more service to their communities in the professions than as college teachers, a choice which itself is explainable in terms of individual reactions to a history of discrimination.

This reply is plausible even if we acknowledge that career choices vary widely among ethnic groups, even among those that have been previously victimized. Thus, whether or not blacks in fact fall under our proposed principle may be more controversial than it might at first appear, but it surely is not unreasonable to think they are in fact covered by it.

What is not so clear is which other groups, if any, also are covered by it. Asians presumably would not be encompassed. Given their achievements elsewhere, the degree, if any, to which they may be underrepresented in the professoriate is best explained by the options available to them elsewhere.

The case of women is especially complex. Women do not seem significantly underrepresented in the lower ranks of the professoriate but are far less well represented among the tenured and as full professors in major research universities. Is the lack of women in higher ranks due largely to past discrimination, to different career paths followed by women, or to some other factor? Will it be remedied automatically as the younger cohort of female professors moves up the academic ladder? Is preference needed at the level of promotion and tenure, rather than for initial appointments, since it is the point of tenure and promotion that seems problematic?

While we have not surveyed all possible or even all plausible criteria for the selection of groups to be encompassed by preferential affirmative action, our discussion does have some general implications. For one thing, it suggests that it is unclear at best just why certain groups and not others should receive preferential treatment. Why include Asians, for example, and not members of white ethnic groups that have been discriminated against?

Of all the groups normally designated as falling under affirmative action, Afro-Americans fit several criteria best, as should be expected in view of the origins of affirmative action. However, even in their case, problems remain. For one thing, preference will not increase the number of black scholars, which is determined by the number successfully completing graduate programs. Moreover, racial preference at earlier stages of the educational system will not solve the problem of the shortage of black scholars either, as long as a large percentage of black graduates of colleges and universities continue to choose nonacademic careers.

Finally, women seem to be an intermediate case. While they tend to concentrate on somewhat different disciplines than men, they are well represented among the professoriate. Their graduate training and scholarly credentials generally are equivalent to those of males, although their career paths may tend to be interrupted more often. Will women advance through the academic ranks, as long as their credentials are judged fairly and the process is nondiscriminatory, or is special preference needed to protect women from lingering and often unconscious or unintentional bias on the part of appointment officers, administrators, and even faculty colleagues? It is unlikely that people on different sides of the affirmative action controversy will agree on whether preference for women is warranted. There is at least room for doubt, critics of preferential treatment will argue, about whether women should be favored over men in appointment and promotion, or whether it is sufficient that special care be taken to ensure that the appointment and promotion process is not discriminatory.

In short, there is a degree of arbitrariness in the selection of just which groups, if any, should receive special preference. Perhaps affirmative action would be on the strongest grounds if preference were extended only to blacks. Although many critics would still find such a practice objectionable, it might still represent a possible compromise between the total elimination of preference for any group and the extension of preference in what at least appears to be a relatively unprincipled way to a wide variety of groups.

Surely it would be useful for philosophers to articulate better the grounds for inclusion or exclusion of groups from the mantle of affirmative action. Without a convincing rationale, selection can seem arbitrary and unfair to groups not covered by the policy. In view of the "significant interest" test, suggested at the end of the last section, the more obscure or less compelling the grounds for extending preference to a particular group, the more unlikely preferential appointment of its members will be justified.

Qualifications, Competence, and Preference

One reason preferential appointment seems so controversial is that it seems to override the claims of candidates based on qualifications and competence. If we assume jobs ought to go to the most qualified, preferential appointment seems wrong. The most qualified candidates can claim to have been wronged if they lose positions to the less qualified. This issue is especially acute where academic appointments, promotions, and tenure decisions are concerned, for these are supposedly made on the basis of the candidates' qualifications as scholars, teachers, and contributing members of an academic community.

Proponents of preferential appointment have responded in a number of ways to the claim that distributing positions on the basis of race or sex wrongs the more qualified candidates. One strategy is simply to deny that the most qualified (or most competent) candidates have a right to the position or deserve it more than others. This approach can be based, for example, on the sort of general critique of desert exemplified by the Rawlsian argument that talents and abilities are arbitrarily distributed as if on the basis of a "natural lottery" of favorable genetic endowments and early environments and so cannot be the basis of desert claims.[16] However, such an approach is highly controversial, since the lottery argument has been criticized on a number of grounds.[17] In particular, it seems doubtful whether the radical separation of the person from all "accidental" attributes and talents can leave much left over to be worthy of the kind of respect and concern to which individuals seem to be entitled. Although this kind of critique cannot be pursued here, general dismissal of desert based on the lottery argument seems hardly less controversial than preferential appointment itself. It is unlikely, therefore, to constitute either an intellectually satisfying or a particularly persuasive defense of preference based on race or sex.

A second approach is to argue that race and sex often are qualifications for academic appointments. For example, if, for whatever reasons blacks and women tend to have different perspectives on a variety of issues, intellectual debate within the academic community is enhanced by their inclusion. Diversity strengthens the academic community intellectually. Thus, an individual's capacity to contribute to a diverse campus is a relevant academic qualification.

This is an important argument for preferential treatment which, as we will see, is not without force. However, it will be considered separately under the heading of diversity, reserving discussion in this section for those views that construe qualifications and competence along more standard lines and then attempt to undermine their force.

A third especially important approach is neither to reject the claims of the most qualified candidates nor to count contribution to diversity as a qualification. Rather, it is to argue that even if we accept (perhaps only for the sake of argument) the principle that positions ought to go to the most qualified, preferential treatment by race or sex is compatible with such a principle, properly understood, and may even be required by it. That is, properly understood, the principle requires that we look not only at actual qualifications but as well at the fairness of the conditions under which they were acquired.

One version of such an approach might be called the argument from counterfactual meritocracy. According to this view, although a black or female candidate may not actually be the most qualified candidate who is being considered for a position, that candidate might well have been the most qualified if not for the effects of past discrimination. As one proponent of this position puts it,

> In a perfectly just world, a world in which blacks and women had fair opportunities to develop their abilities and pursue their interests, many of the minimally qualified blacks and women considered for preferential treatment would be equally or more competent than their white male competitors. . . . We can . . . think of preferential treatment . . . as aiming at picking out candidates who would be deserving of the positions on grounds of competence, were it not for the present effects of past injustice.[18]

This argument is important because it at least attempts to start from premises that the critic of preferential treatment seems committed to accept. Thus, the argument assumes that qualifications and competence should be the basis for decisions about who is appointed (and presumably promoted as well) and appeals only to considerations of individual justice rather than any theory about justice for groups that will itself be highly controversial in this context. It only asks us to rule out the effects of injustice on which people acquire what degrees of various competencies and qualifications.

The argument, however, does rest on two other assumptions that may be problematic. First, it assumes that positions ought to go not to the actually most qualified applicant but to the candidate who would have been most qualified in the absence of past injustice. Second, it assumes that actual beneficiaries of preferential treatment are likely to have been the most qualified candidates in the absence of past injustice. Are either of these assumptions plausible?

It seems implausible to argue that a professorship should be awarded to an unqualified individual simply because that individual would have been the most qualified in a world in which injustice had never taken place. Clearly, the first assumption is best understood as requiring that within the class of at least minimally qualified applicants, a position should go to the person who would have been most qualified if we discount the effects of injustice. But even this modified version has its difficulties. Thus, if factual differences in the qualifications of the candidates are significant, appointment of the less qualified candidate will have deleterious consequences for students, who will receive worse instruction and training than would have been the case if the more qualified candidate were appointed. If some of these students are themselves suffering the effects of past injustice and discrimination, we would be perpetuating the effects of injustice in one area by discounting them in another. In any case, it is not obvious that we *always* should assign higher priority to appointing the counterfactually most qualified candidate rather than providing the best instruction and training available.

While it is unclear how tradeoffs should be made, it would seem that the case for the appointment of the counterfactually most qualified candidate is stronger the closer the actual qualifications of the competing candidates and the better the qualifications of the candidate who is to receive preference. What the proponent of the argument has not shown, however, is that we *always* should give priority to the minimally qualified candidate who would have been most qualified in a just world, *regardless* of the costs in quality of instruction and training such a decision would entail.

If the assumption that we ought to appoint the counterfactually most qualified candidate is not free of problems, the second assumption that beneficiaries of preferential treatment are likely to have been the counterfactually most qualified candidates faces even more serious difficulties.

First, the idea of counterfactual justice itself admits of various interpretations. Are we trying to identify the candidates who would have been most qualified in a perfectly just world or those who would have been most qualified in the absence of certain specific injustices? The passage quoted above suggests both interpretations, but we should not fail to distinguish between the two, since they have different implications and face different problems.

For example, if we adopt the first interpretation, we need to specify what counts as a perfectly just world. Presumably, different conceptions of justice would pick out different social configurations. Moreover, even if we could decide which conception to apply without begging important controversial issues, the kinds of counterfactual calculations needed to determine which individuals would have been most qualified clearly are enormously complex and well beyond present capabilities. Surely, the probability of any actual candidate being the one who would have been most qualified in an ideally just society is exceedingly low.

Suppose, however, we proceed more modestly and try to consider which candidates would have been most qualified if the present generation of women and blacks had been given a reasonably fair chance to develop their capacities. Presumably, a proponent of counterfactual meritocracy would argue that since the actual women and minorities in the applicant pool have done so well under existing conditions, it is reasonable to think they would have done even better if we discount the effects of discrimination. This argument is not implausible. But does it rest on assumptions that beg important issues against critics of preferential treatment?

To begin with, even under the more modest limitation on counterfactual justice, it is unclear whether the candidate who would have been most qualified can be identified with any reasonable degree of probability. Presumably, many more minorities would have been eligible and interested in academic careers in a more just society. However, many other options would have been available to them as well. It is by no means clear what the competitive pool of minorities and women would have been under such circumstances, or even whether many actual candidates would even have been in it, let alone been the best. At the very least, the critic of counterfactual meritocracy would seem to be on reasonable grounds in asking for further evidence that we can reasonably determine the identity of the counterfactually best candidate.

Perhaps more important for purposes of our present discussion, the critic may ask why the relevant counterfactuals are restricted on the grounds of race and sex. That is, why not substitute criteria that are neutral with respect to race and sex? For example, instead of asking who would have been the best candidate if the present generation of blacks and women had had a reasonably fair chance to develop their abilities and capacities, why not ask who would have been the best candidate if all members of the present generation had had such a fair opportunity?

Thus, if the goal of proponents of the argument from counterfactual meritocracy is to meet opponents of preferential treatment halfway, by starting from assumptions common to both positions, it is unclear that they actually have done so. By restricting the relevant counterfactuals in terms of race and sex, they may have begged the very question about the relevance of such features that disturbs the critics in the first place.

One further strategy for defending preferential treatment on the basis of counterfactual meritocracy is available. Perhaps it might be conceded that the actual female or minority candidates are unlikely to have been the most qualified candidates under the specified counterfactual conditions. However, if those conditions have been actualized, the pool of successful candidates would contain a higher percentage of minorities (and perhaps women, particularly at senior positions) than at present. Hence, we can regard the actually most qualified female and minority candidates as stand-ins or reasonable substitutes for the women and minority candidates who would have been most qualified under conditions of fair opportunity.

But while this version of the argument might have some force, it is not clear it should convince the opponent of preferential treatment. Such a critic is likely to respond that while the claims of individuals who probably would have been most qualified under conditions of fair opportunity have some weight against those of the actually most qualified candidates, the claims of stand-ins surely are less compelling. For the claims of stand-ins must be balanced against those of the most qualified candidates, who may themselves have made sacrifices or at least incurred significant costs in order to become qualified, as well as the losses of those students who will be adversely affected if less qualified candidates are appointed. While these factors may not carry the day, they would seem to have greater force against the claims of stand-ins than against individuals who would have been the most qualified under the specified counterfactuals.

Even if this point is ignored, a more important difficulty remains. By appealing to substitutes for the hypothetical most qualified candidates and selecting them only on the basis of race or sex, the proponent of preferential treatment is again assuming the very position about the relevance of race or sex that the critic of preferential treatment rejects. Thus, the critic may ask why, if there is no particular reason to believe the stand-in would have been most qualified under conditions of fair opportunity, we do not select substitutes on some race-neutral or sex-neutral basis, such as degree of economic disadvantage the candidates actually have faced or degree of injustice or discrimination they actually have experienced.

Accordingly, if the defense of preferential treatment based on an appeal to counterfactual meritocracy is supposed to proceed from assumptions that are relatively noncontroversial, it is far from clear that it actually has done so. While the assumptions it rests on may well ultimately be justifiable, the critic of preferential treatment will argue that they are open to serious objections and beg many of the very basic points at issue in the affirmative action debate. It is unlikely, then, that considerations of counterfactual meritocracy form a satisfactory basis for resolving the debate in favor of preferential treatment since they logically depend on the very sorts of premises that opponents of preferential treatment find objectionable to begin with.

So far, we have considered a justification of preferential treatment that does not dispute that positions normally ought to go to the most qualified but attempts to substitute the counterfactually most qualified for the actually most qualified in application of the principle. A more radical approach, however, questions the objectivity of evaluation of qualifications. If the assessment of qualifications is itself liable to prejudice, or if the criteria for "being qualified" are inherently biased in directions unfavorable to women or minorities, the specific claims of some white males to actually be the most qualified candidates would be undermined. Let us consider this more radical approach.

Properly understood, the idea here is not that we ought to appoint less competent candidates instead of more competent ones. Rather, it is that qualifications, as commonly understood, do not generally reflect competence, particularly where women and minorities are concerned, because of the inherent bias built into the very criteria of qualification. As one writer puts it, "Our notion (even our educated notion) of what constitutes a good professional is bound to be partly influenced by features of good professionals with whom we have been acquainted throughout our lives. . . . Thus, in the same way that it is part of our idea of what it is to be a good secretary that the candidate has to have certain features typically associated with women, it is part of our idea of what would make a good lawyer, brain-surgeon, manager, etc. that they should have features typically possessed by white males." [19]

What this argument suggests is that since our conception of qualifications in many areas, presumably including academia, is rigged by racial and sexual stereotypes, the candidate who is most qualified need not also be the most competent. The biased conception of qualifications may illegitimately rule out women and minorities who are in fact the most competent candidates. How should this argument be evaluated?

Although the truth of the claim that qualifications are biased in the way specified may seem debatable, two other points seem of greater interest. First, what is presupposed by the possibility of our knowing that the claim is true?

At a minimum, it must be possible to provide evidence sufficient to convince, or at least to make it seem plausible, to fair-minded people that the most competent candidate is not always the most qualified (according to the standard set of qualifications). That is, it must be possible for many of us to recognize that the standard set of qualifications for many positions, including academic ones, is often biased by sexual or ethnic stereotypes. But that implies that we can sometimes see through those stereotypes and distinguish the candidate who actually is most competent. Otherwise, what reason would we have, other than our political predisposition, to favor the claim that our standards of qualifications are biased over the claim that they are not?

Second, if fair-minded people can detect and see through such bias, in what way does the argument support preferential treatment? Presumably, the intuitive idea is that preferential treatment enables us to appoint people who are perhaps the most competent but who would not have been regarded as the most qualified because of the way the standards of qualification are rigged.

Several difficulties face this approach, however. First, the person appointed through preferential treatment may not necessarily be the one whose competence is misperceived because of stereotypes. Suppose a female candidate, A, who is most competent is not appointed to a position because a white male, B, is wrongly perceived as more competent because of a biased perception of qualifications. How is the wronged candidate, A, helped when C, another female (who may not be the most competent), is preferentially appointed over (a perhaps more competent white male) D, for an entirely different position?

More important, even if we leave the above difficulty aside, it doesn't follow that preferential treatment is the best remedy for the use of stereotypical criteria in appointment. Rather, if we can make plausible judgments about when the qualifications of women and minority academics were underrated because of the illegitimate influence of stereotyping, then we may often be able to correct for such mistakes through such mechanisms as reviews and appeals. Perhaps more importantly, we can reduce the influence of stereotypes through the education of appointing officers and review committees. In other words, the procedural and regulatory forms of affirmative action, in conjunction with procedures used to remedy flaws in the appointment and review process, may be sufficient to reduce significantly the effect of stereotyping without the need for preferential treatment. In other words, if it is reasonable to believe we can achieve much the same gains without preferential treatment, shouldn't we pick the morally least obtrusive means of doing so?

Proponents of preferential treatment may be sceptical, perhaps with justification, about whether and how frequently such methods actually will work, although such scepticism would appear to be less justified, after over a decade of experience in enforcing affirmative action policies, than in the 1970s. However, even if administrative policies designed to promote fairness are not fully effective, they will at least aim at correcting actual injustices, rather than preferring one group of candidates in the hopes of making up for the alleged stereotyping of others. Granted, it is by no means clear which system would in fact be more effective in selecting the most competent candidates and which would minimize overall injustice. That is at least in part to be resolved empirically. The point the critic of preferential treatment can insist upon, however, is that in the absence of such data, the jump from the premise that standard conceptions of qualifications are rigged to the conclusion that preferential treatment is the proper solution is unsupported.

Of course, a deeper scepticism about qualifications is possible. It can be argued that virtually any judgment about which member of an at least minimally qualified set of candidates is more qualified than another is arbitrary. However, I doubt if many proponents of preferential treatment will take this line since, for example, it not only makes it difficult to show that in the past, more qualified women were passed over in favor of less qualified men, but it makes it difficult to understand how we could even identify minimally qualified candidates to begin with. How can we consistently regard judgments about who is minimally qualified as reasonable, while dismissing further judgments about comparative qualifications as unreasonable and totally subjective? Unless some reason can be given why reasonable judgments of the first sort are possible while reasonable judgments of the second sort are impossible, anyone who takes up this line risks being committed to abandoning the notion of qualifications altogether.

Accordingly, the arguments examined in this section are not powerful enough to persuade the rational critic of preferential treatment, often because at crucial points they assume much of what is at issue in the debate over this form of affirmative action. Moreover, concerns have been raised which should trouble both those who are undecided about the morality of preference based on race and sex and even those who tend to support it. For example, if there is at least a moral question of whether racial preference is morally legitimate, is the argument from counterfactual meritocracy or the argument from biased conceptions of qualifications strong enough to override such concerns? Are the premises of such arguments sufficiently well grounded and the reasoning sufficiently cogent to outweigh moral concerns about preference based on race, ethnicity, or sex?

Before dealing with such questions, however, we need to examine what many would regard as perhaps the strongest set of arguments for the preferential appointment of college and university faculty. The arguments, while differing in some respects, fall under the general heading of an appeal to the need for diversity within the academic community.

Diversity and Preferential Treatment

When supporters of preferential treatment appeal to the value of a diverse academic community, just how is "diversity" to be understood? After all, any collection of individuals will be diverse in some respects (e.g., in weight or birth dates) and homogeneous in others (e.g., in being human). Is "diversity" empty of content, then, since any population is diverse in some respect?[20]

Unfortunately, the notion of diversity sometimes does seem to be used in a vague or even vacuous manner, which lends itself to ideological purposes but which is hardly appropriate for the rational consideration of policy. However, we need not accept the dismissive view that the idea of diversity must always function vacuously in a discussion of affirmative action if we distinguish between the *concept* of diversity and *conceptions* of diversity.[21] Diversity as a concept refers to variance among a population in some respect(s) or characteristic(s). But, as we noted, any population varies in some respects but not in others. Accordingly, we need to fill in the respects or characteristics with which we will be concerned.

We also can speak of degrees of diversity. Group A may be more diverse than group B in athletic ability but be relatively homogeneous compared to group C, whose members show enormous variance in athletic talent.

Clearly, claims that a group is or is not diverse are elliptical. They must be filled in by a specification of the characteristics or qualities that are of concern. The very same group can be diverse, if one conception of diversity is applied, but not if another is applied, as when a population is ethnically diverse but religiously homogeneous. A conception of diversity specifies the characteristics according to which diversity is to be measured.

What kinds of diversity, if any, are desirable or even essential in an academic community? In a discussion of diversity in academia, among the kinds of diversity which contribute to the academic enterprise are diversity of methodology within disciplines and sometimes substantive diversity on issues that arise within different fields. These kinds of diversity are important because they sharpen intellectual exchange, allow for challenges to prevailing views, and enhance the process of justification and the search for truth that are central to the academic enterprise.[22]

In addition, ethnic, religious, racial and similar forms of diversity can contribute to intellectual diversity among an undergraduate student body. Students will be exposed, often for the first time, to an enriching blend of cultural differences and be given the opportunity to learn to get along with and respect those from a plurality of backgrounds and traditions.

Can similar considerations justify preference according to race, sex, or ethnicity in the selection of faculty? Perhaps members of minority groups or of groups that have been victimized by discrimination and injustice bring a viewpoint to academic communities different from that of white males and so make a special academically relevant contribution to debate.

In what specific way will greater representation of designated groups contribute to intellectual diversity on campus? Although some writers have suggested such groups may be more suspicious of authority on campus than others, such suspicion probably is already a kind of orthodoxy on many campuses. A more plausible view is that the more members of groups who have been absent from academic dialogue are included, the more likely they will contribute original work in areas not adequately studied by mainstream scholars. Important work in black or African studies and women's studies, as well as the work of feminist scholars in such areas as ethical theory and history, suggests that this is the case. Even when such work is highly controversial, it often has opened up illuminating discussion and challenged received views in ways that contribute to intellectual inquiry.

The argument, then, is that a more sexually and ethnically diverse faculty also will be a more intellectually diverse faculty. Since intellectual diversity is vital to the kind of inquiry the university should support, a candidate's race and sex, which indicate an ability to contribute to diversity, are academically relevant qualities that should be taken into account in appointment.

While this argument is not without some force, several questions can be raised about it. First, even if we grant the premise that members of victimized groups will add a special perspective to the academic community, we need to ask whether that perspective is more important or to be weighed more heavily than other kinds of diversity that individuals also may bring to the campus. How is one candidate's greater potential for original work, surely a contribution to intellectual diversity in the discipline, to be weighed against another candidate's ability to contribute to ethnic diversity and hence possibly to a more diverse range of opinions on campus? What other kinds of diversity, if any, should be given weight in the appointment process? Can arguments similar to the one for ethnic diversity be made for extending preference on other sorts of cultural, religious, or even political grounds? If not, what distinguishes the kinds of diversity it is permissible to count in the appointment process from those it is not permissible to count?

Presumably, a moderate proponent of preferential treatment would reply that many kinds of diversity should count and that the ability to contribute to intellectual dialogue as revealed by one's scholarship should count most of all. But such an advocate of preferential appointment would add that in cases where the other qualifications of the candidates are not significantly dissimilar, the candidate who can contribute to a more diverse campus in terms of race, sex, or ethnicity ought to be chosen.

This leads to a second question. Is it plausible to assume that every member (or even a significant proportion of members) of groups designated to receive preference will contribute to intellectual diversity in the way(s) suggested? Is it insulting, or at least an unjustified form of stereotyping, to assume that every minority candidate or female candidate will espouse particular viewpoints or positions?[23]

The proponent of preferential treatment may reply that we need to look past the individual case. While not every member of a minority group, or every woman, will take perspectives different from those of many white males, the growth of minority and female representation on faculties will tend to produce viewpoints different from those of the dominant white male culture.

A number of questions face such a retort, however. Does it apply to all disciplines? For example, is a black or female physicist or mathematician or geologist likely to hold views different from those of white male colleagues that are traceable to group membership? Is there a dominant white male cultural perspective, or are there highly diverse viewpoints and perspectives that divide white males in important ways? Are there campuses where appointing a political conservative would contribute more to intellectual diversity than appointing a member of a designated group? Is it proper to take such political considerations into account in making appointments? If not, why not? The contribution to intellectual diversity made by such a person might well be direct and significant.

More important, why use group membership as a stand-in for intellectual diversity in the first place? Perhaps when choosing among applicants to the undergraduate body, where the views of applicants are either unknown or very changeable, selection of a racially diverse student body does contribute to intellectual diversity. However, the professional views of candidates for academic positions are well known, are often expressed in publications, and can be taken into account directly. There is no need to assume a member of a designated group probably will contribute to intellectual diversity on the campus when the applicant's work can be directly checked to see if the assumption is warranted.

Moreover, it is possible that an emphasis on groups, and what may become the expectation that members of a group will tend to hold particular positions, may promote conformity rather than diversity. Orlando Patterson is one scholar who has expressed fears that an emphasis on the representation of diverse groups can lead to individual conformity. Patterson maintains that "the greater the diversity and cohesiveness of groups in a society, the smaller the diversity and personal autonomy of individuals in that society. . . . A relatively homogeneous society, with a high degree of individual variation and disdain for conformity, is a far more desirable social order than one with many competing ethnic groups made up of gray, group-stricken conformists." [24]

What Patterson seems to be suggesting is that the greater the emphasis on the selection of group members because of the expectation they will hold particular viewpoints, the greater the pressure on individual members to take those viewpoints rather than shatter the cohesiveness of the group. As a result, there is greater pressure on group members to conform to positions held to be orthodox within that group than on other members of the academic community.

If Patterson's claim is that an emphasis on group diversity must lead to a conformist "group-mind" perspective, it surely is doubtful, although it surely is plausible to think that, particularly among undergraduates, there sometimes will be unusual pressure on members of groups to conform to an overall range of positions attractive to the group. It also is plausible to think, however, that on the faculty level, the interest in women's and minority issues in various disciplines, rather than promoting conformity, has contributed significantly to overall intellectual diversity on campus, often in a particularly stimulating and provocative way.

What seems correct, then is that we are not entitled just to assume that ethnic diversity in given circumstances tends either to promote or to inhibit intellectual diversity. Rather, whether or not emphasis on the representation of groups leads to greater or lesser intellectual diversity on campus is in large part an empirical issue that cannot be resolved here. It is, however, a matter of concern. Whether this concern is warranted and whether whatever degree of conformity results is outweighed by gains in diversity at the group level, I leave for further discussion by other contributors to this volume.

What is important for our purposes, however, is that even if group diversity does lead to gains in overall intellectual diversity, as I suspect it does, it does not follow that preferential treatment is necessary to achieve group diversity. Women are likely to be significantly represented on university faculty without preference, although other forms of affirmative action, as well as special sensitivity to the possibility of bias during the review and tenure process, may well be required to ensure fairness in admission into the upper ranks of the faculty. Given the limited number of blacks in the professoriate, the most preferential treatment can do is redistribute a small number of minority scholars among different schools. Greater racial diversity at one institution will mean less at another. Most important, if intellectual diversity is really what we are after, we can pursue it directly by appointing those individual scholars whose work indicates a potential for unusual contributions of the greatest significance.

Perhaps more important than preferential treatment in promoting intellectual diversity is recognition of the importance of work being done in areas of feminist and various forms of ethnic studies. Investigations in these areas have stimulated inquiry in directions of unusual interest, in which it otherwise might not have proceeded.[25] Colleges and universities that make it clear that they regard work in such disciplines as important, although they are to be judged by the same standards of quality that apply elsewhere, will have taken a major step toward making themselves open to a number of perspectives that contribute to our understanding in a wide variety of areas.

So far, we have considered ways in which greater representation of women and various minority groups on the faculty may contribute to intellectual diversity. Even if other questions about such an approach can be dealt with, however, it remains far from clear whether preferential appointment is needed to secure the kind of intellectual benefits that are at stake.

Perhaps, however, group diversity can be defended along lines other than its direct value for the promotion of intellectual diversity. Thus, although not every black or woman will contribute directly to intellectual diversity, the presence of significant numbers of women and members of minority groups on the faculty will have indirect effects that in the long run should improve the academic community.

For one thing, the presence of minority faculty will help attract minority students, make their adjustment to the campus easier, and decrease the alienation many of them feel due to isolation in predominantly white academic communities. A racially diverse faculty, moreover, can serve as an example to students of the value of pluralistic societies, thereby helping diminish prejudice and discrimination. Moreover, minorities and women on the faculty are likely to be especially sensitive to discrimination in appointment, promotion, and tenure cases, thereby diminishing institutional discrimination.

These and other consequences of preferential treatment would clearly strengthen the academic community. But two questions need to be asked about them nevertheless. Would they actually come about? Is preferential treatment the most morally satisfactory way of achieving them?

There is considerable disagreement over whether the consequences of preferential treatment will be beneficial. Will preferential treatment eventually help reduce racial tensions or will it increase them, especially as less advantaged whites feel the deck is particularly stacked against them? Will minority scholars serve as effective role models on campus, or will their effectiveness be diminished because they are perceived, often wrongly, as less qualified than whites?

These doubts are increasingly voiced by minority scholars, including some who have been classified as conservative critics of affirmative action for many years, but also by others who see both benefits and burdens arising from preferential treatment. One such writer, whose feelings about affirmative action, while ambivalent, have become increasingly critical, worries that since "victimization is what justifies preference, so that to receive the benefits of preferential treatment, one must, to some extent, become invested in the view of one's self as a victim. In this way, affirmative action nurtures a victim-focused identity in blacks and sends us the message that there is more power in our past suffering than in our present achievements." [26]

Should we accept the view that the consequences of preferential treatment are beneficial, or should we reject such a claim? Perhaps other contributors can speak to such issues. I would make only two points regarding this question. First, in view of the concerns expressed by critics, we are not entitled to take for granted that preferential treatment will have the good effects cited by its supporters. Second, if the burden of moral justification is on the proponents of preferential treatment, as suggested earlier, has that burden been met? Or is the empirical case so murky that in light of the presumption against preference by race, sex, or ethnicity we ought to look for alternatives to preferential treatment?

Perhaps, however, it is a mistake to regard group pluralism only as a means to intellectual diversity. Diversity of race, sex, and ethnicity may have value other than as an instrument for advancing academic inquiry. In particular, representation of previously excluded or virtually unrepresented groups on campus can be viewed as a good thing in itself. Perhaps we ought to appoint faculty preferentially simply because we want a reasonable representation of all major social groups on our faculty, particularly those groups that were absent in the past because of discrimination and prejudice.

However, the idea of representation, whether it is "reasonable" representation or the more demanding conception of proportional representation that is at issue, raises disturbing questions. Does it imply, for example, that groups can be overrepresented? If so, are restrictions against entry by overachieving groups, such as the notorious Jewish quotas of an earlier era, to be employed? How are we to tell whether representation is "reasonable"? If proportional representation should be our goal, how do we arrive at the correct proportion? Should we assume that all groups would be proportionately represented in all professions under fair conditions of equal opportunity, even though the available empirical evidence tends to indicate that groups tend to make different career choices under a wide variety of circumstances?

Even if we make such an assumption, how is the goal of proportional representation to be achieved? The proportion of blacks with Ph.D.s or in Ph.D. programs is vastly lower than the proportion of blacks among Americans. If our goal is representation proportional to a group's percentage of the general population, we cannot achieve this for blacks at present if anything remotely resembling present qualifications is employed. As we have seen, preferential appointment appears only to redistribute minority scholars within academia, not substantially add to their number.

For these reasons, few if any philosophical defenders of preferential treatment have attempted to justify the practice by appeal to the idea of representation. Indeed, such an approach would beg the question against the critics of preference since it assumes one of the very points at issue in the debate over alleged reverse discrimination; namely, the moral justification for disadvantaging individuals of one race, ethnic group, or sex in order to improve the situation of another group. Since the appeal to diversity was an attempt to justify preferential treatment by appeal to values, such as intellectual diversity, common to both proponents and critics, the appeal to group representation seems to be a step backward. Rather than attempting to convert critics by appealing to common premises, it starts from the same sorts of assumptions that are at the heart of the controversy to begin with.

Diversity and pluralism undoubtedly sound like attractive values, but rhetoric about them may well be vacuous unless the particular conceptions of diversity and pluralism being appealed to are specified. Once that is done the strategy of justifying the preferential appointment of faculty by appeal to these values may well be promising, depending upon the conception of diversity at issue and the justification provided for it. Yet it is at present unclear that such an appeal succeeds, even when intellectual diversity rather than group representation is the underlying value at stake. Our discussion suggests that we can agree that intellectual diversity is an important component of the kind of inquiry universities should promote and (more controversially) even that racial, sexual, and ethnic diversity are important contributors to intellectual diversity, without agreeing on whether the preferential appointment of faculty is needed to implement it. In particular, those who defend preferential treatment as a means for promoting diversity need to clarify their position on a number of the issues raised above. Without such development, the appeal to an unspecified conception of "diversity" seems vacuous. If instead a specific conception of intellectual diversity is at issue, critics of preferential treatment are unlikely to be swayed until they are persuaded that preferential appointment based on race and sex is the most morally defensible way to promote it.

PREFERENTIAL APPOINTMENT IN PRACTICE

So far, we have not considered ethical problems that may arise from the actual operation and administration of policies of preferential appointment on college and university campuses. However, these problems are of moral significance. If the implementation of the policy involves ethically questionable practices, we need to consider whether it can be revised to avoid them or whether alternatives to preferential appointment ought to be implemented instead.

In their studies of professional ethics, philosophers and other academics often have argued in favor of an obligation on the part of many professionals to tell the truth to those who consult them. Physicians in particular have been criticized for concealing painful truths from seriously ill patients. Although exceptions to the rule are recognized, there seems to be a consensus among philosophers that competent patients should not normally be deceived by their physicians, even for their own good.

How does this apply to the issue of preferential treatment? While the practice of preferential appointment does not necessarily involve conscious deception, it can be argued that it does involve concealing the truth from candidates.[27] As Steven M. Cahn has pointed out, while academic institutions often identify themselves as "Equal Opportunity/Affirmative Action Employers" in job notices, they do not generally specify whether or not they engage in preferential appointment by race, ethnicity, or sex and, if so, to what degree.[28] Thus, some institutions may employ only the procedural and regulatory forms of affirmative action, while others will give preference. In some cases, an institution may fill a position only if a suitable minority or female candidate is found.

Cahn himself recommends that institutions be explicit as to just which form of affirmative action policy they are following.[29] By doing so, we can ensure that candidates are well informed about the criteria used in choosing among applicants, knowledge they are entitled to possess. Of course, it is not necessary that every criterion be filled in on a job description, but surely candidates are entitled to know if race and sex in particular will be used in making the selection. This may raise problems for the institutions, since the legality of voluntary plans of preferential affirmative action at this level of employment still are unclear. But are candidates any less entitled to know the major criteria of selection in this area than patients are entitled to be given basic information about their condition by their physician?[30]

However, the issue of truth telling raises another and in my view a more serious issue. Will colleges and universities even be able to articulate clearly the policy they are following? Since academic departments have a high degree of autonomy in selecting candidates for employment, it is likely that different departments in the same institution, or even the same department at different times, will be following quite different affirmative action policies. Department A may prefer a minority candidate only when that candidate is judged to be as least as good as any other candidate, Department B may do the same for females, Department C may select any minimally qualified minority candidate over all others, while Department D may employ only the regulatory and procedural forms of affirmative action.

If this point is accurate, we need to ask whether fairness in administration requires greater uniformity of policy. Is it fair that a candidate who, if similarly qualified in the relevant disciplines, would have been appointed by one department within a university is not appointed by another because of different forms of affirmative action employed? It would seem that otherwise significantly similar cases are being treated dissimilarly because of what appear to be arbitrary differences in the way affirmative action is understood or implemented. Should one department be allowed to give a certain degree of weight to race or sex, while another within the same institution gives a different weight to such features? Are differences of this kind in the application of affirmative action arbitrary and unfair, or are they simply the kind of flexibility we must allow autonomous departments in the application of any appointment policy?

Clearly, there has been considerable controversy over what consequences preferential treatment will promote. Will it encourage self-confidence on the part of minorities or self-doubt? Will it increase or decrease racial tensions on campus? What has not often been noticed is the effect preferential treatment has on the appointment process itself. Is the fear that policies of preferential treatment lend themselves to highly subjective and variable judgments, made behind closed doors with relatively little review of the degree of preference assigned to membership in a preferred group, or at least to the appearance of such arbitrariness, reasonable or unfounded? The ways, if any, in which race, sex, and ethnicity are weighted in personnel decisions are not only not communicated to candidates, they are seldom reviewed across departments to ensure consistency and fairness. Because they may be based on unstated and perhaps unclear policies, they too easily lend themselves to politicization and other kinds of abuse, and even when appropriate and fair they are seldom known to be so by all those affected.

Is this secrecy and lack of review healthy for academic institutions? Should preference be given in more open and more formal ways? What further problems would openness and explicitness raise? Is preferential appointment at the university level so open to arbitrary interpretation that it needs radical revision?

Whether it is ultimately justified or not, the preferential appointment of faculty in academic institutions raises ethical problems in practice as well as in theory. The former are no less serious than the latter, for they concern how we ought to treat others in such every-day contexts as job interviews and other stages of the appointment process, and the kind of respect owed to persons in one of the major areas of our professional lives.

Preference versus Neutrality

What does our discussion suggest about the justifiability of preferential appointment of college and university faculty? At a minimum, it suggests that the policy of preferential appointment is not obviously morally correct and that in fact it faces serious moral objections. Although this may seem a truism to many and hardly worth mentioning, I suggest it is important to say it anyway. For at least some proponents view preferential treatment as an obvious moral requirement in view of our heritage of racial injustice and hence tend to equate opposition with a kind of covert racism at worst, and at best with a kind of moral blindness to our true situation.

However, to say that there are objections is not to say that they are decisive. While there will be disagreement on how strong such criticisms are, much will depend on how the burden of proof is assigned. Those who believe that preference by race, sex, or ethnicity is at best morally questionable will maintain that the burden of proof will be on proponents of preferential appointment to show not only that the objections to the policy are either misguided or at least not overly significant but also that the reasons in favor are sufficiently weighty to justify a departure from race and sex blindness. But even those who do not assign the burden of proof in such a way still have to face difficulties. How much preference should be given for race, ethnicity, or sex? What weight should be given to the claims of merit and qualifications? Does a policy that discounts the qualifications of candidates on the basis of race or sex equally respect all candidates simply because it expresses no prejudice toward any? What do we mean by diversity? What sorts of diversity are most valuable to academic institutions? How will preferential treatment help us obtain them? These are some of the issues proponents of preferential treatment may want to address, regardless of how they assign the burden of proof in the area.

Critics of preferential appointment also need to address an important issue. They are often told that even if preferential treatment is open to some moral criticism, simply doing nothing is morally worse. Perhaps so. But are the only alternatives preferential treatment or doing nothing?

Our discussion suggests these are not the only alternatives. To begin with, there are forms of affirmative action that do not involve preferential treatment. To be sure, critics have objected that regulatory versions of affirmative action that involve numerical goals involve covert assignment of preference based on group membership. But whether or not goals sometimes turn into the equivalent of covert quotas, this need not be either the intent or the result of regulatory forms of affirmative action. Commitment to kinds of affirmative action that do not involve preferential treatment surely is an alternative to doing nothing and may represent a reasonable compromise that both proponents and opponents of stronger forms of affirmative action may find acceptable.

In addition, special training can be offered to those who sit on tenure and review committees to minimize, and perhaps eliminate, the role of stereotypes and covert biases in the evaluation of qualifications. If we can determine that such factors illegitimately infect personnel decisions, even when made by people of good will, it is plausible to think we can train people of good will to better monitor their own professional judgments. The goal of such training would not be to abandon standards or to politicize them but rather to apply whatever standards are held appropriate in a fair and unbiased manner.

However, these steps by themselves will not increase the small number of black academics who currently teach at American colleges and universities—neither, however, will preferential appointment of faculty. As we have seen, the most preferential appointment can do is redistribute such faculty. In such a context, greater racial diversity at one institution implies less at another.

It doesn't follow that we should do nothing. One possible response is for institutions to set up graduate scholarships for minorities interested in entering the professoriate. Such scholarships could be awarded to minority graduates of each institution, on the condition that upon receipt of the Ph.D., the recipients would return and teach for a certain number of years at the awarding institution. Such a policy, if carried out across the nation, would at least have the potential to dramatically increase the number of minority scholars. Even if it did not, it would at least ensure that black undergraduates were being given a fair chance to enter the academic world and the professoriate.

Is such a proposal no less morally questionable than preferential appointment of faculty, since it too involves the assignment of a benefit on grounds of race? I suggest that it is not. First, it is not clear that any particular white male need bear the cost of the program, since these could be distributed widely.[31] Second, costs inflicted on those who would pay not only could be widely distributed but also would not be prohibitive. On the other hand, preferential appointment could severely harm particular candidates who had already made a heavy investment in a career. In other words, one of the main criticisms of preferential treatment, the unfair and inequitable distribution of the burdens of the policy, would be avoided.

Not all critics of preferential treatment will be satisfied by such considerations. But perhaps two further points may move them. For one, such a program might be another sort of reasonable compromise between the two sides of the debate on the morality of preferential treatment. Critics would acknowledge that such a scholarship program would at least be less objectionable than the preferential appointment of faculty, while proponents would acknowledge that some forms of affirmative preferential treatment are more objectionable than others and hence should not necessarily be defended with full force.

Moreover, it is at least arguable that such a program of scholarships should be administered on racially, sexually, and ethnically neutral grounds, with awards being made on the basis of need and disadvantages faced earlier in a student's development. The greater the need and the more severe the disadvantages faced, the greater the likelihood of being awarded a scholarship. While some might fear that the claims of minorities would be submerged by those of more numerous disadvantaged whites, this should not be true if adequate weight were given to the special problems and disadvantages faced by minorities, particularly by blacks, in our society.

In addition, such a neutral policy would be capable of winning widespread support, since beneficiaries would include members of all groups, rather than divisive, as preferential forms of affirmative action surely have turned out to be. Neutral policies of this kind have the potential to benefit blacks and other minorities both directly, since they should be well represented among beneficiaries, and indirectly, since such policies are likely to draw united support from many liberal groups that have differed over the legitimacy of preferential treatment.

The alternatives, therefore, are not restricted to preferential treatment or doing nothing. Other options, including ones that are group-neutral, deserve consideration.

In any case, our discussion suggests that the policy of preferential appointment of college and university faculty is open to objections that I believe need to be taken seriously. These objections may or may not be decisive. In fact, I myself am unclear about the kind of weight that should be assigned to the different forms of the argument from diversity. Nevertheless, I hope the statement of these difficulties here encourages other contributors to consider just how serious they and others I was unable to consider here really are. Can they be answered or dismissed? Are they sufficiently serious to justify alteration or modification of affirmative action programs? Do they require the replacement of affirmative action, at least in those forms that involve preferential appointment, by activist but group-neutral policies designed to secure social justice through race- and sex-blind means?[32]

The debate over preferential treatment is really a debate about the import of some of our most fundamental political ideals. What do equality and social justice require, in a society striving to overcome a heritage of inequality and discrimination? In particular, how should academic institutions react? Should they be race and sex conscious in the selection of their faculties in order to overcome the invidious use of race and sex, to ensure fair opportunity in the present, and to promote diversity and pluralism in the intellectual community? While my discussion suggests that preferential appointment by race or sex is ethically problematic, I hope it suggests even more the value of the kind of sustained rational inquiry on ethically controversial social policies to which this volume contributes.

It is this kind of rational inquiry that is a primary purpose of the university to foster and that itself involves an appeal by proponents of quite different substantive positions to standards of rational evaluation without which no justification of any view is possible. It is because the university, whatever its faults, is the main protector and preserver of such standards that debate over its role in securing fairness and justice in our land should be of special importance to us all.

NOTES

1. For an argument that goals become quotas, see Alan Goldman, "Affirmative Action," *Philosophy and Public Affairs* 5, no. 2 (1976): 178–95.

2. See Deborah J. Carter and Reginald Wilson, *Eighth Annual Status Report: Minorities in Higher Education* (Washington, D.C.: American Council on Education, 1989), Table 1.

3. *Digest of Education Statistics* (Washington, D.C.: U.S. Department of Education, 1989), Tables 2–3.

4. Derek Bok, *Beyond the Ivory Tower* (Cambridge: Harvard University Press, 1982), p. 111.

5. See, for example, Laura Purdy, "In Defense of Hiring Apparently Less Qualified Women," in T. A. Mappes and Jane S. Zembatz, eds., *Social Ethics*, 3rd ed. (New York: McGraw-Hill, 1987), pp. 227–33; and Dorit Bar-On, "Discrimination, Individual Justice, and Preferential Treatment," *Public Affairs Quarterly* 4, no. 2 (1990): 111–37.

6. Thomas Nagel, "A Defense of Affirmative Action," in Tom L. Beauchamp and Norman E. Bowie, eds., *Ethical Theory and Business*, 3rd ed. (Englewood Cliffs, NJ: Prentice-Hall, 1988), p. 346.

7. Ronald Dworkin, "Why Bakke Has No Case," *New York Review of Books* 24 (1977): 15.

8. Ronald Dworkin, *Taking Rights Seriously* (Cambridge: Harvard University Press, 1977), p. 227.

9. John Rawls, *A Theory of Justice* (Cambridge: Harvard University Press, 1971), p. 3.

10. Dworkin might reply that his right to treatment as an equal differs from utilitarianism in that it does not allow external preferences—preferences which express the bearer's desire for some distribution of benefits and burdens for others—to count in the calculation of consequences. This restriction allegedly rules out biased preferences that would allow a prejudiced majority to dominate an oppressed minority. However, Dworkin's distinction between external and personal preferences (for one's own satisfaction) has been severely criticized in the literature. Perhaps the most telling criticism is that even if we accept the distinction, Dworkin's approach still allows discrimination against minorities when it is based on calculations of self-interest. For Dworkin's account of the distinction between personal and external preferences, see *Taking Rights Seriously*, pp. 234–35. The kind of criticism I have suggested is found in Marshall Cohen's review of *Taking Rights Seriously* in the *New York Review of Books* 24 (1977): 37–39. Other objections are that the distinction between the two kinds of preferences is not always clear (is my preference that my child win the tennis match external or personal?) and that the counting of external preferences may not always be improper (is it improper for utilitarians to count the concern of parents for their children?). For a discussion of Dworkin's views from which I have drawn on for use here, see Robert L. Simon, "Individual Rights and Benign Discrimination," *Ethics* 90, no. 1 (1979): 88–97.

11. It might be objected that we do not object when other inherent properties, such as athletic ability or musical talent, influence outcomes. However, it is doubtful if such abilities are as out of our control as race or sex. For example, innate athletic ability, which may be regarded as out of our control, is by itself probably no more important than dedication and intelligence in its use, which

are to some degree and in some senses under our control, for determining athletic success. Moreover, our developed skills and the character traits that enable us to make effective use of "natural abilities" arguably have a close connection with our moral personhood. Hence, to divorce us from our merits may be to disrespect us as persons.

12. Readers who disagree can simply take the remaining sections of the paper as an evaluation of preferential treatment in faculty appointment as effective social policy, although my own assessment holds it to a higher standard of proof.

13. This standard is less demanding than the Supreme Court's "compelling state interest" test since (a) it requires that the goals promoted be of unusually great significance rather than be compelling and (b) that there be only strong reason to think the policy actually promotes the intended goals rather than the policy being necessary for the goals. Clearly, any policy that fails my "unusually significant interest test" also will fail the "compelling state interest test." However, since the former is less demanding than the latter, imposition of such a standard of proof is if anything more favorable to the case for affirmative action than the Supreme Court has been.

14. An argument for extending preference to women, based on the possibility of stereotyping and bias in evaluation of their qualifications, will be discussed later.

15. It has become notorious that defining the pool of "qualified" applicants may itself raise all sorts of substantive issues. For example, if a department in a major research university generally makes its appointments from among Ph.D.s turned out by the top twenty departments, may it restrict its pool of qualified applicants to such new Ph.D.s, even if, say, a smaller percentage of blacks is enrolled in those departments than among others?

16. See Rawls, *A Theory of Justice*, pp. 100–104, for such an argument.

17. The critical literature on the lottery argument includes Michael Sandel, *Liberalism and the Limits of Justice* (Cambridge: Harvard University Press, 1982), particularly pp. 66–104; George Sher, "Ability, Effort, and Personal Desert," *Philosophy and Public Affairs* 8, no. 4 (1979): 361–76; and Robert L. Simon, "An Indirect Defense of the Merit Principle," *Philosophical Forum* 10, no. 2-4 (1978–79): 224–41.

18. Bar-On, "Discrimination, Individual Justice, and Preferential Treatment," p. 128.

19. Ibid., p. 126.

20. I am grateful to Steven M. Cahn for calling these questions to my attention.

21. Here, of course, I borrow Rawls's distinction between the concept of justice and conceptions of it. See *A Theory of Justice*, pp. 5–9.

22. I owe these points to Alan Goldman's "Diversity Within University

Faculties," in Steven M. Cahn, ed., *Morality, Responsibility and the University: Studies in Academic Ethics* (Philadelphia: Temple University Press, 1990).

23. Critics argue that even worse, there is a tendency for emphasis on pluralism and diversity to become politicized, so that women and minorities who do not take to positions thought proper are not really counted as contributing to "true" diversity after all.

24. Orlando Patterson, "Ethnic Pluralism," *Change: The Magazine of Higher Learning* 7 (March, 1975): 15–16. Goldman also argues that contributions to diversity should be evaluated on an individual, not a group, basis.

25. The stimulating and provocative although quite controversial examination of the claim that women may tend to have a different moral perspective than men touched off by Carol Gilligan's *In a Different Voice* (Cambridge: Harvard University Press, 1982) is a case in point.

26. Shelby Steele, "A Negative Vote on Affirmative Action," *New York Times Magazine*, May 13, 1990.

27. Deception would be involved if an appointments officer told a candidate that race or sex was not a factor in making an appointment when it was, or if an appointment officer told a rejected white male candidate that he was not appointed because, say, "we were under pressure to appoint a woman," when in fact the woman was the best candidate but the appointing officer was not frank enough to say so.

28. Steven M. Cahn, "Colleges Should Be Explicit about Who Will Be Considered for Jobs," *Chronicle of Higher Education*, April 5, 1989, p. B3 (reprinted in the introduction to this volume).

29. Ibid.

30. It might be objected that patients are entitled to information because they must consent to the treatment the physician recommends, and for consent to be valid, it must be informed. Job applicants, however, are not "treated" by prospective employers and hence have no similar need for information. However, prospective academic employers do obtain confidential information about candidates, ask candidates to incur opportunity costs to go to interviews, prepare papers, and the like. It is plausible to think candidates have a right to information about the criteria used in making an appointment before releasing such information and bearing such costs.

31. Perhaps such a program could be funded in part by income that would otherwise have gone to increases in faculty salary. Then at least all faculty would bear at least part of the burden of affirmative action. Senior faculty might even be asked to give up more than juniors, proportionally to their ability to pay. Hence, the costs of the policy would be distributed more equitably rather than, as is the case with preferential appointment, being assigned entirely to arbitrarily selected young white males.

32. This point is relevant to debates about whether liberal policymakers

ought to aim at programs that generate coalitions rather than divide them. A number of black scholars, not easily classifiable as conservatives, have argued for race-neutral but progressive policies as such a coalition-building device. Thus, William Julius Wilson argues that "An emphasis on coalition politics that features progressive race-neutral policies could have two positive effects. It could help the Democratic party regain lost political support, and it could lead to programs that would especially benefit the more disadvantaged members of minority groups—without being minority programs." See Wilson, "Race and the Democratic Coalition," *American Prospect* 1 (Spring 1990): 81.

Affirmative Action and Faculty Appointments

3

Lawrence C. Becker

This essay may be more the product of exasperation than of conviction. At any rate, it is based on a set of assumptions that reflect how little hope I have of being able to say anything both useful and philosophically interesting about affirmative action. My assumptions are these: (1) The philosophical debate about affirmative action is essentially stalled. Over the last fifteen years or so the content, range, clarity, rigor, and soundness of the arguments have remained virtually unchanged. (2) Intellectuals are deadlocked about the justifiability of result-oriented affirmative action programs—especially those involving preferential treatment. (3) Existing empirical evidence and theories of justice are not capable of breaking that deadlock. The affirmative action and abortion debates are alike in that regard: All the relevant material is known to people of good will on both sides; continued discussion of it has very little practical effect beyond educating successive generations of adversaries. (4) The probability of finding new evidence or a new theory or principle that will break the deadlock is remote. (5) That means one's options in writing an essay like this come down to undertaking Quixotic theoretical expeditions in search of decisive new arguments, making incremental improvements in the existing materials, or doing something else.

I have opted for doing something else. Specifically, I have decided to explore the possibility of a political compromise. Here is my reasoning.

REPETITION

We have now had more than thirty years of debate and twenty years of experience with affirmative action. It is disheartening to find so much ambiguity in the empirical record, so much repetition in the continuing political debates, so little evidence of progress toward consensus and political closure. It is even more disheartening to read the normative literature on this subject and to find the same old arguments about equal opportunity, social utility, compensatory justice, quotas, preferential hiring, stigmatization, tokenism, reverse discrimination, burdensome regulation, and so forth repeated nearly verbatim year by year.

Of course, if one pursues a normative argument about affirmative action merely as a means to developing or testing a general theory of justice, then it would be naive to expect closure. As long as the adequacy of the general theory remains in question, so too will its account of the test cases. Similarly, if one pursues the topic of affirmative action as part of a revolutionary or reactionary political project, then again it will be naive to expect closure—at least where (as in Western liberal democracies) there is persistent and quite general resistance to such things. Some of the repetitive quality of arguments about affirmative action may be due to the fact that they are being used as set pieces in larger projects.

In what follows, I propose to hold revolutionary, reactionary, and purely theoretical projects in abeyance and to consider affirmative action in faculty appointments purely as a practical problem. As mentioned at the outset, I assume that knowledgeable people of good will, imagined as a deliberative body, are deadlocked on one crucial issue: preferential treatment. Moreover, I assume there is general agreement (1) that in the past the academy has discriminated against certain groups and that it must be active and vigilant in eliminating such discrimination; (2) that double standards for appointment criteria are demeaning to the people included by them, unjust to the people excluded by them, and damaging to the mission of the academy; (3) that faculties should continue to have the responsibility for establishing criteria and assessing candidates for faculty appointments; (4) that current, legally mandated affirmative action procedures are burdensome; (5) that quota systems are either counterproductive, unjust, or subject to abuse; and (6) that merely removing *formal* barriers to the appointment of target group members is not likely to have a substantial effect on the composition of faculties.[1]

The disagreements are equally familiar. There is disagreement about whether current affirmative action practices have had any significant good effects, about the rationale for them, and about the best means of enforcing them.

The perpetual sticking point, however, concerns appointment criteria: Is mere membership in a disadvantaged class a qualification for appointment, to be considered along with the usual competence criteria in determining who is the best candidate for a position? If so, how much weight should it have in comparison to other criteria? If it is not a criterion for determining the best qualified candidate, may it nonetheless be relevant to deciding which of the qualified candidates to appoint? And if so, how much weight may it be given in such decisions? Tie-breaker weight only? Or enough to allow the appointment of a minimally qualified candidate over a maximally qualified one?

I think it is fair to say that legally, at least since the *Bakke* decision,[2] the distinction between qualifying criteria and additional determinants has been blurred. Suspect-class status is a factor that may be "considered" in making such decisions. That sounds like treating status as an additional determinant. But people engaged in making these policies are very reluctant to concede aloud that target group candidates appointed under them might not be the "best qualified" candidates. Thus there is constant pressure to define qualifications so that they somehow include status. (Arguments about role models and unique perspectives and experience are examples of this.) Yet all such attempts at redefinition for academic appointments remain controversial. The conviction that there must be a sharp distinction between qualifying criteria and additional determinants will not go away. And for many people (perhaps even most), the use of such determinants in addition to qualifying criteria is equally controversial; a heavy burden of proof rests on anyone who recommends passing over the best qualified candidate for a faculty position.[3]

THE NO-NEED/NECESSITY DEADLOCK

A perspicuous way of thinking about these disagreements about preferential treatment is to imagine a continuum between extremes I will call "no-need" and "necessity." At the no-need extreme, we have the view that all the unjust procedural or substantive barriers to the appointment of affirmative action target groups[4] can be identified and eliminated by faculties as currently constituted, and that once such barriers have been removed, there is no need to make an effort to achieve any particular distribution of members of target groups in college and university faculties. There is no advantage to an institution of higher education in having any particular distribution, because matters of the sex, age, race, nationality, or ethnic origin of its faculty members are wholly irrelevant to its teaching and research mission. Competence in teaching and research are the crucial factors, and they are defined independently of such matters. Moreover, there is no need for affirmative action for the purposes of social justice. As long as educational institutions are genuinely equal opportunity employers—that is, impose no unequal barriers on target group candidates for faculty positions—any distribution of men, women, and minorities that results from equal opportunity will be just and will itself, over time, correct distributions that were produced by discrimination.[5] Since there is no need to achieve any particular distribution of members of target groups, any expenditure of effort or resources to that end is unjustifiable at best. And if such an effort violates anyone's rights, expectations, or dignity, then it is not only unjustifiable but flatly unjust.

At the other extreme there is the view that it is necessary (to achieve and sustain social justice and to fulfill the mission of higher education) to have a distribution of members of target groups on faculties that is roughly proportional to their distribution in the society at large. This is necessary for social justice because nothing less will break the self-perpetuating cycle in which underrepresented groups are seen as somehow unfit to be, or uninterested in being, professors—and by extension, unfit or uninterested in high levels of intellectual achievement. It is necessary for fulfilling the mission of higher education because (given what we know about the difficulty of eliminating bias) nothing less will enable us to be confident that our self-defined criteria for professorial excellence are sound. Since a particular distribution is necessary, both for justice and for fulfilling our educational mission, we must take steps to achieve it; we must be result oriented. Moreover, since justice and educational mission are such fundamental matters, we can permit them to override interests and even rights that would otherwise be a bar to affirmative action. For example, just as public health and safety occasionally override private property rights, so too the necessity for results may override our interests in maintaining strictly neutral selection criteria. Preferential criteria may be warranted.

Between those extremes there are indefinitely many positions. This would be harmless enough if we could all agree to rule out large numbers of them as unsound or implausible, perhaps working in from the extremes toward some point of convergence. But even the extremes have respectable defenders, and (my assumption is that) there is currently no net movement toward a convergence point.

The possibilities for breaking this deadlock seem few and remote. It may be (although it seems unlikely) that we will find a new principle, or new theory of justice, or new analysis of existing theories that will yield a generally acceptable convergence point. It may be that we can locate a manageable number of cluster points that are more defensible than any of the positions in their neighborhoods. Then arguments that move people toward the cluster points might eventually yield an intellectually or politically decisive majority for one of them.

More interesting to me is the possibility of a compromise that circumvents the repetitive cycle of argument and counterargument that now characterizes the debate. Such a compromise would begin from common ground, honor fundamental commitments of principle on both sides, and yield the sort of action that both sides can accept, at least temporarily. It would be nice if such a compromise were also clear and easy to administer.

A Modest Compromise

Here is a possibility for compromise. Against the scale of recent practical compromises in Europe, it seems positively timid. In the light of twenty-five years of legislation, lawsuits, committee reports, government regulation, oversight by professional organizations, advocacy group activity, and voluminous public discussion, together with the fact that much administrative, information-gathering, and oversight machinery is already in place, it seems realistic. Item 1 below simply affirms a central part of procedures and policies that are already widely used. Items 2 and 3 are the crux of the matter and are meant to find a safe path between two incendiary practices: setting quotas and giving "extra points" for race, ethnicity, or sex. They are primarily addressed to college and university policymakers, but of course they also have implications for public budgets and therefore have a political dimension.[6] Item 4 deals with enforcement, and is directly political.

1. *The Obvious.* (a) Identify the groups (target groups) whose underrepresentation on faculties is the result of discrimination. (b) Re-

move all procedural barriers to fair consideration of applicants from those groups. (c) Attend to the ways in which discriminatory bias may taint the use of formally neutral procedures and attend to the ways it may taint the definition of substantive criteria of competence. Correct for such bias, and ensure that notices of openings are readily and generally available to members of the target groups. (d) Identify the ways in which members of the target groups, once appointed to faculty positions, may face discriminatory barriers or bias with respect to tenure and promotion and take the necessary corrective action. (e) Monitor (a–d) internally, through an elected committee of tenured faculty members, including if possible target group members, who report to the central legislative body of the institution.

2. *Additional Graduate Fellowships.*   At each institution, for each advanced degree program and target group[7]: (a) Calculate annually the number of additional graduate students from each target group needed to match its percentage of first-year students in the program to its percentage of the relevant baccalaureate degrees awarded nationally in the previous ten years.[8] (b) Guarantee that number of additional graduate fellowships for the following year, and restrict those additional fellowships to members of the target group.[9] (c) Do not alter admission criteria in any way for these additional students. (d) Use the additional fellowships only as needed[10] and only for those who are fully qualified for admission to the program, by standard criteria. (e) Do this each year for a specified number of years[11] and publish the results annually in the graduate catalog.

3. *Additional Faculty Positions.*   For every appropriate aggregation[12] of departments or programs with full-time faculty members: (a) Calculate annually the number of additional faculty members from each target group needed to match its percentage in the faculty to its percentage of the relevant advanced degrees awarded nationally in the previous ten years. (b) Guarantee that number of additional, tenure-eligible faculty positions for the following year, and restrict those positions to members of the target group.[13] (c) Do not alter criteria for appointment, promotion, or tenure in any way for these additional positions. (d) Use the additional positions only as needed, and only for those who are fully qualified for appointment to the faculty, by uniform criteria. That is, if a matching percentage (or more) for group x is achieved in filling the ordinary allotment of positions, then

do not offer any additional (extraordinary) positions for x. If a matching percentage is not achieved in filling the ordinary allotment, then extraordinary positions for x will be available, but if no fully qualified candidates from x apply, those positions will not be filled. (e) Convert extraordinary positions automatically to ordinary ones as follows: Each time an ordinary position of a given rank becomes available in a given department, fill it with the most senior member of that department who holds an extraordinary position of the same rank or above.[14] (f) Do this each year for the specified period and publish the results annually in the academic catalog.

4. *Oversight and Enforcement.* (a) Limit federal and state oversight and reporting requirements to those necessary for establishing compliance with 1–3 above and b–d below and withdraw government funds and/or tax-exempt status from noncompliant institutions. (b) Guarantee a disinterested internal review and a written report of its result to any target-group candidate who is denied a fellowship or appointment and who requests a review. (c) Guarantee a private law cause of action for noncompliance, on behalf of individuals or groups, against both private and state institutions. (d) Guarantee the right of third parties (e.g., advocacy groups, professional associations) to collect, analyze, and publish at their own expense the information published by institutions under 2 and 3 above.

This compromise seems to me to meet the desiderata mentioned above. It begins from common ground. (See discussion below.) And it honors fundamental commitments on both sides: merit criteria remain intact; faculty responsibility for setting such standards is preserved; reverse discrimination is avoided; a powerful remedy for injustice is made genuinely available; and the remedy is not paternalistically imposed on the victims of injustice and is not triggered at all if the injustice does not persist in the form of an inexplicable surplus of fully qualified candidates from the target groups. Whether it is also "the sort of action that both sides can accept" is a more difficult question, but I think the answer to that should be in the affirmative as well. For expository convenience, let me state the reasons as a series of replies to sharply focused objections, as follows.

Discrimination, Quotas, and Injustice

Objection.   This is a proposal for a quota system, both directly and indirectly. It directly specifies a quota of additional positions to be assigned to members of the target groups. It indirectly ensures that target groups will have exactly the specified quota of positions for as long as the program is in place. This is so because every institution will have a strong budgetary incentive to eliminate the need for additional positions. This can be done only if all additional positions are first converted into ordinary ones and then all the ordinary positions held by members of the target groups are somehow retained by members of those same groups. There is a grotesque opening here for injustices of many sorts (expedited resignations, double standards for tenure review, and the like). But the point is that all the incentives are for producing, in the ordinary faculty, a specific quota of positions for members of the target groups.

Reply.   This proposal is certainly not a quota system in a direct way. By definition, a quota sets either a minimum or a maximum. This proposal does neither. It is not "result oriented" in that sense. It does not specify how many or how few people there must be from a given group. If no qualified women or minority candidates apply, none need be found. If only women or minority candidates apply, they may fill all of the ordinary places. This proposal only requires that if there is an excess in the number of fully qualified target-group applicants, together with a deficiency in their representation in the ordinary number of places, then the deficiency should be corrected. This is not a quota system.[15]

To the question of whether this proposed arrangement would indirectly work to establish quotas, the answer is also no. Strictly speaking, the putative economic incentive at issue here is simply to avoid adding members to the faculty, affirmative action plan or not. If no qualified applicants come forward for such positions (or if none accepts an offer for one), then this narrow economic interest is met, and the plan requires no further action. The minimum thus allowed under the plan is by no means fixed by the number of additional positions that must be kept available. It is true that whenever an additional position is filled under the plan, there would be an incentive to convert it to an ordinary position without creating another additional slot. But that hardly amounts to an indirect quota. Quotas are requirements, not mere incentives. To hold that this incentive is an indirect or de facto requirement is to hold that it will regularly be determinative—that it will not regularly face offsetting incentives or countervailing institutional pressures. And that is simply false. Institutions of higher education have powerful professional commitments, as well as economic incentives, for improving and enlarging their faculties. These would surely collide with any cynical or unjust attempt to eliminate additional positions. Moreover, if administrations can be said to have an incentive to eliminate such positions, surely departments can be said to have an incentive to keep them.

Objection.   So then the quota imposed by the plan is simply specified by the point at which all these incentives and pressures reach equilibrium.

Reply.   That equilibrium point is a variable that can take any value from zero to the number of additional positions available under the plan. Surely that is not a quota.

Objection.   But why make *any* additional positions available? Why should we assume that a mismatch in the percentages of advanced degrees and faculty members in the target groups represents a deficiency that we need to address? If opportunity is genuinely equal, then a skewed distribution simply represents (accurately) the career choices competent people make. If opportunity is not genuinely equal, and the inequality is the cause of the skew, then the remedy is to go after the cause directly by equalizing opportunity.

Reply.   Whether opportunity is genuinely equal or not is one of the fundamental issues at stake in the current debate about affirmative action. This proposal concedes to the advocates of affirmative action that there may be a genuine deficiency to correct but concedes to the opponents that we should not simply assume that this is so. Thus the proposal here is for a passive system that can be triggered by a surplus of fully qualified target-group applicants but will not be called into play otherwise. The number of additional places reserved for such applicants seems a reasonable one. It simply insists that until we have clear evidence to the contrary, we ought to assume equal interest in graduate study and the professoriate by everyone who is qualified; it rests on the general agreement that historically, members of some groups were unjustly excluded from such pursuits; and it assumes that opening up the possibility of proportionate representation is a good way to find out whether current distributions are indicative of continuing deficiencies.

Objection.   But reserving positions for minorities, quota or not, is flatly discriminatory. Whole groups are excluded from the opportunity to compete for the additional places.

Reply.   These are "additional" places and are analogous to scholarships restricted to Calvinists or veterans of foreign wars. There is nothing wrong with such arrangements as long as they do not displace other people and do not involve lowering academic standards.

Featherbedding

Objection.   These are not only additional positions, they are by definition supernumerary. Adding to the size of graduate classes creates an overload; appointing additional faculty members amounts to featherbedding.

Reply.   The term "supernumerary" implies a condition of being unneeded or unwanted. I do not think that fairly describes this situation. Surely, as educators, we want to admit all we can of the fully qualified applicants for graduate study. Moreover, we can surely agree that if we get a surplus of fully qualified applicants from groups that have been discriminated against and who remain underrepresented in our programs, it would be a good thing if we could admit more of them. Given the money for extra fellowships, the extra burden imposed by the additional graduate students would surely be offset by the benefits they bring with them (research and teaching assistance, demand for advanced courses, and so on). And of course if there is enough demand to trigger the award of additional fellowships, there will likely (soon after) be enough demand to trigger the additional faculty positions, thus eliminating any vestige of an overload. So the additional students are not supernumerary.

As for the additional faculty, there are two questions: One is whether the additions in a given case create a lower student/faculty ratio; the other is whether a lower ratio is unneeded or unwanted. The answer to the first depends upon what happens to the student population and whether the institution adjusts the size of the faculty to fit falling enrollments. If an increase in faculty is matched or exceeded by increases in student populations (graduate or undergraduate), then the ratio will obviously not go lower, and there is no question about supernumeraries. If enrollments fall while additional faculty positions are added under this proposal, then the institution has a choice: It can decide that a lower ratio is a good thing (e.g., for improving the quality of teaching or research), thus eliminating the question of featherbedding. Or it can make a case for reducing the number of "ordinary" faculty positions to keep its ratio of faculty to students constant—just as it might do for falling enrollments without the complication of additional positions.[16]

That leaves cases in which the ratio of ordinary faculty to students remains constant, but the faculty increases solely through the additional positions available to members of the target groups. Would such extraordinary faculty members in fact be unwanted or unneeded? Quite the contrary, in almost every case. Higher education is not like an assembly line with a fixed number of tasks and work stations. Going from a ratio of 17/1 to 16/1, other things being equal, would surely improve the quality of undergraduate education at a comprehensive university or state college; 15/1 would be even better. And I am not aware of any professional schools at which a comparable enrichment of the student/faculty ratio would be regarded as pedagogically undesirable.[17] So additional faculty at such institutions would surely not be supernumerary. Enrichment of the ratio becomes arguable on pedagogical grounds, I suppose, at those few small liberal arts colleges where the mix is already in the neighborhood of 10/1. If so, and if they do not have the flexibility (given tenure, small departments, and the like) to reduce the ordinary faculty to restore the ratio, then perhaps an exception should be made. But surely those exceptions will be rare. At most institutions, the additional faculty will be a benefit.

Objection. They might be such a large benefit, in fact, that this proposal will be self-defeating. It will be self-defeating if it creates an irresistible incentive for expansion—an incentive to keep percentages of the target groups in the ordinary faculty low, so that departments can get the maximum number of additional positions. This will create and perpetuate an artificial "deficit" in the ordinary faculty that perpetuates and perhaps even magnifies the need for the extraordinary positions.

Reply. Departments regularly pressure deans for additional positions, and deans regularly distinguish genuine need from alarmist,
strategic, or pro forma maneuvers. This proposal adds a new wrinkle
to that game, but not a very difficult one, assuming good will on both
sides. A department attempting to maximize its additional positions
will have to show, each time it appoints someone for an ordinary
position, why it should not appoint one of its target-group applicants
for that position, and then why the target-group applicant it wants
for the additional position is nonetheless fully qualified (by uniform
departmental standards) for a new position in the department. If it
can do this, then its expansionist aims are irrelevant because that sort
of situation is exactly what the proposal is designed to handle. If we
assume bad faith on the part of the department, of course, we can
imagine all sorts of ways the proposed system could be abused. But
that is true of any system (including the current one).

Objection.   It is more subtle than that. Assume a virtual tie between
two candidates for an ordinary position. One is a member of a target
group, the other is not—say, for simplicity, a woman and a man. Isn't
there going to be an almost irresistible tendency to appoint the man
to the ordinary position and the woman to an additional position?
Wouldn't it be best for the department, the future of the profession,
and the future of two fine scholars to do that—rather than to offer the
ordinary position to the woman and nothing to the man? And won't
this make it difficult, even for the most alert and thoughtful people
of good will, to "see" the woman as better than the man whenever it
is a close call? And notice that candidates from the target groups are
actually trapped by this system. Individuals will not be able effectively
to insist that they be considered for ordinary positions only, since that
will simply mean no offer at all. (Departments will look until they find
people willing to take the additional positions.) Still worse, over time,
the incentives in this system will drive all target group appointments
into the extraordinary category. The maximal number of positions for
a department (or division) can be achieved, after all, only when there
are zero members of the target groups in ordinary positions.

Reply.   The last part of this objection rests on a misunderstanding.
Extraordinary positions automatically convert to ordinary ones when
the latter become open. If an ordinary position is added or becomes
vacant, it is automatically filled by one of the faculty members holding

extraordinary positions. So departments will not be able to do much in the way of manipulating themselves toward the maximal number of additional positions. That leaves the cases in which (a) an ordinary position comes open and the department has no extraordinary position to be converted, and (b) it is able to justify getting two for one by appointing a white male (say) to the ordinary position. Is this discriminatory? Is it tolerable? Advocates of the necessity of affirmative action claim that such difficulties exist now and are typically resolved in a discriminatory way. The "no need" wing concedes that this may happen and that historically it has happened very often ("Men need higher salaries than single women," etc.). This proposal at least resolves these difficult matters in a way that minimizes the discrimination. And over time, as the extraordinary positions are converted into ordinary ones, we can hope that the increased representation of the target groups will help correct such discriminatory tendencies. In the meantime, these sorts of close cases may often be resolved with two offers. But that is hardly an objection to the proposal, since at worst it evades a difficult problem of choice and is fair to both applicants.

Objection. It can never be fair to the one who is given the extraordinary position. No matter what the reality, the perception will be that such additional faculty members are inferior and supernumerary. If they are not inferior, why not simply fill all positions according to talent? Any two-track system will stigmatize and demean members of the target group as merely "good of their kind."[18]

Reply. True. The question is whether it is avoidable. If we were to eliminate affirmative action entirely we would eliminate this one excuse for prejudice, but we would surely not eliminate demeaning racial, ethnic, and gender stereotypes. So it is not as though we could free people of invidious stigmas by giving up on affirmative action. And in terms of working out a compromise between the no-need and necessity camps, giving it up is not an option; for the necessity camp, that would be capitulation, not compromise. If there is no need for affirmative action, then of course imposing this sort of additional burden on people is unjustifiable; if affirmative action is necessary, then the burden of it is an unavoidable evil, presumably outweighed by its good. Since that is the fundamental issue in dispute, a compromise can do no more than minimize such burdens. I suggest that they are minimal under this proposal.

Efficacy, Efficiency, and Expense

Objection.   It is hard to predict what the effect of this proposed system would be. The system might be effective in attracting members of the target groups to careers in higher education; it might be damaging to such careers; or it might leave things unchanged. It is hard to predict, but none of the possibilities is satisfactory. (1) If the new system leaves things unchanged, then its costs will have been unjustified. (2) If it does net damage to the career prospects of members of the target groups, then it will be unjustifiable. (3) If it is suddenly and dramatically effective, it will be enormously expensive and inefficient. (Expensive because institutions would immediately be flooded with qualified applicants for all the extraordinary positions, creating a huge, instantaneous drain on budgets that would only gradually decline as the extraordinary positions could be converted to ordinary ones. Inefficient because the sudden bulge in faculty size and the sudden change in budget could not be efficiently absorbed.) (4) Any positive change short of a sudden and dramatic one will be difficult to attribute to the new system (since so many other complex factors are already at work), and the system will consequently be difficult to justify. It will always be plausible to claim that we would have gotten the same change without the expense and inconvenience of the new system.

Reply.   It is hard to see how the proposed system could be damaging to higher education careers for members of target groups, since it guarantees them the availability of a proportionate share of places in graduate schools and positions on faculties. Not all logical possibilities need to be taken seriously for practical purposes.

Moreover, it seems unlikely that the effect on faculties would be sudden and dramatic. It is true that the number of available positions would go up immediately and in some cases dramatically. But it is also true that, except in the case of women, there are not large numbers of people ready to fill them. (For U.S. citizens, there are roughly two thousand doctorates awarded each year to African Americans, Hispanics, Asian Americans, and Native Americans combined—nearly half of them to women. Nationwide, there do not seem to be deficits in the percentages for these groups, except for Hispanics, although the figures for faculty include foreign nationals and may thus be misleading, especially for Asians. At any rate, this rough comparison shows that the percentage of blacks holding full-time faculty positions is roughly 4.1, while the percentage of doctorates awarded to African Americans over the last ten years is roughly 3.9. The corresponding faculty-to-doctorate ratios for the other groups are: Hispanics, 1.7/ 2.3; Asian Americans, 4.0/2.2; Native Americans, 0.4/0.4. See Tables 1–3.) [19] And in any case, the calculations are tied to relevant advanced degrees. A large percentage of target-group doctorates in education will not show up in the calculations made by departments in the humanities.

For women, nationwide, the overall situation is quite different. In graduate schools, the number of women now exceeds the number of men, and U.S. women now receive about 41 percent of the doctorates awarded to U.S. citizens. Their percentage of doctorates averaged over a recent ten-year period is 37.2, but if recent trends continue, that percentage will rise. Women make up roughly 27.6 percent of full-time instructional faculty nationwide. [20] It seems likely that a significant number of the additional positions offered to women under the plan could be filled immediately. But the distribution of available positions and degrees across disciplines is a key factor here, and that distribution is very uneven. In 1986–87, for example, women had under 20 percent of the doctorates in agriculture, computer science, engineering, mathematics, the physical sciences, and theology, but accounted for more than 50 percent of the doctorates in education, foreign languages, health professions, letters, library science, and psychology. [21]

For graduate schools nationwide, the enrollment data for doctoral programs are unfortunately submerged in the overall total for master's and doctoral programs, and those data were sorted only by sex, not by race or ethnic group. [22] In that overall total, the enrollment percentages for women now slightly overmatch their ten-year average percentage of baccalaureate degrees: 52 percent versus 49.2 percent. But much of that comes from counting part-time students. Women make up only 44 percent of the full-time graduate enrollment, whereas they constituted 51 percent of full-time freshmen at the undergraduate level in 1983— almost exactly their percentage of baccalaureate degrees awarded four years later.

Perhaps we can get a rough idea, however, of discrepancies in doctoral programs simply by comparing baccalaureate and doctoral degrees. Such a comparison, averaging baccalaureate degrees over a ten-year period and taking data on doctorates from 1988 (the latest year available) as indicative of enrollment data for that year, suggests

Table 1. Doctorate Awards by U.S. Citizenship, Race/Ethnicity, and Sex, 1978 to 1988

	1978	1979	1980	1981	1982	1983	1984	1985	1986	1987	1988	Percentage Change 1978–88
Total Doctorates[a]	30,875	31,239	31,020	31,357	31,106	31,280	31,332	31,291	31,896	32,367	33,456	8.4
Men	22,553	22,302	21,613	21,465	21,013	20,747	20,633	20,547	20,590	20,941	21,666	−3.9
Women	8,322	8,937	9,407	9,892	10,093	10,533	10,699	10,744	11,306	11,426	11,790	41.7
U.S. Citizens												
All U.S. Citizens[b]	25,291	25,464	25,221	25,061	24,388	24,358	24,026	23,363	23,081	22,991	23,172	−8.4
Men	17,936	17,580	16,875	16,360	15,559	15,119	14,729	14,217	13,633	13,581	13,667	−23.8
Women	7,355	7,884	8,346	8,701	8,829	9,239	9,297	9,146	9,448	9,410	9,505	29.2
White	21,811	21,920	21,993	21,980	21,677	21,699	21,349	20,757	20,626	20,470	20,685	−5.2
Men	15,573	15,261	14,848	14,459	13,987	13,609	13,170	12,805	12,303	12,172	12,296	−21.0
Women	6,238	6,659	7,145	7,521	7,690	8,090	8,179	7,952	8,323	8,298	8,389	34.5
African American	1,033	1,056	1,032	1,013	1,047	922	953	912	823	767	805	−22.1
Men	584	551	499	499	483	413	427	379	322	317	311	−46.7
Women	449	505	533	514	564	509	526	533	501	450	494	10.0
Hispanic	473	462	412	464	535	539	536	561	572	619	594	25.6
Men	317	308	256	275	344	288	314	300	303	333	321	1.3
Women	156	154	156	189	191	251	222	261	269	286	273	75.0
Asian American	390	428	458	465	452	492	512	516	531	542	612	56.9
Men	287	311	313	315	281	312	338	329	348	369	413	43.9
Women	103	117	145	150	171	180	174	187	183	173	199	93.2
American Indian	60	81	75	85	77	81	74	95	99	115	93	55.0
Men	50	56	46	56	44	50	54	39	58	62	51	2.0
Women	10	25	29	29	33	31	20	56	41	53	42	320.0
Non-U.S. Citizens, Total[b]	4,765	4,907	4,935	5,221	5,432	5,774	6,054	6,553	6,707	7,187	7,787	63.4
Men	4,018	4,106	4,126	4,360	4,536	4,825	5,024	5,394	5,481	5,839	6,278	56.2
Women	747	801	809	861	896	949	1,030	1,159	1,226	1,348	1,509	102.0

[a] Includes doctorates with unknown citizenship status and unknown race/ethnicity.
[b] Includes doctorates with unknown race/ethnicity.
Source: National Research Council, Washington, D.C., Doctorate Records File, various years.

Table 2. Full-time Instructional Faculty in Institutions of Higher Education, by Race/Ethnicity, Academic Rank, and Sex: Fall 1985

Academic rank and sex	Total	Race/ethnicity				
		White non-Hispanic	Black non-Hispanic	Hispanic	Asian or Pacific Islander	American Indian/ Alaskan Native
Men and women, all ranks	464,072	417,036	19,227	7,704	18,370	1,735
Professors	129,269	119,868	2,859	1,455	4,788	299
Associate professors	111,092	100,630	4,201	1,727	4,130	404
Assistant professors	111,308	97,496	5,895	1,968	5,469	480
Instructors	75,411	66,799	4,572	1,798	1,806	436
Lecturers	9,766	8,477	631	251	360	47
Other faculty	27,226	23,766	1,069	505	1,817	69
Men, all ranks	336,009	303,953	10,456	5,360	14,846	1,394
Professors	114,258	106,335	2,058	1,206	4,395	264
Associate professors	85,156	77,483	2,595	1,280	3,451	347
Assistant professors	71,463	62,582	2,923	1,316	4,240	402
Instructors	43,251	38,592	2,107	1,141	1,105	306
Lecturers	5,098	4,436	304	117	212	29
Other faculty	16,783	14,525	469	300	1,443	46
Women, all ranks	128,063	113,083	8,771	2,344	3,524	341
Professors	15,011	13,533	801	249	393	35
Associate professors	25,936	23,147	1,606	447	679	57
Assistant professors	39,845	34,914	2,972	652	1,229	78
Instructors	32,160	28,207	2,465	657	701	130
Lecturers	4,668	4,041	327	134	148	18
Other faculty	10,443	9,241	600	205	374	23

Note: Data exclude faculty employed by system offices. Totals may differ from figures reported on other tables because of varying survey methodologies.
Source: U.S. Equal Employment Opportunity Commission, Higher Education Staff Information Report File, 1985, unpublished data. (This table was prepared June 1989.)

discrepancies only for women (8.3 percent) and for African Americans (2.7 percent), for a cumulative total of 11 percent. In 1988, 23,172 doctorates were awarded to U.S. citizens. To deal with the discrepancies, roughly 2,549 additional graduate fellowships would have to be offered nationwide under this plan. If fellowships average $10,000 each, that amounts to a guarantee of some $25.5 million spread over the nearly five hundred institutions that have doctoral programs. Whether all these guaranteed fellowships would actually be awarded would of course depend on the number and qualifications of applicants.

Now of course these nationwide figures are somewhat misleading, since the calculations made by each institution will introduce rounded

Table 3. Bachelor's Degrees Conferred by Institutions of Higher Education, by Racial/Ethnic Group and Sex of Student: 1976–77 to 1986–87

Year and sex of student	Total	White non-Hispanic	Black non-Hispanic	Hispanic	Asian or Pacific Islander	American Indian/Alaskan Native	Non-resident alien
1976–77							
Total	917,900	807,688	58,636	18,743	13,793	3,326	15,714
Men	494,424	438,161	25,147	10,318	7,638	1,804	11,356
Women	423,476	369,527	33,489	8,425	6,155	1,522	4,358
1978–79							
Total	919,540	802,542	60,246	20,096	15,407	3,410	17,839
Men	476,065	418,215	24,659	10,418	8,261	1,736	12,776
Women	443,475	384,327	35,587	9,678	7,146	1,674	5,063
1980–81							
Total	934,800	807,319	60,673	21,832	18,794	3,593	22,589
Men	469,625	406,173	24,511	10,810	10,107	1,700	16,324
Women	465,175	401,146	36,162	11,022	8,687	1,893	6,265
1984–85							
Total	968,311	826,106	57,473	25,874	25,395	4,246	29,217
Men	476,148	405,085	23,018	12,402	13,554	1,998	20,091
Women	492,163	421,021	34,455	13,472	11,841	2,248	9,126
1986–87							
Total	991,260	841,820	56,555	26,990	32,618	3,971	29,306
Men	480,780	406,751	22,499	12,864	17,249	1,819	19,598
Women	510,480	435,069	34,056	14,126	15,369	2,152	9,708

Source: U.S. Department of Education, National Center for Education Statistics, "Degrees and Other Formal Awards Conferred" surveys, and Integrated Postsecondary Education Data System (IPEDS), "Completions" survey. (This table was prepared June 1989.)

numbers which, when cumulated, are likely to differ—perhaps significantly—from the totals given here. And it is true that if a given institution is very attractive to members of the target groups and has very few members of those groups on its faculty or in its graduate programs, it might well face a sudden and dramatic surge of candidates. Of course, if that institution's predicament is due to its discriminatory practices, it is hard to get too exercised about the burden it would have to assume to correct the injustice. If the institution has not been discriminatory but has simply been unable to find qualified applicants from the target groups, then it seems unlikely that there will be a sudden change in that situation at all. In sum, although there is admittedly a good deal of uncertainty here, it does not seem that the costs of the program are likely to be overwhelming.

That leaves the possibility that the new system might have no discernible positive effect at all, either because nothing changes after it is put into place or because the changes cannot confidently be ascribed to the system. The reply to this may be brief. If nothing changes (i.e., if no extraordinary positions are actually filled), then we will have lost nothing but the time and effort of putting the system into place. Given that this proposal calls only for a modification of existing procedures and the creation of some budget reserves that will have been unused, these costs will not have been great. And suppose, instead, that there is a modest, positive change that cannot confidently be attributed to the new system. (Perhaps a slight increase in the target group percentages in ordinary positions, but few or no offers of extraordinary ones.) Again the costs will have been minimal. Either way, the risk seems modest and worthwhile.

Objection.   But what is the probability of success? What is the rationale for making a sweeping change like this in a highly complex, long-established program?

Reply.   There is some evidence that the current system is ineffective.[23] Moreover, the deadlock between the no-need and necessity camps has produced uncertainty and ad hoc compromise throughout the current system—from the confidential meetings of tenure committees and the recruitment policies of departments, to the interpretation of Supreme Court decisions. It seems worthwhile to try to make something of a fresh start that builds on the ground we have gained in the last few decades. That now common ground is considerable and provides a solid basis for a compromise to break the deadlock.

Here is what I take to be the relevant common ground, stated swiftly and abstractly, merely as a set of reminders.

Opportunity is a basic good in our social system, because we have organized many fundamental social institutions around the notion of maximal personal autonomy and initiative. We expect the institutions so organized to be responsive to the activity of individuals but otherwise to be largely passive and unintrusive. In terms of gainful employment, for example, our economic system is mostly passive. There is no legal obligation to work, and the social pressure to work is fairly thoroughly offset for people who stay busy, licit, healthy, and out of the welfare system. By contrast, our educational system is coercive in getting the participation of children from age five to sixteen, rather aggressive through the remainder of high school, and mostly passive thereafter. Mechanistic images are useful metaphors here: Think of passive institutions as complex, hand-operated mechanical devices.

Individuals who, for one reason or another, cannot act to trigger passive social mechanisms either will be excluded altogether from the public goods those mechanisms produce or will get only such "corrective" mechanisms as the welfare system provides. The opportunity to act is of course a necessary condition for action. Thus to be coherent and effective, the parts of a social system premised on such action must guarantee opportunity. And if the social system is also fundamentally committed to principles of equality, then within the scope of those egalitarian principles the guarantee of opportunity must be a guarantee of *equal* opportunity.

Moreover, the opportunity must be "effective" and not purely formal. That is, the guarantee must be that individuals will be able (through their own efforts) actually to trigger the passive social mechanisms if they choose. It is not coherent and effective to set up a passive system meant to serve a given population and then merely to leave its mechanisms unlocked, as it were, if at the same time its levers are out of reach. So the principle of equal opportunity is necessarily a principle of equal effective, as well as equal formal, opportunity.

Equal employment opportunity must be a fundamental commitment for us as long as the employment system is passive and the goods it provides are so fundamental and have so few substitutes.

It is indisputable that large groups of people have been systematically denied equal employment opportunity in our history; that those groups have historically included blacks, women, Native Americans, Jews, Asians, Hispanics, and Catholics; and that such denial of opportunity has occurred in faculty appointments in higher education. Moreover, there is reason to believe that for some groups, including blacks and women, employment opportunities in higher education are still not equal.

Patterns of discrimination in employment are often self-perpetuating. Denial of opportunity leads to diminished ability, which reinforces the denial. This is especially troublesome where entry into a position requires lengthy and expensive preparation, and for that reason (at least) it is troublesome for faculty appointments in higher education.

Where self-perpetuating patterns of discrimination exist, in institutions that are largely passive, sustained affirmative steps may be necessary to break the cycle—affirmative because merely unlocking the mechanism will not bring the levers within reach; sustained because isolated interventions, even if successful in breaking the pattern for one cohort, are unlikely to do much to eliminate the disadvantages that replicate themselves.

That much is clear. What appears to be disagreement about it (e.g., over the justice of redistributive policies designed to implement equal opportunity) is in fact disagreement about one or more of four other things: (1) The scope of our commitments to equality: adults only? citizens? people who are responsible for their own disabilities? (2) The identification of the social mechanisms for which equal opportunity guarantees must be made: housing? medical care? use of wilderness trails by emphysemics? (3) The extent to which mechanisms that have been unlocked de jure actually remain locked in practice: for example, policies designed to produce de facto segregation indirectly. (4) The extent to which the levers of unlocked mechanisms are nonetheless out of reach: for example, available but unaffordable housing and public buildings inaccessible to people in wheelchairs.

The compromise offered in the system proposed here takes seriously all of that common ground and bypasses, as far as possible, the remaining sources of disagreement. It is quite passive, relying heavily on the choices and initiatives of applicants. But it is also more than merely formal. It guarantees fully qualified applicants from the target groups that, until we can be sure the levers are fully within their reach (as indicated by their proportionate representation in graduate schools and faculties), they will not be shut out by the combination of a shortage of positions and subtle forms of personal or structural bias.

Enforcement

The methods of enforcement in this proposal would surely have been naive if put forward thirty years ago—or perhaps even fifteen. The legacy of overt discrimination practiced for so long in higher education, the resistance of faculties to result-oriented policies for change, the newness of the affirmative action policies being proposed, the intellectual windmilling about the justification and implementation of those policies, and the inexperience of peer review committees and professional organizations left the field wide open for evasive and obstructive maneuver.

Times have changed. Sensitivity to overt discrimination has changed as dramatically as sensitivity to smoke-filled meeting rooms. Significant procedural changes have been made to deal with covert and structural forms of discrimination. Peer review mechanisms are in place. Many professional organizations and advocacy groups routinely monitor institutions for compliance with equal opportunity and affirmative action guidelines. The government has elaborate data on these matters. And even though there is a deadlock on the issue of preferential treatment, the intellectual and legal climate is otherwise more settled.

My assumption, therefore, is that in the present circumstances, the operation of a clear, readily observable commitment of resources by an institution can be adequately monitored and enforced with a minimum of bureaucratic machinery. Let the federal legislature specify target groups, define a uniform policy of extraordinary positions (with the necessary exceptions), and define the sanctions for failure to adopt such a policy or to comply with it. Let the Departments of Education and/or Labor concern themselves exclusively with the adoption of the policies in the new system (guarantees of the requisite number of extraordinary positions) and the publication of the relevant data for each school and faculty. Let that data be publicly available and easily accessible to candidates, professional organizations, and advocacy groups. Let members of target groups who are denied available positions be entitled (if they choose to initiate it) to a review of their cases by a disinterested committee of the institution's faculty. Let applicants who are dissatisfied with that review have recourse to the courts for a reversal of the institution's decision (and for costs but not for damages). Let the Department of Justice have the power to launch civil prosecutions for noncompliance.

Objection. Surely the remedies proposed for individuals will be ineffective. Who will sue under those conditions? Since all that would be available is the job itself (in an obviously hostile environment) very few people could afford the legal proceedings. Only those who can afford to pay a lawyer even if they lose (or are able to find one willing to risk getting nothing against the possibility of getting nothing more than ordinary legal fees) and who are at the same time able to wait for the legal process to take its course could afford to do this.

Reply. Any adversarial process concerning affirmative action that is undertaken by an individual will involve delays and expense. And if the aim is to get the position that one has been unjustly denied, one will always have to face the hostility of adversaries among one's colleagues. But several things about this proposal mitigate those problems. For one thing, aggrieved candidates will not be pitting themselves against the (innocent) people who were actually appointed. The argument will not be that those people did not deserve, or should actually lose, their positions. The argument will only be that the aggrieved applicants deserve the available extraordinary positions. Moreover, the case to be decided is relatively free of those notoriously slippery matters of professional judgment that courts are so reluctant to override: There will either be an available extraordinary position or not. If there is, then all a plaintiff will have to show is a set of credentials that is, on its face, fully sufficient as a qualification for admission or appointment to the program or department involved. That will shift the burden to the defendant institution to give cogent reasons for holding either that the credentials are not as good as they appear or that (in terms of some institutional policy adopted prior to the decision at issue and followed in the appointment actually made) the credentials are not sufficient.

Will this work? Consider the range of possibilities. Clear cases—ones in which the institution is clearly in the right or clearly in the wrong—will surely be identified in the institution's internal review and, assuming good faith on the part of everyone, will be settled promptly. That leaves close calls and bad faith.

Close calls—that is, ones in which it is plausible to believe that the institution might have made a mistake in its evaluation of the candidate—will also be identified in the internal review. And an institution acting in good faith may well decide to make an offer to the candidate at that point. This is so because, by hypothesis, there is a strong likelihood that the candidate is in fact fully qualified and will serve the institution well (especially if not forced into court to prove it). And the legal expenses involved with making a dubious decision stick may be considerable. If the institution does proceed to court in such close cases, it is true (given current practice) that it is likely to prevail. Plaintiffs who know this and who recognize that the institution also has a strong case may decide not to go to court. But it is not clear that this is regrettable—as long as the institution is acting in good faith.

As for bad faith, plaintiffs should be able to get a good deal of help. Manipulative, duplicitous, and frankly noncompliant institutions will get attention from many sources, including the Justice Department. But it seems to me that the guarantee of enforcement for this system will come primarily from the pressure of accrediting bodies, professional associations, advocacy groups, media attention, and peer pressure. And that is something we could not have said thirty years ago.[24]

In sum, the compromise outlined here appears to be a promising way of circumventing the central controversy about preferential treatment. It recognizes the powerful, subtle, and persistent effects of injustice; it offers a genuinely powerful and enforceable remedy; it makes that remedy available when, and only when, there is reason to believe it is justified; it leaves merit criteria and faculty responsibility for them intact; and it avoids reverse discrimination. Such a compromise does nothing to help settle the underlying philosophical issues. But until we have such a settlement, it seems a reasonable basis for action.

Notes

1. This last point is important, because it shapes the nature of the debate on affirmative action so dramatically. Merely dropping male-only admissions policies did have an immediate and large effect on the composition of student populations at prestigious colleges and universities that went coed between 1965 and 1975. The affirmative action required to produce that change was minimal and in some cases concerned efforts to ensure an "adequate" population of males. Note also that "at least since *Green v. County School Board* 391

U.S. 430 (1968), it has been clear that a public body which has itself been adjudged to have engaged in racial discrimination cannot bring itself into compliance with the Equal Protection Clause simply by ending its unlawful acts and adopting a neutral stance." Opinion by Justices Brennan, White, Marshall, and Blackmun in *Regents of the University of California v. Bakke*, 438 U.S. 265 (1978), at 362.

2. *Regents of the University of California v. Bakke*, 438 U.S. 265 (1978). Justice Powell, writing for the court, rejects quotas (307) but holds that race may be considered as one factor among many in university admissions policies (318, 320). Justices Brennan, White, Marshall, and Blackmun hold that there is no constitutional difference between setting aside a certain number of places for minority candidates and giving them a certain number of additional points in the application process. Either method is in principle permissible (378). Justice Stevens, with whom Justices Burger, Stewart, and Rehnquist concur, holds that it is impermissible in these cases ever to say yes to one candidate and no to another solely on the basis of race (418).

3. It is often conceded that additional determinants may be used to break ties between candidates. And in a closely related move, it may be conceded that preferential treatment of various sorts (for veterans, women, minorities) is appropriate where there is not much difference between minimal and maximal job performance and hence between minimal and maximal qualifications. The former (tie-breaking) is relevant to faculty appointments; the latter is not.

4. I use the abstract term "target groups" rather than the familiar "women and minorities" to indicate that this discussion is meant to be independent of decisions about which groups are marked for affirmative action. But the sort of affirmative action considered here is meant to respond to the persistent injustices of discrimination. Thus target groups will necessarily be drawn only from those groups that continue to suffer from such past or present injustices. The standard list, for a national frame of reference, includes women, African Americans, Asian Americans, Hispanics, and Native North Americans.

5. Compensation for victims of past injustice is appropriate, especially where adjustments can be made to overturn specific injustices (i.e., an identifiable individual denied an identifiable, merited position in favor of a less qualified candidate). But that sort of compensation is irrelevant to affirmative action policies designed to select candidates from an equal opportunity pool.

6. In trying to find this safe path, I have drawn ideas from many sorts of plans, ranging from attempts to reserve a certain number of "places" for minorities (e.g., U.C. Davis Medical School) to various incentive systems with explicit numerical goals (e.g., the "Madison Plan" at the University of Wisconsin).

7. The proposal here is to do this department by department, to encourage a more uniform distribution across disciplines. If the calculations were made simply for each institution, a huge percentage in one or two fields might

satisfy the criteria and effectively stop affirmative efforts in other fields. For reasons explained in Note 11, I recommend aggregating data for the faculty calculations, and if those reasons turn out to be applicable here as well, I would certainly yield to them.

8. Ten is a somewhat arbitrary figure, chosen in part to match the way such data are often reported (for example in the *Digest of Education Statistics*). It is clear that we would not want to tie these calculations to yearly oscillations. We want to deal with relatively stable trends, so the frame of reference must cover several years at least. On the other hand, we do not want the frame of reference to be so large that recent trends will be lost in the calculations. Thus we wouldn't want to take twenty- or thirty-year samples. But why ten years rather than five or fifteen? Nothing in my argument hinges on the number. I assume demographers are the ones who should settle such issues.

9. There are various ways of making these calculations. The simplest, and least expansionary, is to take each target group in turn and compare it to the current first-year graduate class in the program, with the object of finding how many places in the class it "lacks." So, for example, if 10 percent of the relevant baccalaureate degrees nationally have gone to each group, but the current population of each in the local program is only 5 percent, then we would guarantee as many additional fellowships for each as it "lacks" in the current distribution. Thus: if k, l, and m are each represented by five students of a total of one hundred, but each has 10 percent of the baccalaureate degrees, then each "lacks" five students of the hundred. Thus five additional fellowships should be guaranteed for each, for a total of fifteen.

10. That is, if the percentage of target-group students in the current first-year class matches or exceeds the standard without the use of additional fellowships, then no additional fellowships should be offered.

11. Here, as below under number 3, I do not even make a tentative proposal for a time period because I am so uncertain about how to argue for one. With respect to faculty appointments, my temptation is to assume (absent evidence to the contrary) that in order to be sure of breaking the self-perpetuating cycle, we would have to run the program long enough to have one complete turnover in the population of current faculty. That means, I suppose, something like forty years. But I am unsure whether that assumption makes sense, whether the figure should be adjustable in terms of how rapidly or slowly the proposal gets results, and whether the figure for graduate fellowships should be higher or lower than the figure for faculty positions.

12. By "appropriate aggregation" I simply mean that, for the purposes of the calculations outlined here, it may not be wise to proceed department by department. Rather, we may wish to pool the data from groups of related departments (e.g., into the typical academic divisions or schools) or even to treat a whole college or university as a unit (see Note 11). But all departments should be included.

13. Whether these calculations should be made for each department separately, for each academic division and school, or for the institution as a whole is an interesting question. The institution-wide approach has two very unattractive features. First, it introduces the sort of administrative complexity that virtually guarantees everyone's dissatisfaction. Departments will compete for the additional positions by proffering candidates. Someone will then have to decide between candidates in this very heterogeneous pool (studio artists, classicists, accountants, chemists, lawyers), in terms of their absolute academic merit, the staffing needs of the various departments involved, budgetary or tenure considerations, or some combination of factors. All of this is open for manipulation, misunderstanding, and outright abuse. Under those conditions it would be very difficult to establish that an institution has been noncompliant, even if it has refused to fill any of its available positions. Second, if all or most of the additional positions are filled, the institution-wide approach will tend to entrench current patterns of specialization among members of the target groups. It will do nothing to address the problem of whole disciplines in which minority participation is now negligible. And departments added several years after the program has gone into effect may be locked out of it altogether. At the other extreme, department-by-department calculations seem outlandish in cases where numbers are small. Say there is a three-member classics department, with no minority members, at a small college. The data on percentages of doctorates awarded show that 3.9 percent of the members of the department should be African Americans. Adding one full-time position is obviously a large overcorrection. Adding an appropriate fraction consigns the affirmative action operation for this department to the (usually exploitative) practice of hiring adjunct faculty course by course. It thus seems necessary to pool this department with some others. As long as the pool stays within some sensible boundaries (say, in this case, the humanities, or languages and literature) the administrative difficulties can be minimized. It may be that the best uniform approach would be to adopt a rebuttable presumption in favor of aggregation by academic division or school, with exceptions for institutions that can justify an institution-wide, departmental, or mixed system.

14. In cases where the vacant ordinary position must be reserved for a particular subspecialty within the department, and there is no one among the extraordinary faculty with the requisite subspecialty, the conversion will not be possible.

15. In a thoroughly unconvincing footnote in the *Bakke* case, Justice Powell dismisses this sort of reply as follows:

> Petitioner [the university] defines "quota" as a requirement which must be met but can never be exceeded, regardless of the quality of the minority applicants. Petitioner declares that there is no "floor" under the

total number of minority students admitted; completely unqualified students will not be admitted simply to meet a "quota." Neither is there a "ceiling," since an unlimited number could be admitted through the general admissions process. On this basis the special admissions program does not meet petitioner's definition of a quota.

The court below found—and petitioner does not deny—that white applicants could not compete for the 16 places reserved solely for the special admissions program. 18 Cal. 3rd at 44, 533 P. 2d, at 1159. Both courts below characterized this as a "quota" system. (*Regents of the University of California v. Bakke* 438 U.S. 265, at 288–89)

This conflates two issues: the concept of a quota and the practice of offering certain benefits exclusively to members of a given group. Surely the university's definition of a quota was on the right track, if overstated. A quota is a required minimum or maximum (or both), although it need not lower qualification criteria. One may offer a certain number of places to qualified women or blacks without establishing anything that could reasonably be called a quota. Of course if we are prohibited from offering any benefits exclusively to members of the target groups, then all efforts at affirmative action are prohibited. That is not what Justice Powell intends to do.

16. Since the availability of the additional positions is linked to the percentages of target-group representation in the ordinary faculty, everyone will bear the consequences of such a reduction in a roughly proportional way. (A reduction in the number of white males, for example, will necessarily increase the percentages of target groups and thus reduce the availability of additional positions for them.)

17. I am leaving aside, for the moment, the possibility that institutions might not get extra funding to cover the cost of the additional positions, thus forcing them to sacrifice other parts of their operations to run the affirmative action program proposed here.

18. Stephen L. Carter, "The Best Black, and Other Tales," *Reconstruction* 1, no. 1 (1990): 6–48. I am indebted to Steven M. Cahn for calling my attention to this article.

19. Unless otherwise noted, all data on doctorates were drawn from the National Research Council, Doctorate Records File, as published in Deborah J. Carter and Reginald Wilson, *Eighth Annual Status Report: Minorities in Higher Education* (Washington, D.C.: American Council on Education, 1989). All other statistics are drawn from the *Digest of Education Statistics (1989)* (Washington, D.C.: U.S. Department of Education, 1989).

20. I say "roughly" throughout, not only because the data from 1982–83 are unaccountably omitted in some of the tables in the *Digest of Education Statistics*, but because collection methods are somewhat obscure to me—par-

ticularly with respect to how much is "imputed" to compensate for incomplete responses.

21. *Digest of Education Statistics (1989)*, pp. 249–50.

22. See *Digest of Education Statistics (1989)*, p. 179.

23. Blacks, in particular, are losing ground in numbers of baccalaureate and doctoral degrees conferred. See Table 1. And among full-time faculty members, the 20-percent disparity in tenure rates between men and women has been constant during the 1980s, even though there have been steady increases in the number of women in doctoral programs and on faculties. (Roughly 70 percent of the men are tenured, while only 50 percent of the women are tenured.) See the *Digest of Education Statistics (1989)*, p. 216.

24. For discussion of the proposal in this chapter, I am grateful to many deeply sceptical colleagues and friends. Special thanks go to Charlotte Becker, Allie Frazier, and Robert Sulkin, whose help should in no way be construed as an endorsement.

PART II

4 *What Good Am I?*

Laurence Thomas

What good am I as a black professor? The raging debate over affirmative action surely invites me to ask this searching question of myself, just as it must invite those belonging to other so-called suspect categories to ask it of themselves. If knowledge is color blind, why should it matter whether the face in front of the classroom is a European white, a Hispanic, an Asian, and so on? Why should it matter whether the person is female or male?

One of the most well-known arguments for affirmative action is the role-model argument. It is also the argument that I think is the least satisfactory—not because women and minorities do not need role models—everyone does—but because as the argument is often presented, it comes dangerously close to implying that about the only thing a black, for instance, can teach a white is how not to be a racist. Well, I think better of myself than that. And I hope that all women and minorities feel the same about themselves. It is a credit to the authors of this volume that they do not make much of this argument.

But even if the role-model argument were acceptable in some version or the other, affirmative action would still seem unsavory, as the implicit assumption about those hired as affirmative action appointments is that they are less qualified than those who are not. For, so the argument goes, the practice would be unnecessary if, in the first place, affirmative action appointees were the most qualified for the position, since they would be hired by virtue of their merits. I call this the counterfactual argument from qualifications.

Now, while I do not want to say much about it, this argument has always struck me as extremely odd. In a morally perfect world, it is no doubt true that if women and minorities were the most qualified they would be hired by virtue of their merits. But this truth tells me nothing about how things are in this world. It does not show that biases built up over decades and centuries do not operate in the favor of, say, white males over nonwhite males. It is as if one argued against feeding the starving simply on the grounds that in a morally perfect world starvation would not exist. Perhaps it would not. But this is no argument against feeding the starving now.

It would be one thing if those who advance the counterfactual argument from qualifications addressed the issue of built-up biases that operate against women and minorities. Then I could perhaps suppose that they are arguing in good faith. But for them to ignore these built-up biases in the name of an ideal world is sheer hypocrisy. It is to confuse what the ideal should be with the steps that should be taken to get there. Sometimes the steps are very simple or, in any case, purely procedural: instead of A, do B; or perform a series of well-defined steps that guarantee the outcome. Not so with nonbiased hiring, however, since what is involved is a change in attitude and feelings—not even merely a change in belief. After all, it is possible to believe something quite sincerely and yet not have the emotional wherewithal to act in accordance with that belief. It is this reality regarding sexism and racism that I believe is not fully appreciated in this volume.

The philosophical debate over affirmative action has stalled, as Lawrence C. Becker observes, because so many who oppose it, and some who do not, are unwilling to acknowledge the fact that sincere belief in equality does not entail a corresponding change in attitude and feelings in day-to-day interactions with women and minorities. Specifically, sincere belief does not eradicate residual and, thus, unintentional sexist and racist attitudes.[1] So, joviality among minorities may be taken by whites as the absence of intellectual depth or sincerity on the part of those minorities, since such behavior is presumed to be uncommon among high-minded intellectual whites. Similarly, it is a liability for academic women to be too fashionable in their attire, since fashionably attired women are often taken by men as aiming to be seductive.

Lest there be any misunderstanding, nothing I have said entails that unqualified women and minorities should be hired. I take it to be obvious, though, that whether someone is the best qualified is often a judgment call. On the other hand, what I have as much as said is that there are built-up biases in the hiring process that disfavor women and minorities and need to be corrected. I think of it as rather on the order of correcting for unfavorable moral head winds. It is possible to be committed to gender and racial equality and yet live a life in which residual, and thus unintentional, sexism and racism operate to varying degrees of explicitness.

I want to return now to the question with which I began this essay: What good am I as a black professor? I want to answer this question because, insofar as our aim is a just society, I think it is extremely important to see the way in which it does matter that the person in front of the class is not always a white male, notwithstanding the truth that knowledge, itself, is color blind.

Teaching is not just about transmitting knowledge. If it were, then students could simply read books and professors could simply pass out tapes or lecture notes. Like it or not, teachers are the object of intense emotions and feelings on the part of students solicitous of faculty approval and affirmation. Thus, teaching is very much about intellectual affirmation; and there can be no such affirmation of the student by the mentor in the absence of deep trust between them, be the setting elementary or graduate school. Without this trust, a mentor's praise will ring empty; constructive criticism will seem mean-spirited; and advice will be poorly received, if sought after at all. A student needs to be confident that he can make a mistake before the professor without being regarded as stupid in the professor's eyes and that the professor is interested in seeing beyond his weaknesses to his strengths. Otherwise, the student's interactions with the professor will be plagued by uncertainty; and that uncertainty will fuel the self-doubts of the student.

Now, the position that I should like to defend, however, is not that only women can trust women, only minorities can trust minorities, and only whites can trust whites. That surely is not what we want. Still, it must be acknowledged, first of all, that racism and sexism have very often been a bar to such trust between mentor and student, when the professor has been a white male and the student has been either a woman or a member of a minority group. Of course, trust between mentor and student is not easy to come by in any case. This, though, is compatible with women and minorities having even greater problems if the professor is a white male.

Sometimes a woman professor will be necessary if a woman student is to feel the trust of a mentor that makes intellectual affirmation possible; sometimes a minority professor will be necessary for a minority student; indeed, sometimes a white professor will be necessary for a white student. (Suppose the white student is from a very sexist and racist part of the United States, and it takes a white professor to undue the student's biases.)

Significantly, though, in an academy where there is gender and racial diversity among the faculty, that diversity alone gives a woman or minority student the hope that intellectual affirmation is possible. This is so even if the student's mentor should turn out to be a white male. For part of what secures our conviction that we are living in a just society is not merely that we experience justice, but that we see justice around us. A diverse faculty serves precisely this end in terms of women and minority students believing that it is possible for them to have an intellectually affirming mentor relationship with a faculty member regardless of the faculty's gender or race.

Naturally, there are some women and minority students who will achieve no matter what the environment. Harriet Jacobs and Frederick Douglass were slaves who went on to accomplish more than many of us will who have never seen the chains of slavery. Neither, though, would have thought their success a reason to leave slavery intact. Likewise, the fact that there are some women and minorities who will prevail in spite of the obstacles is no reason to leave the status quo in place.

There is another part of the argument. Where there is intellectual affirmation, there is also gratitude. When a student finds that affirmation in a faculty member, a bond is formed, anchored in the student's gratitude, that can weather almost anything. Without such ties there could be no "ole boy" network—a factor that is not about racism, but a kind of social interaction running its emotional course. When women and minority faculty play an intellectually affirming role in the lives of white male students, such faculty undermine a nonracist and nonsexist pattern of emotional feelings that has unwittingly served the sexist and racist end of passing the intellectual mantle from white male to white male. For what we want, surely, is not just blacks passing the mantle to blacks, women to women, and white males to white males, but a world in which it is possible for all to see one another as proper recipients of the intellectual mantle. Nothing serves this end better than the gratitude between mentor and student that often enough ranges over differences between gender and race or both.

Ideally, my discussion of trust, intellectual affirmation, and gratitude should have been supplemented with a discussion of nonverbal behavior. For it seems to me that what has been ignored by all of the authors is the way in which judgments are communicated not simply by what is said but by a vast array of nonverbal behavior. Again, a verbal and sincere commitment to equality, without the relevant change in emotions and feelings, will invariably leave nonverbal behavior intact. Mere voice intonation and flow of speech can be a dead giveaway that the listener does not expect much of substance to come from the speaker. Anyone who doubts this should just remind her- or himself that it is a commonplace to remark to someone over the phone that he sounds tired or "down" or distracted, where the basis for this judgment, obviously, can only be how the individual sounds. One can get the clear sense that one called at the wrong time just by the way in which the other person responds or gets involved in the conversation. So, ironically, there is a sense in which it can be easier to convince ourselves that we are committed to gender and racial equality than it is to convince a woman or a minority person; for the latter see and experience our nonverbal behavior in a way that we ourselves do not. Specifically, it so often happens that a woman or minority can see that a person's nonverbal behavior belies their verbal support of gender and racial equality in faculty hiring—an interruption here, or an all too quick dismissal of a remark there. And this is to say nothing of the ways in which the oppressor often seems to know better than the victim how the victim is affected by the oppression that permeates her or his life, an arrogance that is communicated in a myriad of ways. This is not the place, though, to address the topic of social justice and nonverbal behavior.[2]

Before moving on let me consider an objection to my view. No doubt some will balk at the very idea of women and minority faculty intellectually affirming white male students. But this is just so much nonsense on the part of those balking. For I have drawn attention to a most powerful force in the lives of all individuals, namely trust and gratitude; and I have indicated that just as these feelings have unwittingly served racist and sexist ends, they can serve ends that are morally laudable. Furthermore, I have rejected the idea, often implicit in the role-model argument, that women and minority faculty are only good for their own kind. What is more, the position I have advocated is not one of subservience in the least, as I have spoken of an affirming role that underwrites an often unshakable debt of gratitude.

So, to return to the question with which I began this essay: I matter as a black professor and so do women and minority faculty generally, because collectively, if not in each individual case, we represent the hope, sometimes in a very personal way, that the university is an environment where the trust that gives rise to intellectual affirmation and the accompanying gratitude is possible for all, and between all peoples. Nothing short of the reality of diversity can permanently anchor this hope for ourselves and posterity.

This argument for diversity is quite different from those considered by Robert L. Simon. I do not advocate the representation of given viewpoints or the position that the ethnic and gender composition of faculty members should be proportional to their numbers in society. The former is absurd because it is a mistake to insist that points of view are either gender- or color-coded. The latter is absurd because it would actually entail getting rid of some faculty, since the percentage of Jews in the academy far exceeds their percentage in the population. If one day this should come to be true of blacks or Hispanics, they in turn would be fair game.

Francis rightly observes, though, that the continued absence of any diversity whatsoever draws attention to itself. My earlier remarks about nonverbal behavior taken in conjunction with my observations about trust, affirmation, and gratitude are especially apropos here. The complete absence of diversity tells departments more about themselves than no doubt they are prepared to acknowledge.

I would like to conclude with a concrete illustration of the way in which trust and gratitude can make a difference in the academy. As everyone knows, being cited affirmatively is an important indication of professional success. Now, who gets cited is not just a matter of what is true and good. On the contrary, students generally cite the works of their mentors and the work of others introduced to them by their mentors; and, on the other hand, mentors generally cite the work of those students of theirs for whom they have provided considerable intellectual affirmation. Sexism and racism have often been obstacles to faculty believing that women and minorities can be proper objects of full intellectual affirmation. It has also contributed to the absence of women and minority faculty which, in turn, has made it well-nigh impossible for white male students to feel an intellectual debt of gratitude to women and minority faculty. Their presence in the academy cannot help but bring about a change with regard to so simple a matter as patterns of citation, the professional ripple effect of which will be significant beyond many of our wildest dreams.

If social justice were just a matter of saying or writing the correct words, then equality would have long ago been a *fait accompli* in the academy. For I barely know anyone who is a faculty member who has not bemoaned the absence of minorities and women in the academy, albeit to varying degrees. So, I conclude with a very direct question: Is it really possible that so many faculty could be so concerned that women and minorities should flourish in the academy, and yet so few do? You will have to forgive me for not believing that it is. For as any good Kantian knows, one cannot consistently will an end without also willing the means to that end. Onora O'Neill writes: "Willing, after all, is not just a matter of wishing that something were the case, but involves committing oneself to doing something to bring that situation about when opportunity is there and recognized. Kant expressed this point by insisting that rationality requires that whoever wills some end wills the necessary means insofar as these are available."[3] If Kant is right, then much hand-wringing talk about social equality for women and minorities can only be judged insincere.

NOTES

1. For a most illuminating discussion along this line, see Adrian M. S. Piper's very important essay, "Higher-Order Discrimination," in Owen Flanagan and Amelie Oksenberg Rorty, eds., *Identity, Character, and Morality: Essays in Moral Psychology* (Cambridge: MIT Press, 1990).

2. For an attempt, see my "Moral Deference," *Philosophical Forum* (forthcoming).

3. Onora O'Neill, *Constructions of Reason: Explorations of Kant's Practical Philosophy* (Cambridge University Press, 1989), p. 90.

5 Who "Counts" on Campus?

Ann Hartle

The need for "diversity" is the only specifically academic argument for affirmative action in faculty appointments. According to this view, education is an enterprise in which the student learns by being exposed to different perspectives on the world, or at least on the human world. The educationally valuable perspectives, we are told, are those of gender, race, and ethnic background.

There is an underlying supposition about human rationality that is expressed in this view of what education should be. The supposition is that each of us is born into a certain limited perspective on the human world. Each sex, race, and ethnic group has its own perspective, and if I simply remain within my own perspective, I cannot really learn what it means to be a human being. Indeed, it is supposed that I cannot clearly understand my own perspective from within; I must see it from another perspective. Then it will appear as arbitrary as it really is. Thus, the ability to step into other perspectives is what a "liberal" education should aim at: the student must be set free from his own narrow, exclusive perspective, that is, from his own given set of prejudices. This process will be made possible by constituting a faculty and a curriculum in which many perspectives are represented.

It seems to me to be perfectly plausible that most scholars of Islam might be Islamic, that most scholars of Latin American literature might be Latin American, and so forth. This is plausible because interest in these subjects could well have nontheoretical roots in such things as family life and religion. There is even a certain plausibility in the notion that being brought up in a culture gives one a kind of immediate access to an affective dimension of that culture. But those who argue that diversity is essential are committed to the much stronger claim that the "givens" of nature and culture are necessary for understanding the products of human thought and culture, for example, that one must be black in order really to understand black history and literature, that one must be a woman if one is to have access to a crucial dimension of human experience.

Do we not, then, have an incoherent view of what education should be or can be? On the one hand, we are told that it is essential to step outside one's native perspective and into another arbitrary perspective. On the other hand, we are told that only an "insider" can really understand the native perspective. In either case, education would be impossible.

The very idea of "education" entails the need for somehow going beyond the givens of biology and ethnic background. But it is difficult to see how anything is to be gained by trading one arbitrary perspective for another. If education does proceed by introducing the student to different perspectives on human life, these should not be the arbitrary perspectives of sex, race, and ethnic origin, perspectives tied to the very native domains we are trying to transcend.

Having granted the possibility of noncognitive influence on academic interest, it must be said that factors of sex, race, and ethnic background do not determine success in understanding anything about what it means to be human. The ability to understand an author is not "in the blood" or in the chromosomes. It is difficult to think of anyone who has shown a more profound understanding of Dante than Charles Singleton or T. S. Eliot. And Italian students have to work just as hard at trying to understand the human meaning of Dante's poem as Americans, black or white. If the only thing an author (or a teacher) did was to express a perspective of sex or race, he would not be worth our trouble. The very possibility of "education" implies that it is both difficult and possible to move beyond the limits of these perspectives.

The goal of faculty diversity as it is pursued in affirmative action policies has nothing to do with the only kind of diversity that is academically relevant. Differences of sex, race, and ethnic background do not guarantee differences in intellectual perspective. On the contrary, while diversity of appearances is pursued as the highest academic value, diversity of thought is avoided and discouraged. So, for example, blacks who are not "politically correct" and women who do not share the feminist perspective often find that they do not "count" on campus.

Reflections on Affirmative Action in Academia

6

Robert G. Turnbull

The reflections in this essay can be briefly summarized as follows:

1. The special racial, ethnic, cultural, and religious makeup of the American population requires for a number of reasons that this diversity find an appropriate counterpart in those academic institutions most responsible for the cultural, scientific, and reflective life of the nation, namely, the colleges and universities.
2. There is no legitimate reason for our colleges and universities to recruit and encourage any but competent persons in their several fields of teaching, research, and service.
3. The appropriate determiners of competence for the purpose of employment and promotion of persons in the several fields are recognized experts in the relevant fields (usually faculty members of the recruiting and encouraging institution).
4. The standard criteria for academic performance—namely, teaching, research, and service—remain appropriate (in the recruitment of beginning faculty, the promise of satisfaction of those criteria). To these must be added collegiality or the promise of it.

Quite obviously 1 may be at odds with 2, 3, and 4. And 2, 3, and 4 may be thought inconsistent with advocacy of affirmative action programs in academia. The remainder of this essay will be an attempt to remove these apparent inconsistencies. In so doing I hope to be able to make a case for the continuation—even the enhancement—of affirmative action programs in academic institutions.

1. Diversity

The United States, despite lapses from moral and constitutional grace, is a special nation. By constitution and historical encouragement of immigration and naturalization, it is committed to the recognition and preservation of the individual rights of a racially, ethnically, and religiously diverse population. And there is a judicial and legislative history of efforts, again despite occasional lapses, to allow for maximum diversity while safeguarding those individual rights.

Given the historical and legal encouragement of such diversity, members of diverse groups may, *ceteris paribus*, reasonably expect equal access to advanced educational institutions and, given appropriate education and performance, equal access to appointment to and continuation in positions on the faculties of those institutions.

It is reasonable to assume that members of diverse groups will seek employment in positions that carry with them status, monetary reward, relative permanence, and continuing interest and satisfaction. Despite standard complaints about low faculty salaries, status, and power, faculty positions in colleges and universities generally have these advantages. Absent good reasons to the contrary, it is reasonable to assume that such faculty positions would be distributed in rough accordance with general population diversity. As everyone knows, there are neither good reasons nor any such distribution.

Three groups in particular are seriously underrepresented: women, Hispanics, and African Americans. At least partially because of affirmative action programs and certainly as a result of the women's movement, the proportion of women faculty is definitely increasing. Not so the proportions of the other two groups. Indeed, the proportion of African Americans is, if anything, decreasing.

The Special Case of African Americans

Since American history includes the moral blot of black slavery and its continuing aftermath, the addition of African Americans into academia is a special problem. And it is part of the major problem of full incorporation of African Americans into American life. Considerable progress has been made. Even so, as the phenomena of the "black underclass" and certain recent political developments suggest, there is a long way to go. Especially relevant to the issues of this essay are the dismal statistics concerning high school dropouts, performance on nationally normed tests, and low percentages of African Americans in college enrollments (including the percentage of those enrolled in Ph.D. programs).

Generally the "pool" of appropriately educated African American candidates for academic positions is so small that colleges can and do readily rationalize most of their failures to appoint black faculty members. Clearly the major problem lies in increasing the size of the pool, and that requires attention to a number of issues: (1) improvement in primary and secondary education of African Americans; (2) fostering a belief in young African Americans that they can do excellent academic work; (3) motivating capable young African Americans to enter careers in academia; and (4) increasing the opportunity for such young people up to and through the level of graduate Ph.D. work. Efforts have been and continue to be made on all of these fronts, but they are pitifully small and have had relatively little effect on increasing the pool. In some areas, notably those that also qualify persons for nonacademic employment (e.g., law, medicine, social work, clinical psychology), there has been considerable progress. And in some more strictly academic areas, such as sociology and political science, there has been moderate progress, largely as the result of special programs.

In most of the standard academic areas (e.g., the physical sciences, engineering, biological sciences, experimental psychology, mathematics, languages, history, English literature, philosophy) progress has been slight to non-existent. Clearly, if there is to be movement toward proper academic mirroring of the black contribution to the diversity of America, much needs to be done—and not simply by way of removing prejudice in the employment of African Americans in colleges. Increasing efforts (1)–(4) is largely a political, economic, and motivational matter, although affirmative action as such may play a role in (4). In most of the standard academic areas a qualified black student can not only secure admission to a Ph.D. program; s/he is virtually assured of fellowship or assistantship support (although the student may have to accept admission to a program that is not top-rated). The problem is increasing the number of African American students who are both qualified for and desirous of admission to Ph.D. programs. To increase the number who are both qualified and motivated, there is urgent need for the continuation and enhancement of affirmative action programs. And there is little reason to fear a Bakke-type case in an affirmative action program in these areas.

The Special Case of Hispanics

Except for the special history of American slavery and the language barrier, the situation of Hispanics is much the same as that of African Americans. Indeed, there is a considerable overlap of the populations, since a large number of Hispanics are African Americans at one remove. The major problem in adding them into the faculties of colleges and universities is getting an appropriate pool of qualified people.

The Special Case of Women

There has been definite and continued improvement in the graduate education and faculty appointment of women. Here more than elsewhere programs of affirmative action have increased the pool as well as the academic employment of a targeted group. Except for African American and Hispanic women the issues of precollege education, confidence, and motivation play no large role. Bias remains, and, thus, the need for affirmative action programs, but the improvement of recent years is clear.

Other Groups

There may be some problems concerning some Oriental Americans and Americans with Middle Eastern backgrounds, but they are slight when compared with those of African Americans and Hispanics. Native Americans are rare in graduate programs and college and university faculties. Efforts should continue to get them into college and graduate programs, and affirmative action can help with both.

2. COMPETENCE

American post-secondary education is remarkably complicated. There are many, many two-year institutions with a variety of missions, commonly providing practical and/or preprofessional training and usually teaching some general education courses. A great many four-year institutions have a similar mission but normally provide a greater variety of introductory and middle-range courses in standard academic areas. There are as well all of the "regular" four-year colleges offering standard baccalaureate programs, many of them state supported, many church related, and many independent. A number also offer various certification and master's degree programs, some of these professional and quasi-professional degrees, and others offer "standard" degrees in recognized areas of post-secondary teaching and research. Finally, there are the universities that offer large numbers of programs including Ph.D.s and a variety of professional doctoral programs. In all of the programs offered by all of these institutions there is need not only for competent persons to offer direct instruction in the programs but also for instruction in appropriately related areas and, normally, in general education courses.

What I have just gone through is, of course, well known, and I have really only hinted at the variety of levels of instruction, fields, specializations, subspecializations, and so on for which competent persons are needed in American post-secondary education. What I am trying to suggest by this rehearsal of the obvious but often ignored is that the matter of competence is extremely complicated in higher education. While possession of an appropriate degree or certificate may be a necessary condition for competent instruction or service in an academic institution, the matter of which degree or certificate is appropriate for a given position at a given institution forbids any sort of simple generalization. And this formal requirement of competence leaves out experience, ability to teach effectively, ability to work with colleagues, complementing existing personnel in a program, and so on.

The whole point of my comments under the heading of "competence" is to stress the complicated nature of the judgment of competence in academia. I have in mind the often-stated criticism of affirmative action that it requires the employment of less competent persons than others seeking that employment. I believe that the criticism may in any given case be confused, but the likelihood of its being confused is enhanced when applied to an academic position.

When one keeps in mind the levels and variety of academic positions, it becomes clear that the likelihood of there being no academic employment for one possessing an appropriate degree or certificate, barring financial exigency or aberration in the employment market, is small. What is more to my general point is that there is no need for an institution to offer employment to anyone who is less competent than the competing candidates. And it must equally be kept in mind that this point is not made simply on behalf of the abstract or societal need for faculty proportions approximating the diversity of the general population; it is made rather in recognition of the practical problems of academic appointment and continuance.

Having made these claims, I wish to go on to stress the need for continuation and even enhancement of programs of affirmative action in academia. There is a great deal of anecdotal evidence of bias in academia against the hiring and retention of minority candidates, especially African Americans and women. This alone gives sufficient reason for continuation in academia of affirmative action goals and consequent advertising and reporting of attempts to meet them when filling academic positions.

As noted above, the present situation is a dearth of persons in the candidate pools from the groups most in need of affirmative action. As long as the shortage continues, there will be obvious need for affirmative action in the recruitment and support of graduate students. And, especially in the case of African Americans and even if all of the candidates in the pools were to receive appropriate academic appointments, it is important that recommending and appointing authorities remain under the constraining conditions of affirmative action. There are two reasons for this: (1) Increase in the pool of qualified candidates depends heavily upon the perception that, should they work to acquire the appropriate credentials, African Americans and Hispanics have the assurance that their candidacy for academic positions will be taken seriously. (2) Academic institutions need the constant reminder that academia cannot justify itself in America as a racially exclusive club.

In the competence connection it is worth noting that the presence of women, African Americans, Hispanics, and other minority groups in academia has an important bearing on the topics of research and teaching. Obvious examples are to be found in the correction and expansion of the historical record concerning African Americans, women, and Hispanics (to say nothing of Native Americans and other minorities). Less obvious ones are to be found in research attention to medical, economic, educational, and cultural matters peculiar to minority groups; increased attention to legal and moral issues concerning minority groups; and outreach teaching of minority persons whose life coping skills are less than adequate. Finally, I must mention the salutary effect of academic role models on depressed minorities.

3. Appointing and Continuance Authority

The standard forms of academic governance are commonly a mystery to outsiders, who tend to think of the administrative structure (department chair, dean, dean of faculties or provost, president, and board of trustees) on the model of unrestricted private businesses. The idea that faculty appointment and continuance begins with a department faculty recommendation and proceeds on up with recommendations to the board of trustees is unfamiliar, especially when it is understood that administrators uncommonly ignore the recommendations of faculty members and faculty committees and then only in accordance with rules approved by the general faculty and the board of trustees. The details of academic governance, especially their institutional variations, are not, however, relevant to this short paper. What is relevant is the recognition that the appropriate persons to recommend appointment and continuance are those faculty members who are presumptively the most competent in the area of those being considered for appointment or continuance.

It is virtually impossible to deny that they are, again presumptively, the appropriate persons. But there are some interesting caveats. First, it is the duty of administrators to conduct periodic reviews of the recommendations (for appointments and continuations) of academic departments, using (among others) external experts in the relevant fields. Such reviews may lead to and have led to exposures of bias (intellectual or social), cronyism, and incompetence.

Second, and germane to this essay, the existence of affirmative action programs has significantly influenced the recommendation of departments, if only in requiring faculty members to attend carefully to applications of women and minority candidates. Usually an affirmative action program requires a department to make an estimate of the appropriate pools of available candidates and, when authorized to recommend an appointment, to assure the administration that it has considered seriously the applications (if any) of candidates in those pools.

Although a department may for several years correctly report that there are no properly prepared candidates in a pool, the existence of the affirmative action program, as I noted earlier, remains a constant incentive for women and minority persons to seek appropriate education in given fields. And there have been and will continue to be published reports and articles urging them to consider graduate work in those fields. Indeed, graduate programs have attempted and will attempt to recruit students in at least some of those fields with a view to approximating both local and national affirmative action goals for higher education faculties. The existence of such opportunities gives added incentive to recruiting and motivating programs in schools and colleges.

4. STANDARD CRITERIA

The standard criteria for appointment, continuance, and promotion in academia are teaching, research, and service. Since institutions, departments, and academic missions vary considerably, no one is prepared to give any precise weighting to these. And most academicians are reluctant to drive a wedge between teaching and research, regarding them in most situations as complementary. It is reasonably clear, however, that research is less important to colleges and junior colleges whose primary mission is teaching and that the judgment of competence will be appropriately affected. Although service is multifaceted (including work on committees, editing journals, work with national organizations, as well as community outreach) it is also reasonably clear that institutions or departments with community service missions will count it more heavily. At the other end of the spectrum, institutions whose mission is primarily graduate instruction and research will emphasize research more heavily.

The moral of these considerations is that the judgment of competence, while remaining largely in the hands of appropriate faculty members and requiring some minimum knowledge of a field, is not appropriately based on a single factor and varies considerably from institution to institution and program to program. There is yet another factor to be considered in this connection, and that is collegiality. I have two things in mind here: (1) the likelihood that a candidate will get along in the academic setting and (2) the fit of a candidate's special qualifications with those of existing personnel. Once again competence must be recognized as relative to existing or potential circumstances.

Since a candidate who is most competent for a graduate and research program may not be most competent for a program emphasizing beginning and service courses as well as an outreach program and vice versa, close attention to candidates from the pools is indicated. (And other situations are easily imagined.) If an affirmative action program with the requirement of attention to candidate pools is not in force, an institution may well overlook the most competent candidate in a given situation and thus exacerbate a morally disturbing problem.

Summary Comments

I have been at pains in these reflections to point out that, on the assumption that diversity is a desideratum in higher education faculties, the issue of appointing and encouraging the most competent persons is a complex one. With that complexity in mind, it is clear that continuation of affirmative action programs in academia is indicated. The grounds for such continuation are intellectual, moral, and political. Once the complexities are noted, one can readily defend affirmative action along with the obvious requirement that, as far as possible, the most competent should be appointed and continued. Affirmative action grows out of moral need and legal enactment and is directly related to what I have called the "desideratum" of diversity. The political desirability of successful affirmative action in academia is as clear as the need for a population that has not soured on the American dream.

A Postscript Concerning the Lead Essays in This Volume

I find Lawrence Becker's proposal impractical and cumbersome. And, although I share some of his cynicism about the arguments of philosophers concerning affirmative action, it is not clear to me that the obvious requirements of the American "experiment" are not worth reaffirmation (sans most of the niceties of attempts to get around counterexamples in moral casuistry). I agree with Ronald Dworkin that the right to treatment as an equal is both morally and constitutionally fundamental but disagree with Robert Simon that, in the defense of affirmative action, this entails or even supports unmodified utilitarianism. The disagreement is muted, however, by my agreement with Simon that procedural and regulatory affirmative action (and not preferential affirmative action) is clearly not only justifiable but needed. At least this is what I think Simon defends in his concluding remarks. I do disagree with his remarks concerning diversity. Here what is controlling for defending affirmative action is the fact of continuing racial, ethnic, and sexual discrimination. Other sorts of diversity may be helpful for the academic enterprise but are not relevant to the issue of affirmative action. I am in agreement with Leslie Francis's principal aim, namely, to show "that affirmative action is morally justified as a corrective for discriminatory employment processes" and with her endorsement of "process-directed rather than outcome-directed methods wherever possible to end discrimination."

The Injustice of Strong Affirmative Action

7

John Kekes

The context of affirmative action is the selection of people for prized, scarce, and competitive jobs, opportunities, or honors. It is customary to distinguish between two forms such a policy may take. The aim of the weak form is to ensure both open access to the initial pool from which people are selected and selection in accordance with fair procedural rules that apply to everyone equally. The aim of the strong form is to go beyond the weak one by altering the procedural rules so as to favor some people in order to increase the likelihood that they rather than others will achieve the desired position. The strong form of affirmative action, therefore, involves preferential treatment, while the weak one does not. The claim for preferential treatment is that it is morally justified because those favored by it belong to groups many of whose members have been unjustly excluded from achieving desired positions simply because they were members of one of these groups.

The moral justifiability of preferential treatment has been debated since the 1964 Civil Rights Act. Its defenders and opponents somewhat wearily continue to restate their familiar cases, but the controversy appears to have come to a standstill. There are tactical victories and losses on both sides. The resolutions thus reached, however, are unstable, short-lived, and unsatisfactory because they are not the products of principle but of political in-fighting that is symptomatic of a failure to face the underlying deep moral disagreements.

Given this background, it may seem foolhardy to advance the claim that one side has it right and the other is mistaken, but, for better or worse, that is the claim this essay intends to defend. Its strategy, however, is not to work over yet another time the details of the usual arguments, nor is it to offer original objections to them; the strategy is rather to present an overview that sums up state of the controversy. What emerges from it is that the preferential treatment favored by the strong form of affirmative action is unjust.

II

Perhaps the most useful way to begin is to impose some restrictions on the scope of the discussion and then proceed to enumerate some assumptions that form part of the common ground among the contending parties. The issue of preferential treatment arises in many areas of life, but we shall restrict the discussion of it to universities and colleges. And within that context, it will be restricted further to the consideration of preferential treatment involved in hiring, granting tenure to, and promoting people who belong to certain unjustly treated groups.

Turning now to the assumptions, we should notice first of all that the people whose proposed preferential treatment gives rise to the controversy are acknowledged by all parties to belong to some group, many of whose members have been victims of injustice, such as American blacks, Native Americans, Hispanics, and women. The fact that injustice has occurred is not doubted; the question is rather whether the injustice warrants preferential treatment.

Second, the controversy centers on the strong form of affirmative action, involving preferential treatment, and not on the weak one whose aim is merely to make entry into the initial pool open to members of the unjustly treated groups and to ensure the fair application of the procedural rules guiding the selection process. A more precise formulation of the controversy therefore is whether it is morally justifiable to go beyond the weak form of affirmative action and accord preferential treatment to the appropriate people.

Third, it is also agreed by both sides that under normal circumstances preferential treatment is morally wrong. This does not mean that it cannot be justified in unusual circumstances, but it does mean that it must be justified because the initial presumption is against it and that the burden of justification rests on those who advocate it. The procedural rules governing the selection of people in a competitive context normally ought not to be altered in favor of some of the competitors. But what holds normally does not hold necessarily. The required justification must therefore show that the circumstances surrounding the preferential treatment involved in the strong form of affirmative action are in some ways sufficiently unusual to warrant doing what normally it would be wrong to do. And, of course, defenders of preferential treatment do offer justifications of this sort. If the controversy is conducted reasonably, it hinges on the adequacy of these justifications. These three assumptions are generally held explicitly; the next three tend to be implicit, implied rather than articulated by participants in the controversy.

Fourth, one reason why preferential treatment is favored by its defenders is that without it members of the unjustly treated groups would be less likely to gain desired positions than members of other groups who have not suffered injustice. If access to the initial pool is open and the application of the procedural rules is fair, then the greater likelihood that members of the unjustly treated groups will be at a comparative disadvantage should be attributed to handicaps suffered as a result of injustice. It ought to be noticed that although injustice is one explanation of this disadvantage, it is not the only one. Other explanations may be that there are genetic differences or that it is psychologically impossible to overcome the effects of injustice. But since there are serious empirical and moral questions about these alternative explanations, the common ground between defenders and opponents of preferential treatment may be interpreted as concern with the conditionally formulated question that if the difference in qualifications were due to injustice and it could be overcome, would preferential treatment be then just and justified?

In case it is found to be offensive to expect comparatively lower qualifications merely on the basis of membership in a group, it should be noticed that this expectation is central to the case *for* preferential treatment, the case being opposed in this paper, since if there were no such expectation, there would be no perceived need for preferential treatment.

Fifth, it is acknowledged by both sides that the result of preferential treatment is not merely that it favors some people who otherwise would be less likely to gain desired positions but also that it makes it more difficult for fully qualified people to gain the positions they would be likely to have if difficulties were not put in their way. Preferential treatment consequently entails that part of the cost of benefiting some is harm to others. The justification of preferential treatment, therefore, must not only show that it is reasonable to confer the benefits that follow from it, but also that it is reasonable to inflict the harms that it inevitably produces.

Sixth, as we have already noted, the context in which the issue of preferential treatment arises most acutely is higher education. It is generally assumed that the two chief functions of universities and colleges are teaching and research. That assumption follows from the deeper one that these institutions have the responsibility of being guardians of knowledge. The responsibility is discharged by advancing knowledge (through research) and by handing down knowledge from generation to generation (through teaching). Knowledge should be understood quite generally to include the fields of the natural and social sciences, as well as the humanities, and being both pure and applied, theoretical and practical, descriptive and normative, historical and contemporary, taking as its scope the lasting achievements of humanity.

The kind of higher education a society provides for its young tends to reflect and perpetuate the forms of knowledge valued in that society. It is not surprising, therefore, that the nature of higher education should be as controversial as the question of what forms of knowledge should be valued. After all, the nature of higher education has a strong influence on the nature of society when the young come to occupy the positions for which they are supposed to be educated.

The issue of preferential treatment arises against this background. Its defenders claim that since members of some groups have been systematically and unjustly excluded from higher education, they ought to be preferentially treated so that they too might influence the direction in which society will go. By contrast, opponents of preferential treatment, while conceding injustice, deny that it could or should be remedied by preferential treatment.

III

Bearing in mind the assumptions just discussed, we can pose the question: What justification is there for the preferential treatment of prospective or actual academics who belong to some group, many of whose members have suffered injustice merely because of their membership? An alternative way of posing the question is: What justification is there for going beyond the weak form of affirmative action, which is aimed at ensuring open access and procedural fairness, and adopting the strong form, which is aimed at the preferential treatment of people belonging to the appropriate groups?

The questions are moral because they deal with how benefits and harms ought to be distributed. And they arise in a particularly acute form because they concern a proposed policy of distribution that goes against what would normally be regarded as fair. It exacerbates the controversy that what is at stake is not merely how benefits should be distributed but also the unavoidable consequence of the proposed policy that it will cause harm to those who would have received the benefits under the apparently fair distribution scheme that is to be abandoned.

Defenders of preferential treatment have offered three types of justification based on compensation, redistribution or correction, and diversity. Each begins with the generally acknowledged fact of injustice, but they differ because they offer different justifications for adopting the policy of preferential treatment as a remedy.

The idea of compensation as a justification for preferential treatment is that of doing what we can to balance the moral scales so as to make them as even as they would have been if past injustice had not occurred. Since injustice has harmed members of some groups and benefited others, we can achieve a just balance by favoring those who were harmed in the past at the expense of those who have benefited. Preferential treatment is the means by which this is accomplished.

Compensation is a backward-looking strategy of justification because it is grounded on past injustice. Redistribution or correction often assumes an atemporal attitude to injustice. The guiding thought motivating it is that it is unjust that members of some groups should receive a greater share of scarce, prized, and competitive benefits than members of some other groups, and this judgment holds true quite independently of whether the injustice is past, present, or future. It is injustice per se that is being opposed. By redistributing the benefits evenhandedly, this injustice would be corrected. The reason redistribution or correction requires preferential treatment is that a newly introduced and more just method of distribution is unlikely, by itself, to be effective, since the chances are that its implementation will be obstructed by the same prejudices against members of some groups as motivated the previous method of unjust distribution. Preferential treatment as a policy is needed to counteract the force of prejudice that may not be conscious or malicious but merely an unexamined habit of thought. A legally mandated policy of preferential treatment thus coerces people to act as they would act were they not prevented by prejudices.

The justification of preferential treatment derived from diversity concentrates on the future; its claim is that preferential treatment has generally beneficial consequences and that these go far beyond the benefits received by those who are favored under the policy. These general benefits are associated with pluralism. Part of the reason why pluralism is regarded as attractive by many people is that it enriches human possibilities by being hospitable to a multiplicity of different ideals, values, and conceptions of good life. Analogously, part of the reason why racial or sexual prejudice is unreasonable is that it injures not only its victims but also the society informed by it, since prejudiced people impoverish their own prospects by excluding from their lives possibilities represented by members of the unjustly treated groups. Preferential treatment is generally beneficial because it enriches higher education and thus the future, by providing an important forum for voices that otherwise would be doomed to remaining unheard.

These arguments, of course, have been developed in far greater detail than what has been presented above. The details, however, are irrelevant to our main purpose, which is not to reconsider these arguments but to show how damaging are the objections against them and to persuade those who support preferential treatment either to stop doing so or to find better arguments for it.

IV

We shall now consider two general objections directed against all three types of arguments advanced to justify preferential treatment. The first starts by asking whether the arguments for preferential treatment are intended to benefit unjustly treated individuals *qua* individuals or *qua* members of some group. To put this more concretely: Is the preferential treatment of, say, a particular black person or a woman supposed to be justified because of the harm they themselves have personally suffered or the benefits their preferential treatment may produce, or is the proposed justification rather that through their preferential treatment the position of the unjustly treated group to which they belong would be improved? In the first case, the justification of preferential treatment must depend on the circumstances of *individuals* who happen to be members of a group; in the second case, the justification concentrates on what has befallen the relevant *group*, and the individuals in question could then be replaced by other members of the same group. The objection is that neither alternative can be reasonably defended.

According to the individualistic interpretation, the preferential treatment of individuals is justified by the injustice they have personally suffered and/or by the benefits that favoring them over others would produce. In view of this, it is extraordinary that the strong form of affirmative action does not mandate or even recommend finding out whether the individuals in question have actually suffered any injustice that would warrant compensation or redistribution. Nor is there any attempt to find out whether these individuals would contribute to diversity by holding ideals, values, or conceptions of a good life other than those already represented.

It may be said in reply that conducting such an investigation would be a formidable task. But that, of course, merely strengthens the doubts about the feasibility and justice of preferential treatment. Or, alternatively, the rejoinder may be that the investigation is unnecessary because we can assume that individual members of some groups have been unjustly treated and that they would enhance existing diversity, since exceptional circumstances would have to be postulated for this assumption not to hold. But this reply will not do either. The individuals being considered for preferential treatment are likely to be selected from among those members of the unjustly treated groups who are least likely to have suffered and who are most likely to have been acculturated to the views prevalent in their society. After all, we are typically considering prospective or actual young faculty members, both male and female, who have received many years of undergraduate and graduate education and who are normally quite different from impoverished slum dwellers who live without hope and who are the strongest candidates for being victims of injustice.

But it is not merely that the individualistic interpretation selects people for preferential treatment without ascertaining whether the injustice that would supposedly justify it has actually occurred to them; it is also that by conferring unjustified benefits on them it harms other specific individuals. The ones harmed are those who have been excluded from the benefits they would normally have earned so that people less qualified than they could be favored. And there is no reason provided, and none sought, for supposing that these excluded individuals have done anything to contribute to the groundlessly as-

sumed injustice preferential treatment intends to remedy. The consequence of this interpretation of preferential treatment, therefore, is to
institute a policy that arbitrarily favors some individuals while it deliberately injures innocent ones. Even if good reasons were provided
for favoring some individuals, the policy would merely substitute one
set of innocent victims for another set of equally innocent ones. As it
stands, this interpretation merely assumes that just because a particular individual is, say, black or female he or she has suffered injustice.
And that assumption, without the evidence to back it, is as much a
prejudice as the assumption that a particular individual is inferior just
because he is black or she is a woman.

There are, therefore, strong reasons for abandoning the individualistic interpretation and turning to the group interpretation. According
to the latter, the object of preferential treatment is to improve the position of the unjustly treated groups; individuals are favored, as it were,
not on their own behalf, but on behalf of the group to which they
belong. The reasons for proceeding with this interpretation, however,
are no better than the reasons for the previous one.

For one thing, the selection of the groups for preferential treatment
is arbitrary. It is true that American blacks, Native Americans, Hispanics, and women have suffered injustice as a group. But so have
homosexuals, epileptics, the urban and the rural poor, the physically
ugly, those whose careers were ruined by McCarthyism, prostitutes,
the obese, and so forth. There is no good reason for selecting some
of these groups over others for preferential treatment. The arguments
given to justify preferential treatment apply equally to all.

There have been some attempts to deny that there is an analogy
between these two classes of victims. It has been said that the first
were unjustly discriminated against due to racial or sexual prejudice
and that this is not true of the second. This is indeed so. But why
should we accept the suggestion implicit in this attempt at finding a
disanalogy between the two classes of victims that the only form of
injustice relevant to preferential treatment is that which is due to racial
or sexual prejudice? Injustice occurs in many forms, and those who
value justice will surely object to all of them.

The same arbitrariness pervades the attempt to justify preferential
treatment by an appeal to the benefits of diversity. It is nothing but
cant to praise diversity when it is taken to consist of the differences
in the degrees to which people move to the left of the left wing of the
Democratic party. No effort is made to contribute to diversity by ac-

cording preferential treatment to religious fundamentalists, antifemi-
nists, political conservatives, defenders of the desirability of American
primacy in international affairs, or to those who advocate research into
genetic racial differences. As it now stands, diversity is a code word
for individuals or views that find favor with left-wing academics.

Moreover, the identification of the groups whose members are supposed to be victims of injustice is intolerably vague. No account is
taken of socioeconomic status; thus upper-middle-class women or
blacks may be favored over the sons of impoverished white migratory
workers. It is not recognized that there have been waves of immigration and that many blacks and Hispanics, both male and female, have
come and are coming to this country voluntarily. It is most implausible to assimilate eager immigrants to those groups whose ancestors
were transported here as slaves or as migratory workers. Nor is there
any systematic attempt to distinguish between those members of the
unjustly treated groups whose lower qualifications are due to injustice and those whose personal defects are responsible for them. Also,
it is often and fallaciously assumed that since there is a statistically
significant correlation between injustice and the lower qualifications
of members of a group taken collectively, there will also be a like
correlation when members of the group are taken individually.

What makes matters much worse, however, is that the preferential treatment of members of these unacceptably identified groups not
only subverts the original intention of remedying injustice, but it actually produces similar injustice by creating a new group of victims.
For every benefit provided by preferential treatment, there is a corresponding injury inflicted on those who have been penalized so that
some members of the unacceptably identified group could receive the
benefits to which, for all we know, they may not be entitled. And are
these new victims also to be entitled to preferential treatment? And
are the victims of the new preferential treatment? And if not, why not?

V

This leads to the second general objection against the arguments
attempting to justify preferential treatment. The objection focuses on
three morally undesirable consequences of the policy: the situation
of academics whose appointment, tenure, or promotion was due to
preferential treatment; the situation of prospective or actual academics
who would have received the positions that have gone to their pref-

erentially treated colleagues; and the way in which preferential treatment is likely to affect the responsibility of universities and colleges to act as guardians of valued forms of knowledge.

Assume, then, that a policy of preferential treatment is in place and that there is a group of academics at a university or college who have been its beneficiaries. This means, of course, that these people would be unlikely to hold the positions they hold if it had not been for the preferential treatment they have received. That this is so is a straight implication of the assumptions upon which preferential treatment rests; namely, that unjustly treated people can be expected to have lower qualifications than nonvictims do. If this were not the case, preferential treatment would lose whatever warrant it has. The fact of lower qualification, on this assumption, would be common knowledge and, as such, known by the people who benefited from the policy, by those who were injured by it, and by those who have been affected by it only because they have colleagues who have been favored or injured as a result of preferential treatment.

What would be the attitude of reasonable and decent individuals toward the knowledge that they have received their positions through preferential treatment and would not have received them without it? It seems likely that their attitude would be a mixture composed of resentment, shame, guilt, embarrassment, pride, self-doubt, and a desire to prove themselves. Depending on their character and circumstances, in some cases one, in others a different component would assume a dominant role in this mixture. But whatever happens, their position would not be that of a normal academic, and the obstacles in the way of achieving normalcy would be formidable.

There would always remain nagging questions about how they would have fared without the preferential treatment they have received and whether their colleagues are responding to them as individuals or as victims of injustice who could just as easily be replaced by some other victim of the same type. And, naturally enough, these questions will nag not only at them but also at their colleagues. Everybody will know that if it had not been for preferential treatment, their positions would probably have been occupied by others with better qualifications. This cannot but produce bad feelings. It could be hypocritically disguised, but genuine and reciprocal trust and good will would be unlikely to obtain due to perfectly realistic obstacles existing on both sides. In light of this, it is legitimate to wonder whether coming to occupy positions through preferential treatment is indeed a benefit that would remedy past injustice. It seems much more likely that it would rather perpetuate its memory by putting its victims in an extremely difficult position through this clumsy attempt at social engineering.

But we must not forget about the consequences of preferential treatment for those who have been injured by it. These people will feel unjustly harmed, and they would be right in so feeling. They have not been responsible for the past injustice, or, at the very least, no more so than other people in their society, and yet the effect of the policy is to force them to bear an unfair share of the burden of it. The victims in this group will typically be actual or prospective academics who have invested many years of their lives and considerable financial resources in order to have an academic career, and they have foregone prospects of a different career. And, by hypothesis, the likelihood of their doing well at an academic career is higher than the likelihood of those who ended up getting the appointment, tenure, or promotion which they sought and which they would have received if it had not been for the preferential treatment of others. It is natural, therefore, for this new class of victims to be as indignant and resentful as the old class of victims who are now being favored at their expense. And, of course, this class of new victims will increase at exactly the same rate at which the supposed benefits are bestowed through preferential treatment on the old class of victims.

Let us finally turn to an indirect consequence of preferential treatment: its effect on the capacity of universities and colleges to discharge their responsibility as guardians of valued forms of knowledge. This responsibility involves teaching and research. It is essential to the welfare of our society that both activities should be done as well as possible. For the welfare of a society is essentially connected with the information, skills, understanding, and values its citizens possess. Through these forms of knowledge, people endeavor to make good lives for themselves, and a good society is one that is hospitable to their endeavors and so provides these endeavors with a reasonable chance of succeeding. In a good society, therefore, the interests of individuals and the interest of the society are inseparably intertwined.

It is against this background that we should evaluate the unavoidable consequence of preferential treatment that the people favored by it are less qualified for the positions they receive due to the policy than the people whom they displace. No one would voluntarily choose the services of a physician, a lawyer, an architect, or a dentist if a better one were available on comparable terms. What preferential treatment does is to make it a policy to do what no one would consider doing when acting individually on his or her own behalf. Moreover, by focusing on higher education, preferential treatment imposes this policy not on any particular area of life but on all areas within which the acquisition of the relevant forms of knowledge depends on higher education. For preferential treatment is the policy of favoring the appointment, tenure, and promotion of less qualified victims of injustice over those of better qualified nonvictims. The inevitable result is that as the policy is implemented so the vital functions of teaching and research already compromised by other causes are further weakened.

It will be objected that this way of putting the matter misses the salient point that preferential treatment is not a perverse attempt to weaken our society, with whose welfare the welfare of all of us is intimately connected. Preferential treatment, rather, is a policy of remedying injustice, and it is not the aim, but one of the incidental outcomes, of the policy that less qualified victims are favored over better qualified nonvictims. It will be said that injustice ought to be remedied, and preferential treatment is the policy that attempts to do so. Like all policies, it too has its acknowledged costs. The benefits, however, are said to outweigh the costs because the removal of injustice is more important than the occasional violation of the fair procedures that normally ought to govern academic appointments, tenures, and promotions.

But this rejoinder is unconvincing. It fails to recognize that protecting fair procedures is far more important than remedying injustice. One indication of their differing importance is that if the already existing injustice were permitted to continue to exist without remedy, our society would not be harmed more than it has already been. It is true that there would remain one or two generations of victims, but if we concentrate on guaranteeing open access and fair procedures, no new victims would be added. Injustice is bad, of course, and it ought to be remedied, but the point is that the welfare of the large majority of nonvictims would not be appreciably affected if no feasible remedy were available.

By contrast, if fair procedures were not protected, the consequences would be much more far-reaching. These consequences are, first, that a new class of unjustly treated people would replace the old class, so that the amount of injustice in society would not decrease. Second, the policy contains no feasible way of identifying victims of injustice. It unjustifiably assumes that all members of some groups have been victims of injustice, and its selection of the groups themselves is arbitrary. Thus the policy offers no procedures that would present a feasible alternative to the ones that it is designed to replace. Third, the essential process of expanding and transmitting valued forms of knowledge would be weakened by favoring less qualified people over better qualified ones. This would not only shortchange the next generation who would not receive what it could and should have, it would also injure generations thereafter by transmitting to them less knowledge, less well taught, by less qualified people as their inheritance. The policy intended to strengthen society by remedying injustice would consequently end up weakening it by undermining its system of higher education. Fourth, preferential treatment is intended to remove the causes of injustice, namely, lack of open access and fair procedures. But if fair procedures were suspended, the same causes of injustice would be perpetuated, and thus the policy would be inconsistent with the intention behind it.

VI

To sum up, the logic of the argument is as follows. The weak form of affirmative action is intended to guarantee open access and fair procedures guiding the competition for academic positions. It has been assumed throughout this essay that this policy is morally justified. The question we have concentrated on is whether it is also morally justified to violate fair procedures in order to overcome the disadvantage injustice has caused to members of some groups. We have briefly presented three well-known arguments intended to support the affirmative answer: compensation, redistribution or correction, and diversity. And we have summarized in the previous paragraph the reasons for the claim that none of these arguments succeeds. It is reasonable to conclude therefore that the strong form of affirmative action or preferential treatment is an unjust and unjustified violation of fair procedures.[1]

NOTE

1. Readers wishing to have references to the literature on preferential treatment will find them in the chapters by Leslie P. Francis and Robert L. Simon in this volume. It would have been pedantic to duplicate here what they have admirably supplied.

Preferential Treatment Versus Purported Meritocratic Rights

8

Richard J. Arneson

Controversy persists in the United States over whether affirmative action hiring policies are an effective means of achieving legitimate social goals. Some query the moral legitimacy of any of the goals that affirmative action might be thought to serve; others believe that if there are any such legitimate goals, affirmative action will not help to achieve them. These controversies are important, but I intend to focus on a different issue in this chapter.

Consider the norm that, other things being equal, it is morally undesirable if some persons are worse off in life prospects than others through no fault or voluntary choice of their own. An implication of this norm is that, other things being equal, it is morally undesirable if some persons are worse off than others in life prospects on account of their race or skin color. Call this implication the norm of racial egalitarianism. Although this latter norm is controversial, I suppose that many more persons would assent to it than to the broader egalitarian principle. The force of assenting to it will vary, of course, depending on what one packs into the proviso of other things being equal. Leaving this matter aside, I assume that most citizens of modern democracies correctly believe that compliance with the norm of racial egalitarianism is a legitimate goal that governments should seek to pursue by reasonable and morally permissible means. I would also claim that there is a broad consensus in support of a somewhat stronger assumption: The goal of achieving racial egalitarianism is a requirement of justice, hence a morally mandatory, not merely morally permissible goal.

Assuming all this, I will address a narrow question: whether or not policies of weak preferential treatment or reverse discrimination that are agreed to be effective means to the morally mandatory goal of racial egalitarianism are nonetheless unjust in that they violate the moral rights of disfavored applicants. Weak preferential treatment occurs when a more qualified candidate for a job or post is passed over in favor of a less qualified (but still qualified) candidate on account of the race or ethnicity of the applicants (or their sex—but for convenience I limit my discussion to the racial application).

In Chapter 3, Lawrence Becker explicitly assumes that there is a wide agreement today that preferential treatment ("double standards for appointment criteria") is unjust. In Chapter 2, Robert Simon argues vigorously toward the conclusion that preferential treatment is in fact unjust. I say that Simon argues "toward" this conclusion rather than to it because he does not commit himself as to whether his arguments compel this verdict of injustice that they attempt to support. Both writers work to convey the impression that there are powerful philosophical arguments capable of rationalizing the ordinary person's "common sense" opinion that preferential treatment is unfair. But nothing could be further from the truth. The philosophical arguments against preferential treatment are nonstarters. Recent shifts in political opinion in the United States regarding affirmative action policies are not tracking a reasonable philosophical consensus any more than the fact of the Compromise of 1877 ending hopes for Reconstruction was any sort of signal that new and powerful philosophical arguments for Jim Crow laws were informing public discourse at that time.

The discussion to follow proceeds within the following deontological constraint: If a policy proposed as a means to promote a morally required goal is in itself wrongful or unfair, the policy should be rejected even if it is necessary for the achievement of the goal. In other words, the constraint holds that if preferential treatment is unfair in itself, then that policy is morally forbidden even if it turns out that it is the only way to achieve the obligatory goal of racial nondiscrimination. (The constraint would in that case condition the obligatoriness of the goal.) This constraint is nontrivial. Indeed, it is very likely false at least in this sense: If the only alternative to imposing an unfair burden on one person is allowing greater unfair burdens to be imposed on other persons, then imposing the unfair burden is the lesser evil and hence ought to be chosen. For example, if the *only* way to prevent two murders is to commit one comparable murder, then committing the one murder is morally right, because on a scale of injustice two murders are worse than one. So even if preferential treatment should turn out to be wrongful reverse discrimination against white males but is nonetheless required to prevent greater discrimination against black females, such reverse discrimination needed to avert worse evil would be justifiable according to consequentialism.

This "consequentialism of rights" position tends to be submerged in Simon's discussion. He seems to have difficulty distinguishing the rights consequentialist component in the arguments by Ronald Dworkin and Thomas Nagel that he considers from the plainest Benthamite utilitarianism (which would justify murdering white males if murdering rather than refraining from murder would produce even a small net gain in human happiness, say by providing the pleasure of eating an ice cream cone to a very large number of people). However, the moral choice between a consequentialism of rights position and a strict deontological constraint against unfair treatment of persons is evidently a matter of controversy about which reasonable people are deeply divided. It would be nice to discover that arguments for preferential treatment need not rely on any assumption as problematic as the correctness of consequentialism. Fortunately, less controversial arguments are ready to hand. The fact that it is possible to argue successfully for preferential treatment while eschewing any support from consequentialist premises—as it were, with one hand tied behind one's back—illustrates my point that the sense that there is considerable rational force behind the arguments against preferential treatment is an illusion produced by the strong countervailing political winds blowing now across the United States.

The claim to be defended is that weak preferential treatment policies are not unfair to unsuccessful job applicants who are thereby rendered worse off. I focus on the case of faculty employment in universities, but this case readily generalizes. Why might one think that a best qualified job applicant is wronged if he is denied a job that is given to a less qualified applicant for reasons of preferential treatment? One must be supposing that if one applies for a post and is best qualified for it, one has a right to be selected for the post. An ancillary right of fair treatment would hold that if one applies for a post, one has a right that one's qualifications for it should be tested by a reasonaly reliable procedure impartially applied to all applicants, with the outcome of the fair procedure determining who is to be selected for the post. Is this norm of careers open to talents plausibly regarded as an individual right?

It will be useful to consider two cases of university faculty employment: a private employer and a public-sector employer.[1] And we should straightaway concede that if the employer solicits applications on the express or implicit understanding that the post will be awarded to the best qualified candidate, it would be wrong for the employer to treat the applicants otherwise than she promised to treat them. So we should be asking whether it is wrong for an employer who announces in advance that she is following a weak preferential treatment policy to treat those who apply in accordance with that announced policy. We might also be worried about the "legitimate expectations" of applicants who began to prepare themselves for a university career in the reasonable belief that eventually they would be considered for employment on the basis of careers open to talents. So to clarify the issue we should suppose that the employer announces now that after an appropriate time lag sufficient for legitimate expectations to be met she will be accepting applications for employment under a policy of weak preferential treatment. In these circumstances, does preferential treatment wrong the best qualified applicants who will be hurt by it?

In response to this question, one might voice skepticism as to whether there exist clear, unambiguous, reasonable standards of qualification for university professor positions that are not heavily distorted by the prejudices and cultural presumptions of the white males who have defined these standards for many years. This skepticism raises interesting issues but strictly speaking this line of thought is irrelevant to the issue of the justice of preferential treatment. Skepticism about existing standards of qualification introduces doubt as to whether those hired according to prevailing standards really are best qualified in the true sense, whatever that is. But a policy of preferential treatment is a policy of preferring a less qualified applicant over a more qualified applicant, in order to achieve a racial or ethnic balance in hiring, where "best qualified" refers to whoever really is best qualified according to the best set of standards and the best tests for judging these matters. Accordingly, no appeal to skepticism will succeed in justifying a policy of preferential treatment as construed for purposes of this discussion.

A private-sector university, like any private-sector firm, is morally free to pursue its own purposes by means of its policies, including its hiring policies, within the broad limits of legitimate state law and policy. Each firm is free to seek out its own market niche. A religiously chartered university might have as its announced goal the provision of adequate education to members of its faith in an environment that is supportive of the faith. Such a university might sensibly seek to hire faculty who share (or are sympathetic to) that religious faith besides meeting academic qualifications. Such a school might give weight to the religious faith of the applicant along with academic qualifications, so that a qualified Roman Catholic is preferred over an atheist or Trotskyist who is better qualified on academic grounds. Against the claim of the better qualified atheist that he is wronged when he is passed over for the job on religious grounds, a satisfactory reply is that those who own the university are entitled by virtue of their private ownership to use it to further their preferred purposes, including religious purposes, as they see fit.

Similarly, the legitimate governing authorities controlling a privately owned university might decide that the university shall be administered in such a way as to promote the social goal of racial egalitarianism along with its educational mission. In pursuit of this mixed goal they might inaugurate a policy of weak preferential treatment. This can be viewed simply as a legitimate exercise of prerogatives of private ownership. To deny that such a preferential policy would be legitimate is to hold that independently of conventional arrangements the most talented applicant for an advertised job has a natural right to be selected for the post that constrains the terms on which an owner can offer employment. The ideal of meritocracy or careers open to talents is just that—an ideal, one among many, which we are at liberty to accept, reject, or partially accept as a compromise with other competing values. Why suppose that the talented have special rights of access to property owned by others via a right that the most qualified applicant shall be selected for any job slot that an owner might wish to define and fill? One way to appreciate the strength and oddity of the right that is being claimed is to ask why this meritocratic right of access, if accepted at all, should be limited to the right to be chosen in competitions for job slots designed by legitimate owners. Suppose that one could construct a procedure that would elicit applicants for the role of designer of job slots and that the best qualified applicant for the post of designer could devise a set of roles that would more efficiently further the objectives of the private university as given in its charter than the set of roles that the university's private governors are likely to devise. One wonders why, if there is a right of meritocracy, it does not include the right of the most qualified designer to design job slots that would then be filled by the most qualified applicants. One could go further. No doubt the charters of private universities and the interpretations of these charters by university governers could be improved upon. Why not implement a fair competition to select the best qualified applicant for the role of interpreting the purposes of private universities? The logic of meritocracy, after all, would have it that the best qualified have a natural right to be given whatever jobs there are to be done. There is no reason internal to meritocracy to limit this right to applicants for jobs that happen to be constituted by nonmeritocratically established decision procedures such as private ownership prerogatives. But to imagine the right of meritocracy expanding in this way—and to appreciate the craziness of the proposed expanded rights—is just to exhibit the arbitrariness of the initial claim that the best qualified have a right to be selected for the job.

The argument just given does not presuppose any very robust commitment to the rights and prerogatives of private ownership. After all, it might be the case that from the correct moral standpoint private ownership rights will be perceived to be rather weak, capable of being overridden without a trace by many sorts of moral considerations. That does not matter. The argument just given should be convincing whatever one's views on private ownership rights, just so long as those rights, whether weak or strong, are deemed strong enough to take priority over the claimed right of the most talented applicants to be selected for any jobs they apply for—regardless of the announced terms of the job competition. An advocate of capitalism who believes that private ownership rights take priority over virtually all competing moral considerations and an advocate of socialism who believes that private ownership rights take priority over very few moral considerations might both agree—and be right to agree—that private ownership rights trump the claimed right of meritocracy.

My argument from the right to private ownership to the right to administer weak preferential treatment in faculty hiring policies is intended as a moral argument. The argument does not address the issue of whether or not preferential treatment policies are legal under current U.S. law or constitutional under currently prevailing interpretations of the U.S. Constitution. In brief, my view is that in this area morality should guide the law, so if weak preferential treatment is morally right then the law should implement it and constitutional interpretation should accommodate it.

Someone might object at this point that the 1964 Civil Rights Act prohibition of employment discrimination on grounds of race, color, religion, sex, or national origin encodes an obvious moral principle of nondiscrimination that preferential treatment policies obviously violate. A utilitarian might countenance some discrimination now in order to lessen discrimination in the long run, but any such strategy runs afoul of the right of each and every person not to suffer discrimination (this right being understood as a deontological constraint).

This objection fails in a way that is instructive. There is nothing morally wrong per se with discriminating in one's treatment of persons on grounds of race, religion, sex, and so on. One might have innocent preferences to associate with those who are similar to oneself, and race, sex, religion, and so on can be either significant bases of similarity or proxies for similarity of a significant sort. Consider the desire of women to attend an all-women's college or the desire of Afro-Americans to attend a college attended only by Afro-Americans. Discrimination becomes morally invidious only when it either (a) expresses hatred, contempt, or the like against those who are excluded or (b) has a serious negative impact on the life prospects of those excluded. Recall that the norm of racial egalitarianism postulated at the outset of this comment holds that it is morally undesirable if some persons are worse off than others in life prospects on account of their race or skin color. Notice that this norm could conceivably be fulfilled in a race-conscious society in which people of the same race tend to share a common culture and tastes and tend to club together in many institutional settings, but in ways such that these associational divisions do not cause any inequalities in life prospects. Such a society might be less than ideal according to norms we might hold of racial integration, but the society as envisaged has achieved racial egalitarianism. Clearly the case for a legal ban on employment discrimination of the sorts singled out by the 1964 Civil Rights Act is that in the United States today these sorts of discrimination tend to cause or perpetuate unjust inequalities. But then preferential treatment effectively designed to ameliorate unjust inequalities based on race does not prima facie fall into the category of unjust discrimination that an antidiscrimination statute should be striving to eliminate. Preferential treatment should then be a permitted exception to any law forbidding discrimination in employment. Preferential treatment is no more in conflict with the goal of ending unjust discrimination than priming a pump is contradictory to the goal of drawing water from it.

So far a case for the moral permissibility of weak preferential treatment at universities that are substantially privately owned has been considered. But essentially the same point applies in the case of a university under public ownership. The public then has the same right to set policies for a university it owns that a private owner has to set policies for a university she owns. To simplify a complicated point, if democratic decision-making procedures are in place and are deemed a legitimate mode of policymaking for public ownership, then if the public owners of a public university by duly constituted majority-rule procedures set a policy of preferential treatment and see that it is administered fairly and impartially, no best qualified applicant who fails to be selected for a job is wronged. Meritocracy is no more than an ideal that the public is at liberty to embrace, not a right belonging to each potential job applicant that is a constraint of justice on public policymaking.

The argument in this comment has been limited to the contention that weak preferential treatment in faculty hiring is a morally permissible policy. My own opinion is that preferential treatment is morally mandatory, not merely permissible. But another argument, and one that would not be merely an extension of the argument given so far, would be needed to sustain that stronger conclusion.

Finally, I would not wish to exaggerate the significance of the preferential treatment issue in relation to the larger problem of how to achieve racial justice in the United States. Preferential treatment is a small part of a large strategy, the major elements of which would surely include humane social democratic policies that would ensure jobs and education and decent lives to racially disadvantaged Americans. We do not lack the knowledge necessary to formulate and implement intelligent and humane policies, but tragically, for the present at any rate, we apparently lack the will.

NOTE

1. The line of argument that I pursue in defense of preferential treatment was developed in Judith Jarvis Thomson, "Preferential Hiring," *Philosophy and Public Affairs* 2, no. 4 (Summer 1973): 364–84.

Faculties as Civil Societies: A Misleading Model for Affirmative Action

9

Jeffrie G. Murphy

Should faculty appointments at colleges and universities be based, at least in part, on considerations of affirmative action for such targeted groups as women and members of racial minorities? Many, particularly those who favor such affirmative action, see this question as one of distributive justice—as an attempt to make sure that certain benefits (in this case, the benefits of holding a university position) are spread throughout society in such a way that they conform to a pattern thought to be appropriate. On this model, affirmative action is not discussed simply as a matter of policy—that is, in terms of whether it is likely to produce a balance of good over bad social consequences—but rather as a matter of right. Members of targeted groups are thought to have rights, based on considerations of distributive justice, to some representation on university faculties; and universities that do not hire the appropriate numbers may be said not simply to show bad judgment but actually to wrong (perhaps by failing to show proper respect for) at least some members of the groups in question.[1]

My purpose in this brief essay is to express my skepticism about the relevance of distributive justice to faculty appointments at colleges and universities. I am inclined to think that considerations of distributive justice have no direct bearing on the issue and that the common belief that they do have a bearing is based on a defective model of a college or university faculty—namely, that it is to be conceived as a miniature civil society. Space limitations will not allow me to present my view in all the details and with all the qualifications that would ideally be desirable, and thus I shall content myself simply with sketching the broad (and thus partially distorted and inaccurate) outlines of my view—a view of the framework that should structure the debate on the issue of affirmative action for faculty appointments.

A just and rational civil society exists, I would argue, to secure basic rights and benefits for those persons who are its members. Meritocracy as a principle defining its basic structure is thus out of the question, and all members of such a society should have an equal vote and share equal rights as citizens with respect to all issues that importantly affect them. This is because, in a very real sense, the society exists only for them. It does not, for example, exist as a professional association (which might properly be meritocratic) to serve an external set of goals or to provide benefits for an external constituency. It is its own reason for existing and is its own constituency. Given the nature of a civil society as an agency to secure basic rights and benefits, banishment from the society will be the severest of punishments and refusal of membership (e.g., through unreasonably restrictive immigration policies) will be the gravest of rejections.[2]

Civil society, as conceived above, is often used as a model for the institutions that exist within civil society—that is, arguments that are relevant to civil citizenship are used as though they are equally relevant in other contexts. I think that much confusion and much mischief can result when this happens. Consider, for example, the issue of whether untenured faculty members (or even academic professionals and graduate students) should be allowed to vote on important issues of departmental or college policy (including policies having a bearing on tenure) and on new faculty appointments. Such voting was not common when I first entered the world of university teaching, but today it is almost universal. The change was not, in my experience, brought about by policy arguments (e.g., by the claim, perhaps true, that untenured faculty will bring to bear a fresh and useful perspective) but rather by an appeal to misplaced notions of egalitarianism and rights to equal citizenship. The argument (or rather the 1960s slogan) "people who are affected ought to have a vote," an argument or slogan so exactly right when general issues of citizenship in a true civil society are at stake, was confusedly used to extend the voting rights of faculty members to a group of persons who had not yet proved their worthiness to be permanent members of the very institution the permanent future of which their vote was affecting. Such a development (more appropriate, in my view, to the ideology of a welfare agency than to a profession) involved a failure to see that a university faculty is not a miniature civil society but is rather a service profession (a noble calling, I once would have said) whose reason for existence is defined, not by the interests of its own present and future members, but by external goals and an external constituency. It exists, in short, to provide the best teaching possible and the best research possible; and it fails in its mission if it forgets these objectives and focuses instead on the personal needs and desires of its members or of those who would like to become its members.[3]

The point I wish to make is particularly compelling, I would argue, for tax-supported colleges and universities. Why, we may ask, might a rational citizen be willing to pay taxes in order to create that association of persons called a university faculty? Surely it is not to create career opportunities for those few persons who will wind up being university faculty members. ("Let's create a university so that a few people called faculty members can have nice lives and a few extra rights" is hardly a slogan that is likely to be a big vote-getter.) Rather it is because of a belief that this group of persons will provide a benefit that the citizens themselves can (if rational) see is of value *to them*— primarily the quality education of their children and, to a certain lesser extent perhaps, the pursuit of truth in research. For this reason, few things make the public angrier (and rightly so, in my judgment) than the perception that the colleges and universities for which they pay are being operated more for the benefit of the faculty than for the students—e.g., some high-salaried professors having zero or nearly zero teaching loads—perhaps even spending much time away from campus—while undergraduates are being "taught" mathematics by beginning graduate students who cannot speak English.[4]

Having outlined my general thoughts about the primarily external mission of a college or university faculty, let me now return to the topic of affirmative action for faculty appointments—a topic I find useful to discuss in contrast to affirmative action for undergraduate admissions. Because undergraduate institutions exist in large measure to provide the kind of education increasingly necessary to allow individuals to lead meaningful lives as useful and informed citizens, there are arguments of distributive justice that might support programs of affirmative action for admission to some educational programs beyond the high school level. This is because the more closely an educational program is tied to the possibility of being a full member of civil society the more will arguments clearly applicable to civil society apply to that program as well. Undergraduate programs do exist, like the civil society of which they are a part, to confer benefits and opportunities on those students who are a part of them; and thus any person excluded from such programs—particularly when they are tax-supported—may understandably claim that he or she has been unjustly treated. Such claims may in particular cases be without merit (e.g., the person making the claim may, sadly, simply lack the intelligence necessary to benefit from any level of education beyond high school), but they are not claims that are in principle misplaced. They are claims that must be taken seriously and evaluated on their merits, because any program that exists to confer a benefit or opportunity must meet the test of distributive justice in the allocation of that benefit or opportunity.

Such arguments of distributive justice, however, even if compelling with respect to undergraduate admissions, have so far as I can see no direct relevance to faculty appointments and thus are misplaced in principle when so applied. University faculties exist not to confer benefits and opportunities on the actual or possible members of those faculties but rather to serve the external goals of excellence in teaching and research. Thus the only relevant question for faculty appointment, in my judgment, is this: Is the college or university hiring the person best able—in terms of talent, training, values, and temperament—to attain these goals? All other considerations are either irrelevant or secondary (e.g., of potential use in resolving cases where competing candidates equally satisfy the primary criteria).[5]

My main point, in summary, is simply this: Considerations of distributive justice have a bearing only with respect to social practices that exist to confer benefits and opportunities upon their participants. Where a social practice is justifiably conceptualized primarily in terms of external values (e.g., providing a certain complex and expert service), however, considerations of distributive justice should have no direct bearing on the decision of how to fill the positions and offices within that practice. Since I regard university and college faculties as groups defined by practices of the latter sort, I see no direct bearing of issues of distributive justice on the matter of faculty appointments and thus regard a distributive justice rationale for affirmative action with respect to such appointments to be not simply wrong but wrong-headed.

Does my argument entail that affirmative action with respect to faculty appointments is always a mistake?[6] No. I have been attempting to undercut one common rationale for such action, but it is, of course, possible that such action is to be justified by some other rationale.

One could, for example, attempt to show that a college or university will do a better job of attaining its goal of educating all of its students if its faculty exhibits diversity with respect to gender and race—perhaps because this will enrich the number of views and perspectives to which students will be exposed (a silly argument for physics or mathematics, no doubt, but perhaps not so silly for philosophy or literature) or perhaps because more students will be able to see, in some faculty member, a role model for his or her own aspirations. These arguments are empirically complex and tend to depend rather heavily for my taste on anecdotal and normative sociology.[7] They are, however, the kind of policy arguments that need to be considered carefully and honestly if we are to get beyond the misplaced rhetoric of distributive justice and discuss the values—and the hard value choices—that really are at stake in the issue of affirmative action for faculty appointments.[8]

As I read over my remarks in this essay, I am painfully aware of how much they need to be refined and qualified in many ways—how much they need the kind of space for expansion and nuance that the present format simply does not allow. I have tried to make one major point—that affirmative action must be assessed against a background theory of the nature and purpose of the institution to which it is to apply—and I hope that this point may be of some use in structuring discussion on the topic of affirmative action for faculty appointments. There are, I know, those who will argue that the modern college and university serve and should serve many more purposes than the narrow ones of teaching and research that I have emphasized. Others will be skeptical of my rather old-fashioned assumption that it is possible to articulate objective standards for what constitutes teaching and research and what counts as excellence in those endeavors—the lunatic fringe of modern academic life no doubt simply insulting my assumption as "Eurocentric, phallocentric, and racist," but a more reasonable group actually giving arguments on this issue that intellectual honesty would force me to take seriously. I cannot, of course, further explore these matters here; so I shall simply close off my remarks by raising one final question: If there are no objective standards in these matters, then what are we doing in this business and what could conceivably justify us in expecting other people to pay the bill for it?

NOTES

1. I once attended a law school faculty meeting where it was suggested that affirmative action advantage be given in admission to persons who are handicapped or disabled. I expressed some skepticism about this suggestion (in part because I feared that the targeted class was so vaguely specified that it might include alcoholics, drug addicts, psychotics, and persons who are mentally retarded) and asked why the group of "handicapped persons" should be singled out for special consideration. Supporters of the suggestion (presumably having examples other than mine in mind) told me it was because such persons are "underrepresented in the legal profession." But what, I asked, does that mean and why should I care about it? Was it for policy reasons (e.g., is there evidence that there are handicapped persons going without legal services that they would likely receive if there were more handicapped lawyers?) or for some other kind of reason? I was told that it was because many such persons have a strong desire to have a legal career and that their handicaps make it harder for them to compete on an equal basis with all others and that affirmative action for them is thus needed. This was clearly an argument of distributive justice. Although the context of the argument was admission to a professional school, I have heard similar kinds of arguments given in support of faculty appointments—given even by persons who are properly skeptical of arguments of compensatory justice in this matter. (See, for example, the essay by Leslie Francis in this volume.) Ronald Dworkin has exposed some of the problems in using such arguments in the context of admission to professional schools, and I think that some of his arguments have a bearing on faculty appointments as well. See Ronald Dworkin, *Taking Rights Seriously* (Cambridge, MA: Harvard University Press, 1977), chap. 9; and *A Matter of Principle* (Cambridge, MA: Harvard University Press, 1985), Chaps. 14, 15, and 16.

2. Denying immigration to one who is fleeing tyranny (e.g., a totalitarian society lacking in respect for basic human rights) seems much graver (and thus much harder to justify) than denying immigration to someone who wishes to leave one just civil society simply because he believes he would derive greater pleasure from living in another one. In the former case, denial of immigration may well make it impossible for the individual to live the kind of autonomous and meaningful life that is properly demanded by any self-respecting person. In the latter case, the person still has ample opportunity to live such a life— even though it will not take the form he might ideally desire. For these reasons I would reject meritocracy, not simply as a principle for rights and benefit assignment within a just civil society, but also as a principle for deciding who deserves to be admitted as a member of such a society. There is, of course, an elaborate Rawlsian story that could be told to justify some meritocratic institutions within societies that reject meritocracy as a principle for assigning the

rights and benefits that define what Rawls calls the "basic structure" of the society. My following remarks will assume such a story, but I do not have space here to tell it.

3. Sometimes, of course, university faculties—indeed, members of any profession—will fail in their mission unless certain of their own personal needs and desires are met. Such policy arguments for caring about such matters are, in my view, quite appropriate. What I tend to resist are justice-based arguments for such considerations. Even the special rights we associate with faculties—for example, the rights of academic freedom—are surely accorded faculty members because of a belief that these rights are vital to their activities as teachers and researchers, *not* because of a belief that university faculty members are intrinsically more worthy of certain freedoms and satisfactions than are other members of society. For more on the distinction between policy and worth/respect-based arguments for rights and opportunities see Jeffrie G. Murphy and Jules L. Coleman, *The Philosophy of Law: An Introduction to Jurisprudence*, rev. ed. (Boulder, CO: Westview Press, 1989), chap. 2.

4. Very low teaching loads can, of course, often be justified because of the important research productivity of the faculty members in question. Just because the university in general must serve the dual missions of teaching and research, it is not required that each particular faculty member fulfill those dual missions in exactly the same way. However, can anyone with an insider's familiarity with the modern university honestly deny that low teaching loads are frequently sought and awarded to serve the values of employee job satisfaction (given a choice, who doesn't prefer to work less instead of more?) rather than in genuine support of valuable research? And can anyone honestly deny that supremely gifted teachers will often receive fewer rewards in the realm of promotions and salary raises than some boring journeymen academics who grind out, under the heading of research and scholarship, the proper number of trivial little "contributions" to their fields of learning? Self-deception is rampant within the modern college and university, and actual and potential faculty members (e.g., advanced Ph.D. students) sometimes find it very difficult to accept that these institutions do not exist for *their* benefit. This is why muckracking books such as *ProfScam*—for all their shrill overstatements—should be read and soberly reflected upon by all of us in the academy who genuinely care about the integrity of our profession and its public mission. See Charles J. Sykes, *ProfScam* (Washington, DC: Regnery Gateway, 1988).

5. It is, I think, a tragedy if a person who could benefit from the education that is instrumental in preparing that person for a meaningful and useful life as a self-respecting citizen is not given an opportunity for such education. Thus I am inclined to favor some affirmative action and other applicant-biased admission policies for at least some of the public institutions that provide such education. (I must here ignore the problems posed by the fact that admission

places will be finite—a fact most obvious for professional schools, where the finite number tends to be very small, but still a nontrivial fact with which even many undergraduate schools must cope.) Better to err on the side of admitting and ultimately failing some (even many) lost causes than to run a substantial risk of excluding those who could indeed benefit. It is typically not a tragedy, however, for someone simply to suffer the disappointment of not becoming a college teacher, a lawyer, or a physician—or a member of any other profession that exists to provide a complex and expert service rather than to enhance the lives of its own members. Professional vocations and the educational preparations for them are unlike high school education (and increasingly college education) in this regard, and they are thus not to be defended as stepping stones toward allowing a person to lead a meaningful and satisfying life and to assume the full status and respect of a free and responsible citizen. Because of this I think it is reasonable here to be biased in favor of the standards that define the integrity of the professions and thus to give primary place to the goal of reducing the risk of inflicting second-rate teachers, lawyers, and doctors on their publics even when this involves disappointing certain applicants (who might well have made it if given the chance) by setting high standards that they may be unable to prove they meet (even if in fact they do). Here it is, I think, better to err on the side of excluding some who might have high merit (but cannot prove it) than on the side of risking the appointment of any who do not and the serious harm that such persons will very likely cause. "He doesn't seem very good but, what the hell, let's give him a chance" is an appeal that has a certain sentimental attractiveness and might properly carry the day when admitting a student or hiring a custodian. Such an appeal would be utterly irresponsible, however, if adopted as an appointments policy by a profession that exists to provide a highly complex and expert service to the public. Academics, lawyers, and doctors are not fungible; and it seems to me that a rational society would want members of these professions to be, not simply adequate or minimally competent, but the best possible. (All jobs are in some sense task or service defined; but I am here making the assumption—admittedly controversial—that external goals and the needs of an external constituency are more controlling for some professions than for others or for jobs in general. I think this has something to do with a presumption of complex expertise and potential for harm—including harm to the mind and spirit—that is not present in all professions and jobs.) I certainly have no illusion, by the way, that the academic world was a perfect meritocracy before the pressures of affirmative action came along; but I am reluctant to accept the fact that a profession has already partly abandoned its ideals as an argument to abandon them even further. I would rather argue for an attempt to roll back whatever unfortunate departures have already taken place.

6. I should make it clear, if it has not been made clear already, that by "affirmative action" in this essay I mean something more than merely the non-

controversially important attempt to eliminate unfair discrimination that keeps the best qualified persons from attaining faculty appointments. Attempts to end unfair discrimination are usually conceptualized under the heading of "equal opportunity" and will have a bearing on affirmative action—for example, actual preference for minority candidates who may, given traditional indicators, seem less qualified—only for someone who holds the belief (which I do not share) that such action is the only way to correct discrimination. (One might more properly attempt to correct discrimination, in my judgment, by assigning an extra-departmental or extra-college antidiscrimination officer to each faculty search committee.) The demand for formal equality of opportunity is sometimes conceptualized as an aspect of distributive justice. In this sense I am, of course, happy to concede that distributive justice *is* relevant to faculty appointments.

7. Robert Nozick has defined normative sociology as the study of what the causes of social problems ought to be. He uses Marxism as an example of normative sociology.

8. If a case can be made that students are shortchanged by a faculty that does not manifest gender and racial diversity, then an argument of distributive justice can be made on behalf of those students and thus will have an indirect bearing on faculty appointment. When I say, as I do in the essay, that considerations of distributive justice have no direct bearing on affirmative action for faculty appointments, I mean to deny that such arguments can be made on behalf of actual or potential faculty members themselves.

Facing Facts and Responsibilities: The White Man's Burden and the Burden of Proof

10

Karen Hanson

The three lead essays in this volume display an admirable commitment to uncovering common ground between opposing sides of the affirmative action debate. Each essay is attentive to the theoretical and practical issues of individual and social justice generally at stake in the controversy and to the particular inflections of those issues when the institution whose policies are in question is one with reasonable claims, or aspirations, to being meritocratic. I share the authors' sense that the broad outlines, and many of the details, of the arguments for and against various forms of affirmative action are by now fairly familiar and that the most appropriate approaches to continued discussion are those that recognize the strength of each side's case.

My own judgment is that the balance of considerations weighs in favor of some forms of affirmative action—including, in some circumstances, specific efforts to achieve targeted employment goals and including the allocation of admittedly limited resources for special employment programs of the sort described by Lawrence Becker. I cannot, in this short comment, examine each point at which I agree or disagree with the arguments and proposals detailed by Leslie Francis, Robert Simon, and Becker. Instead, I hope to support the push for practical compromise by raising a few questions about our conceptions of academia and higher education.

As the lead essays note, one of the continuing intellectual problems in the debates about affirmative action is determining where the burden of proof should lie. If women and minority group men are not employed in academia in numbers and at levels proportional to their numbers in qualified applicant pools, are we entitled to assume the likelihood of unfair hiring and promotion practices and to insist that opponents of affirmative action prove opportunities really are equal for all? Or should we suppose that all racial and gender biases must be identifiable, so that, absent any specification of a problematic practice, we are entitled to rely on the fairness of sex-blind and race-blind employment procedures? If we admit that there has been racial and sexual injustice in the past, and we want to give some special treatment to those who have been disadvantaged, is it reasonable to extend this special treatment to all members of a racial group and to all women? Or should we proceed to attend immediately to disadvantage, formulating race- and sex-neutral policies that respond more directly to the specific disadvantages that are the ground of our concern? Although I grant that no general formula can be given concerning where, in discussion of actual circumstances and proposed policies, the burden of proof must lie, it seems to me that we should be inclined to doubt equality of opportunity and inclined to think race and sex are relevant categories to attempted amelioration. This inclination may be more widely shared if we begin our discussion of affirmative action only after open reflection on a couple of very basic, very general, very simple questions: Do we think our society, as a whole, has eliminated all traces of racism and sexism? And do we take the academy—and ourselves, as members of the academy—to be isolated from, or insulated against, the practices and institutions of the larger society?

I do not think we can responsibly deny that racism and sexism are still very much a part of American life; and, once we admit that, it becomes difficult to insist that we must always begin in a race-neutral and sex-neutral fashion as we try to attend to the "disadvantages" of some members of our society. An important part of the evidence of continuing racism and sexism is economic, but we must not reduce these problems to their economic markers and associated deprivations. An African American boy whose parents can afford to send him to a fine private prep school will still be exposed, throughout his life, to vicious racial epithets. As a young man, even after he has completed college and graduate school and has begun a promising professional career, he may not be able to jog in old clothes through an affluent white neighborhood without attracting undue attention and unpleasant suspicion. A young girl's interest in science may be encouraged and supported by her family, and they may, when the time comes, pay her tuition to, say, MIT. But she will grow up in a society rife with special contests for women only—those, for example, where young women parade about in swimsuits and evening gowns, seeking appearance points from their judges, and where, perhaps in quirky response to feminist criticism, more points can be earned for the appearance of "poise." She will notice, with or without rueful hilarity, that the events themselves are now often dubbed "scholarship pageants." And however our young woman finances her years at MIT, she may still be reasonably reluctant, as her male colleagues are not, to walk alone to the library at night. Even these sketchy examples should remind us that we cannot simply dissolve all the problems of racism and sexism into, in Simon's words, "some race-neutral or sex-neutral basis, such as degree of economic disadvantage . . . or degree of injustice or discrimination" a given individual has actually experienced.

Thus, while I in fact share most of Simon's worries about proposals to staff universities according to a counterfactual meritocracy (and I would certainly reject the proposals themselves), and while I agree with the general consensus that affirmative action hiring is not adequately grounded on the notion of compensation, I find untenable the suggestion that we can address the injustices of racism and sexism without taking special account of race and sex. Ethnicity and gender play important roles in the social experience of every American, and racism and sexism are special, distinctive difficulties for all women and all members of some minority groups, whether or not there is, in an individual case, economic deprivation as well. This of course does not mean that every African American male and every woman has suffered more or had to overcome more in life than any white male. It does mean, however, that it is inappropriate to insist on a common category of generic "disadvantages" in our initial consideration of and responses to the problems of racism and sexism. The distinctiveness of racism and sexism also suggests that it may simply be a red herring to note, in these discussions, that many white men have had to suffer and overcome economic and other disadvantages. There are indeed other structural injustices in our society—as well as plain individual misfortunes—and perhaps there should be, from the academy, an institutional response to these problems. But if the topic on the table is racism and sexism, and the question being pursued is whether the academy should use any form of affirmative action to attack *these* injustices, we do not show that it should not by noting that the world may already contain other injustices as well.

The adversion to other injustices would not be irrelevant if it could be shown that all forms of affirmative action must exacerbate these other standing problems. It is, however, exceedingly unlikely that such a demonstration could ever be made. What unbreakable link could there possibly be between attempting to improve the lot of women and minority group men and positively worsening the condition of, say, economically exploited white males? That these groups may sometimes be pitted against one another is one thing. It would be quite a different matter to show that in all social and economic arrangements these groups' fortunes must be inversely related. In fact, the usual worry about other injustices is rather different. The concern is that affirmative action may generate new injustices. White males, especially young white males, may suddenly be deprived of equal opportunity and fair treatment; and women and minority group males may be freshly stigmatized by being treated once again in terms of group identity and as if they were in need of special allowances, help, or protection. Raising these possibilities of injustice opens wider questions about the conditions for equal opportunity and about the nature of fair treatment, and we may once again be barred from progress by disagreements about the appropriate location of the burden of proof.

While I do not deny that there could be policies of preferential treatment for women and minorities that would be unjust to white men and harmful to the academy, and I do not deny there could be affirmative action procedures that would treat white men unfairly, it seems to me that we should be able, in each such case, to identify precisely the elements we judge unjust, harmful, or unfair. (Are white men's applications being solicited but never read or taken seriously? Are men with demonstrably superior qualifications being passed over in favor of women and minority group males lacking even minimal credentials?) We do not, however, need such specific worries to feel intellectually respectable anxiety about the extent to which our employment and promotion practices provide fair opportunity for women and racial minorities. To arouse that anxiety we should, I suggest, ask ourselves the second of my two very general questions: Is the academy—and are we, as members of the academy—untouched by the sexism and racism pervading the surrounding society?

What could be the ground of the requisite confidence that we— and all our colleagues on hiring and promotion committees—have escaped the pernicious social influences that maintain racism and sexism? We might want to insist that our disciplinary training and our allegiance to a meritocratic academy force judgments free of racist and

sexist taints. But the fact that the academy has in the past undeniably practiced unfair discrimination and the fact that many academic
disciplines have in the past undeniably supplied specious theoretical
underpinnings for racism and sexism should give us pause. Are the
social and economic pressures on the academy—and the psychological pressures on its inhabitants—entirely different from those at play
in the larger society?

The academy's reaction to the infusion of women and minorities
into its ranks has not been dissimilar to the reaction to integration
elsewhere in the world of work. There has been, from some quarters,
a begrudging attitude and a diffuse sense that white males are being
denied fair treatment and equal opportunity. Does anything beyond
an unwarranted sense of entitlement stand behind this sense?

Leslie Francis, in her defense of affirmative action, says, "When academic jobs were scarce, concentration on affirmative action appointments virtually foreclosed some white males from academic careers."
Is there statistical evidence to substantiate the claim that white males
shut out of academic careers in the 1970s and early 1980s have affirmative action appointments to blame for their plight? Were women and
minority group members appointed to academic jobs in numbers far
exceeding their proportions of the applicant pools? And was the employment of women and minorities, in whatever numbers, the major
factor in leaving so many white males without academic jobs? Francis
herself notes other factors pertinent to the disappointment of many
white male candidates. Simon, in criticizing preferential treatment as
a form of compensation, speaks, as others often do, of a white male job
candidate facing a compensatory hiring program as suffering the "loss
of a position." Again, although I share Simon's sense of the inadequacy of arguments for academic policies of affirmative action based
on ideas of compensation, to speak of white males "losing" jobs is to
suggest that those jobs were, somehow, already theirs. It is a rhetorical
hint of entitlement.

A bit of distemper should be expected. If a pie once enjoyed by our
group alone now must be shared with individuals from groups formerly denied a piece, then unless we can make a bigger pie, some of
us are going to get less than before or none at all. Even if we are now
making an equitable distribution, if the field of distribution has been
enlarged, the expectations of individuals in the group with a once exclusive claim will have to be lowered. Is this all that has happened
with extant policies of affirmative action? Perhaps not, but when we

have seen the morally indefensible resistance to integration in various other segments of the work world, can we simply assume that all academic uneasiness is a product of sound reasoning?

Whether or not we are willing to entertain the idea of an academic parallel to the meanly self-interested opposition to integration in other sections of society, we should attend not only to the similarities between the academy and other institutions but also to the articulation of our own institution with others. Even if we cherish some ideal of an ivory tower, we must recognize that the denizens of the tower in fact live in ordinary communities and in ordinary families; that work done in the tower affects the nation and the world; that the tower and its staff are visible to those outside it. Even if we could be certain that the hiring and promotion procedures within academia were fair and untinged by racism and sexism, if conditions outside the tower clearly tend to impede participation by women and minority group males, should we rest content that we have done our bit for equal opportunity? In her discussions of childbearing and of community service, Leslie Francis touches on some of the differential effects of the interpenetration of academic and extra-academic life. If we continue and extend that sort of discussion, what will we take our responsibilities—our academic responsibilities—to be, if we want to make real our formal equality of opportunity? Our institutional self-reflection cannot be undertaken from a perspective wholly within our institution, and our reflection on society is not from a point outside our society. Facing the fact that the professoriate is mainly white and male, we may show some proper respect for individual autonomy when we explain this profile by alluding to the "different choices" made and "alternative career paths" taken by women and minority group males. But it is a shallow morality and a faulty analysis that portrays these "different choices" as made, the "alternative paths" as taken, in circumstances unrelated to the legacy and the continuing existence of racism and sexism.

Insofar as we want to end racism and sexism and insofar as we value academia and believe in the social and personal importance of our enterprise, we should want to see a fair proportion of women and minority group males participating in our profession. It is not just the content of our courses and our research results but also the structure of our institution that teaches lessons to our students and to the wider society. Until recently, one of the lessons we taught was that higher education is conducted mostly by white men, that the professionals who are equipped to train our society's professionals are mostly white men, that the keepers and extenders of a significant portion of our society's intellectual tradition and activity are mostly white men. When an argument for affirmative action adverts to the value of diversity within academia, the rationale need not be only the assumption that women and minority group men are likely to bring fresh and different perspectives to the academy's search for truth. The idea may also be that our society now has a stale perspective *on* women and minority group males and that the visible faculty diversity encouraged by policies of affirmative action could be properly edifying.

The haste with which opponents of affirmative action contend that what will be visible is a stigma on all women and minority faculty, the quick assurance that affirmative action hiring will brand as inferior the women and minority males thus hired, should provoke a further moment of institutional and personal self-reflection. If we have granted that members of these groups are, in our society, already stigmatized by sexism and racism, what, exactly, do we think will be added by our proposed procedures? Are we sure that we are, in our claims about stigmatization, doing more than expressing our resolve not to see women and minority males as full members of the academy? For most of the life of American higher education, white men have been hired to the faculty not through the fairest and most open procedures but through friendships and old school ties. Prestigious all-male colleges have had special "legacy" admissions, and family connections have meant more than individual merit. Did these practices ever stigmatize all white males? Did they even cast general doubt on the competence of the specific white males who were their specific beneficiaries?

I raise these questions not to suggest that we should, for the sake of a crude balance, replace one flawed system with another. I suggest instead that, as we take up the issue of whether there are genuine flaws in various policies of affirmative action, as we consider the need for affirmative action at all, we ask ourselves again: Are we sure that we— in our individual consciousnesses and judgments and in the academy as a whole—have left behind the unfairness of a racist, sexist past?

Affirmative Action: Relevant Knowledge and Relevant Ignorance

11

Joel J. Kupperman

Affirmative action is one of those disturbing issues of our time, like that of abortion, about which reasonable people can disagree. The issue never is resolved, partly because what look to some like brute facts turn out to be highly interpreted; and the interpretations can be called into question. Part of the reason also for the stubbornness of disagreement is that essentially contestable terms, such as "right" or "justice," are part of what is being contested. The struggle is philosophical as well as political and ideological.

Nevertheless, progress of a sort can be made simply by becoming clear about the obstacles to progress and about the character of the best arguments on both sides. The worst misconception about affirmative action is that it is primarily concerned with redress or compensation for individual human beings who have been victimized. Robert Simon is surely correct in suggesting that the best justification is as a means of strengthening the position of disadvantaged groups. The best case in favor of affirmative action must be understood in relation to the empirical requirements of a kind of social engineering. This case then, as Simon also points out, is vulnerable to empirical doubts. Will the desired consequences actually come about?

The victimization of a group can take a variety of forms. At one extreme, a large number of members of the group can actually be killed. The group can be repeatedly exposed to hostile words and deeds. Groups also can be denied opportunities, kept in isolation, treated with contempt, deprived of opportunities for initiative, "treated like children," and so on. None of these forms of behavior is excusable, and perhaps all call for compensation. But many of these raise issues that are far removed from the territory of affirmative action. What

Turks owe Armenians and Germans owe Jews has nothing to do with any claim (absurd on the face of it) that Armenians and Jews have been placed at a competitive disadvantage in modern industrial society or that there is a systematic cultural legacy of discouragement. The discouragement that is connected with demands for affirmative action is typically rooted in experiences of contempt and avoidance rather than hostility and confrontation and indeed is compatible with traditions of being the objects of benevolent, patronizing, and dismissive attitudes.

If we look at data such as, for example, the significantly higher school dropout rates among Mexican-Americans and Puerto Ricans than among Cuban-Americans, it is tempting to form the following hypothesis. Some groups, because of historical factors (the circumstances in which they found themselves in America and their early treatment here), carry around sociological and psychological baggage that impedes their educational and economic performance. Two facts about this hypothesis should be noted immediately. One is that it might seem to the careless reader like a claim of victimization that calls out for compensation. But that is to read in a one-dimensional way the account of the group's misfortune; whatever happened to Mexican-Americans in this country was bad but certainly not as bad overall as genocide (although in one or two limited respects related to affirmative action it was actually much worse). Furthermore, the damage is not evenly distributed, and in any affirmative action program the first to benefit will be those individuals who were hardly damaged at all. Second, insofar as a group's baggage is linked to low group self-esteem, which can be counteracted in part by group pride, there is a conflict between the things the group will want to report as supporting a need for affirmative action and the things in its past that the group will want to dwell on. A careful account of the psychological and social damage wrought on the black family by slavery and Jim Crow will provide, on my view, strong support of the need for affirmative action. But the account itself, to the extent that it is persuasive, will also be demoralizing. Conversely, African Americans have a strong need for narratives of slaves who asserted their autonomy, slave revolts, slave families that held together despite obstacles, and so on. Those outside a group may underestimate how important it is for the group to have a version of the past that can ground positive developments in the future. But they may also underestimate how a different version of the past grounds persistent failures within the group.

The empirical data that support the hypothesis that some groups are at a competitive disadvantage because of psychological and social legacies from the past fall under three or four main headings, which should be referred to briefly. Fear-of-success studies pioneered by psychologist Matina Horner showed that there was a frequent tendency among women to shy away from conspicuous academic or professional success. This is not to say that such tendencies were to be found among all women or were absent among men; but they were more common among women than men. Interestingly enough, Heming and Horner found an exception to this in that, among blacks, fear of success was more common among men than women.[1] There also are studies that show that some groups are more self-critical and less self-confident in relation to their own performance than are others. A recent study of discouragement among women science majors at Harvard is a good example.[2] The two assistant deans who prepared the report concluded that the higher attrition rate among women could be attributed at least in part to the fact that women in scientific fields believed only "extra good" could be good enough. There are studies that suggest that, among some black and Hispanic groups, development in the teenage years is affected by the influence of an "oppositional culture" that discourages academic success.[3] Finally, there may be evidence, although I do not know a good source, that low expectations of the careers or rewards that are open to one may inhibit academic or career-related performance among certain groups.

Some readers may be inclined to respond as follows: "All of this is unfortunate, but it has nothing to do with the justice of affirmative action programs. Justice is a matter of giving each person what he or she deserves, and what you have reported are factors that cause some people, in the end, to deserve less." This is an arguable response, but of course counter-arguments are available. One centers on the claim that handicaps should be taken into account in gauging desert. I have already indicated my sense that this is not a promising line of counter-argument, in that the main beneficiaries of affirmative action programs typically have been hardly handicapped at all. Another line, which seems to me more promising, is to insist that it makes sense to reduce questions of justice to questions of individual desert only in some limited kinds of case—ones that involve fair competition by reasonable, agreed-upon standards and in which no social goals of overriding importance are at issue. In Book I of Plato's *Republic* it is suggested that justice is to give to each what is owed to him, but the view then does not survive dialectical examination. Our reasons for considering it inadequate may not be quite the same as Plato's, but there are similarities. An individual-desert model of justice cannot readily avoid being an uncritical endorsement of a social status quo, including the accepted view of what counts as individual merit and what counts as a reward. If we are willing to be reflective, it makes sense to raise questions about what would count as a just social order. It then would, in my view, also make sense to support policies that will move us in the direction of a just social order. The best case for affirmative action takes this form.

The most intelligent supporters of affirmative action are driven forward, it seems to me, by a hypothesis such as the following. Fear of success and low expectations of the sort of success that is possible can be counteracted by persistent images of people one can identify with who are very successful and who do not seem to be paying any special price for their success. To the extent that fear of success and low expectations are problems among groups, then highly successful role models from afflicted groups are what is needed. Such role models also can help young people from those groups feel good about themselves and their possible relations with mainstream culture, thus disarming tendencies to be excessively self-critical or to gravitate to "oppositional" forms of behavior.

If it turned out that affirmative action programs did actually accomplish what they are designed to do, they might well accomplish it in different ways for different groups. One of Francis's many perceptive observations is that one may need to think differently about the issue of affirmative action for women and for African Americans. As she points out, there have been recent improvements for women in many areas, but not for African Americans. One way of seeing this is to recognize that problems for African Americans (especially African American men) are more closely tied to a general pattern of discouragement at all levels of education. It may be that patterns of discouragement for women are operative chiefly when a certain (fairly high) threshold of excellence has been passed, and then mainly in the context of higher education. This suggests, on the one hand, that the need for righting the balance is far more acute for African Americans as a group than for women as a group, but on the other hand that programs for women have a better chance of immediate success.

Indeed those of us in higher education have opportunities for visible immediate accomplishments in empowering women as a group. We can especially encourage our best women students and allow them to feel good about themselves when they express original ideas, and we can facilitate the psychologically crucial transition from the situation in which many faculties have an isolated woman scholar here and there to the one in which there are groups of secure women scholars in many departments. Psychologists of women have offered the opinion that this transition (from isolated individuals to cohorts) is crucial in diminishing the influence of a "fear of success" factor, although I do not know of research that shows this.

No doubt we can—and I think we should—attempt to do all of this for African American students. But here we are struggling much more obviously against problems that predate higher education. If we want to appoint, say, more African American philosophy professors, then we will need more African American philosophy Ph.D.s, which in turn will call for more African American undergraduate philosophy majors; and our prospects here will depend in part on what happens in primary and secondary education. To say that the problems here are far more difficult is, of course, not to counsel resignation. But it does mean that we may need to look for a larger variety of remedies and that more patience and determination may be required.

It also means that there is more room for worries as to just what the consequences of various policies will be. It is a truism of conservative political theory (especially the school of F. A. Hayek) that public policy departures from tradition generally have unintended consequences, which may well not mirror the intentions of the policymakers. It could be argued, for example, that one consequence of the movement for women's equality of the last few decades has been a deterioration in the quality of primary and secondary schools, as many of those intelligent and energetic women who traditionally would have become schoolteachers have found a more attractive set of alternative career paths available to them. (This should not be taken as showing that what was, after all, a major gain in social justice was a mistake, but rather as suggesting that when we improve one part of the social fabric we should see whether compensatory adjustments are needed elsewhere.) A number of African American scholars recently have pointed out that the civil rights legislation of the 1960s and 1970s has had negative consequences in the African American community, by emphasizing the gap between successes and failures and by draining effective role models away from the inner cities.[4] Can we have any genuinely clear idea of what the major consequences will be of affirmative action policies we implement?

In my view, this is a reason to maintain some degree of scepticism and irony in relation to the policies we favor and is not a reason to do absolutely nothing.[5] Is there a way to pursue the goals of affirmative action while minimizing the risk of negative side effects and at the same time minimize the impact on young white males (who may come to feel that they, disproportionately, pay for affirmative action in terms of diminished career opportunities)? Lawrence Becker's ingenious proposal seems to offer this hope. Why not have categories of additional graduate fellowships and additional faculty positions, for the benefit of "target groups" such as African Americans and Hispanics? Becker seems to offer the hope of a moral free lunch. The realities of budgeting in times of limited resources suggest, though, that at least some of the additional graduate fellowships and faculty positions would have been (if we were entirely indifferent to affirmative action) regular fellowships and positions, and it is hard to believe that in practice they would not be viewed in that light.

One difficulty I have with Becker's proposal overlaps with reservations about Steven M. Cahn's suggestion that institutions should display greater openness about the criteria they employ in job searches. Becker speaks of institutions' "admission criteria" and criteria for appointment, promotion, or tenure as if these are both clear and reasonably precise; he advocates that they not be modified for target groups. In practice, of course, committees may favor candidates who (for a variety of reasons) they think may be expected to display energy and independence of mind, or may favor candidates who remind them of themselves at that age. The factors that produce these expectations or impressions may well be both vague and "subjective," and it may well be that different committees will respond differently to the same folders. Conceptions of the subject also may play a part. An undergraduate applicant to a graduate program or a job applicant may have done well at what a committee judges to be "not really philosophy" (or too far removed from the canon of English literature, or whatever). In practice, stretching a point for a member of a minority group may be not so much stretching one's standards of accomplishment as it will be a matter of stretching one's sense of what counts as an appropriate area of study or research.

Academic positions are typically filled on the basis of recommendations made by committees to department heads and other administrators. Should committees be, in job advertisements, as clear as possible about what the criteria for appointment will be? There is the practical objection that what the committee thinks are morally and legally appropriate criteria may be vulnerable to lawsuit. The most practical legal advice may thus be to say as little as possible. But even apart from this consideration (which may seem cowardly to some) there is a worry about whether a typical committee knows what its criteria are and whether anything is served by attempting in advance to arrive at a precise and assured sounding formulation of what is at best both vague and tentative. What will count as "equally qualified" candidates for a position as an assistant professor of philosophy? A committee may start with the thought that it will favor women or minority candidates if and only if their credentials are at least equal to those of the best qualified white male. But, in making this assessment, how does one compare the twenty-page essay in *Hypatia* or *Signs* with ten pages in *Public Affairs Quarterly*? How does one factor in various clues that might help one predict future energy levels and, indirectly, future growth as a scholar? My experience is that committees by and large do not know what they think until they think it, and that any attempt in advance to provide a precise-sounding formulation of committee standards is likely to be resented as a limitation on the committee's ability to reflect on what it is doing. What this suggests is, at best, a mixed message in relation to affirmative action, in part because it suggests the very real possibility that committees that think they will pursue a "liberal" agenda in appointing women and minorities will in the end, in part because of highly traditional screenings of what is looked for and considered important, arrive at results that some would argue favor white males.[6]

NOTES

1. Matina Horner, "The Motive to Avoid Success and Changing Aspirations of College Women," in J. Bardwick, ed., *Readings on the Psychology of Women* (New York: Harper and Row, 1972).

2. "Female Science Majors Said to Face Strong Pressures," *Chronicle of Higher Education*, February 29, 1984, p. 2.

3. See, for example, Signithia Fordham and John U. Ogbu, "Black Students' School Success: Coping with the 'Burden of "Acting White," ' " *Urban Review* 18 (1986); reprinted in Diane Ravitch and Gilbert T. Sewall, eds., *Educational Excellence Network News*, April 1987.

4. See, for example, Roy L. Brooks, *Rethinking the American Race Problem* (Berkeley and Los Angeles: University of California Press, 1990).

188 Joel J. Kupperman

5. There is a more general worry here about the use of empirical evidence in relation to personal and public policy decisions. Philosophers, partly because most of them do not normally work in areas driven by empirical research, may overestimate the availability of empirical evidence. Compare my *Character* (New York: Oxford University Press, 1991), Appendix 1, "The Tradition of Moral Psychology." Much useful evidence would require longitudinal studies and highly intrusive methods of investigation and may be unavailable because of costs, risks of legal liability, or the difficulties of observing subjects at appropriate moments. The difficulties are compounded if what is wanted is evidence of the likely future consequences of a departure from established policy. Anyone who thinks this is a decisive reason for doing nothing should ponder the amount of empirical evidence typically available to an individual deciding whether to get married (and to whom) or what career to pursue.

6. I was helped by presenting some thoughts on this subject to my department's weekly "Brown Bag Seminar" on February 6, 1991. Comments by Margaret Gilbert and Jerome Shaffer were especially useful.

12 Remarks on Affirmative Action

Andrew Oldenquist

A premise with which I and most supporters of affirmative action almost certainly agree is that groups that previously have been mistreated and excluded ought to be well represented on a university's faculty. They ought to be represented in such numbers and proportions that reasonable members of these groups do not complain. It is easy, especially if one thinks that active discrimination in university hiring is largely a thing of the past, not to appreciate the importance, to women and African Americans, of just seeing black or women professors, or just knowing they are there, and of having them voting at meetings and otherwise participating in university business. Individuals who belong to and identify with groups that have been treated poorly in the past are extremely sensitive to how members of the group are treated today. Even the least militant are inclined to count faces, be indignant at what appear to be slights, and feel proud or vindicated when a woman or African American receives an honor or overcomes some obstacle. These group loyalties and rejection anxieties are deeper than many people realize and they ought to be respected, for almost everyone would feel the same way in similar circumstances.

The goal of reasonable representation would seem to call for some form of affirmative action, unless we think the problem is rapidly correcting itself. While I believe the problem is correcting itself for women, it is not for African Americans, and there is not much that can be done about it on the level of faculty recruitment. One kind of measure thought to be effective is preferential hiring, by which I mean hiring a member of a target group when another applicant, who is not a member of the group, better satisfies, overall, the standards and acknowledged qualifications for the position in question. I shall argue that preferential hiring of African Americans will not produce reasonable representation and preferential hiring of women is unnecessary. Affirmative action without preferential hiring, in the form of imaginative and conscientious searching and recruitment, can hardly be faulted, but it is not easy to find significant and effective measures short of preferential hiring. There are some things we can do, of course, such as, in the spirit of Leslie Francis's remarks in this volume, giving a woman, on request, an extra year to earn tenure if she has a child during that period. Another measure is defining an open position so that it includes new, needed, and academically legitimate fields or courses that make the position more attractive to women and black candidates.

Measures such as these, if adopted by one university and not by another, may help that university recruit at the expense of the other. If they are generally adopted, they will not affect the competition among universities for target group members, nor will they increase the number of target group members in the profession, except to the extent, if any, that such measures influence the decisions of women and African Americans to enter the profession. When part of a general practice, these measures probably should not be thought of as part of affirmative action but merely as common sense and decency.

We should not talk about "minorities" but about African Americans. No one needs to worry that Jews or Chinese Americans are underrepresented on university faculties, and while Hispanics are indeed underrepresented, a large proportion of Hispanics are also black, and those better represented in universities tend to be more nearly European. The problem of minorities is about African Americans (and in some parts of the country about Native Americans too). African Americans are the primary focus of our racial history, our racial guilt, our concern with racial justice, and in the universities our fear of doing anything that might leave us open to being called racist.

I want to suggest that preferential hiring for academic positions is ineffective and in the long run likely to be harmful to those hired by that means. Also, preferential hiring does seem to be unfair to white males, and this remains as an argument against it even if a case could be made that it does more good than harm. As Robert Simon argues in his essay, rejected white males are not being treated "as equals" in the relevant sense, that is, as equals in respect of rights and fair treatment, if all "as equals" means is that white males are given equal consideration in a utilitarian calculation. Justice requires that we not use anyone as a means to a good end, except perhaps in extreme cases, and that we not do the sort of thing to white males that we did to African Americans and women in the past.

Assume, in field X, that each year five new Ph.D.s are awarded to African Americans and one hundred to women. It is reasonable to assume that all of the African Americans who want academic jobs in field X will get them, without a need for preferential hiring or special new positions. In a field where, say, nearly 50 percent of the new Ph.D.s are women, and during times when there are three applicants for every job in that field, there will be jobless female and male Ph.D.s. Here, women join men as victims of market conditions, not discrimination. This is not to say that there are no departments that discriminate against women—a topic I shall take up—but that there is no longer a pattern of discrimination that prevents women from finding more and better departments that do not discriminate and which, in fact, tilt toward women candidates, other things being roughly equal.

Some of these women and African American candidates will not get jobs as good as they would have under widespread preferential hiring—someone hired at a major state university by preferential hiring might otherwise go to a small private college or a community college. But they will get jobs of the sort white male candidates with similar qualifications would get. It is not plausible to suppose that without preferential hiring or special positions, but with the current level of vigilance against negative bias, some of those black and women Ph.D.s would go jobless as a result of discrimination.

Preferential hiring does not give target groups *more* jobs but *better* jobs than they would get under race- and gender-blind policies. The result is that higher prestige schools rob relatively lower prestige schools of the benefits of having a faculty with enhanced proportions of African Americans and women. If the more prestigious schools get 20 percent more of the available black and women assistant professors, and the less prestigious schools accordingly get 20 percent fewer, is that a social advance?

It may be thought that this is nit-picking and that it misses the big picture. Do not good will and common sense say, just do it? That is, create positions when necessary and hire African Americans and women almost up to their proportion in the population, in order to show good will, compensate for past injustice, and provide the reassurance and role models women and black students need in order to feel secure and do well in American universities. The approach of many administrators shares this bluntness. They in effect say, "Don't argue, just get more blacks and women in your department and we will give you money for it." This approach can make one school look good at the expense of others. But it makes no sense as a national practice. There is no pool of black Ph.D.s driving taxis that would fill these new positions, and no women either except in those fields that have produced too many Ph.D.s altogether for the prevailing job market. During the past twenty years the number of women entering graduate programs in many fields has increased dramatically, and consequently so has the number of women Ph.D.s. Has affirmative action, by publicizing and perhaps also by preferential hiring, moved women to enter graduate programs who otherwise would have done something else? Or is the influx of women into academia just part of the more general movement, during the past twenty years, of women out of the home and into careers? I find the second alternative a little more plausible.

If my argument is right, preferential hiring of university faculty has no national effect and produces no social gain. It is reasonably certain that every African American Ph.D. who seeks an academic position will be offered one, usually several. This is compatible with the existence of colleges and departments that still discriminate, although those institutions are unlikely to have the opportunity to reject black Ph.D.s because these Ph.D.s will be avidly courted by better schools. Preferential hiring is hard to justify or even make much sense of when demand greatly exceeds supply, which is the case with African American Ph.D.s.

The ingenious plan offered by Lawrence Becker in this volume, by contrast, would not redistribute people. If it creates new positions without lowering standards, and there is no additional supply of candidates, these positions simply will not be filled. However, I question whether there is a significant disparity between the percentages of Ph.D.s in the last ten years earned by African Americans and women (who wanted academic jobs) and the percentages of faculties today that are black and female. That is, I am surmising that almost all black and women Ph.D.s who wanted to be professors *are* professors. If this is so, Becker's formula would not call for additional positions, quite apart from the question of whether they would be filled. It is still unclear to me why we should peg the number of special positions in, say, chemistry to the proportions of chemistry Ph.D.s awarded to African Americans and women, as though there were unemployed black and women Ph.D. chemists, and as though all of these Ph.D.s wanted to be professors.

If Becker's plan is adjusted so that departments do offer more positions than there are qualified applicants, but still without lowering standards, would this vacuum for African American and women chemistry or engineering Ph.D.s stimulate more African Americans and women to pursue Ph.D.s in chemistry and engineering? I don't know; career choices of this kind are complex and personal. However, might Becker's proposal to offer additional graduate fellowships earmarked for African Americans and women have the potential to fill the vacuum? Some questions arise. How many additional African Americans and women would win fellowships, given that the criteria for winning them are not relaxed? Does any black applicant today, who satisfies color-blind criteria for admission and support and is known to be black, fail to be offered a fellowship or teaching associateship? I doubt it. For the plan to work there must be a surplus of fully qualified black applicants; but there isn't a surplus, there is a great deficiency. Most colleges and universities, and especially the more distinguished ones and the state schools, are on the lookout for black and women graduate students.

The heart of the problem is how to increase the number of fully qualified black applicants and, with lesser acuteness, the number of fully qualified women applicants in traditionally male fields, and this cannot be solved on the college level. In most fields the number of African Americans with Ph.D.s is so small that affirmative action consists of bidding a known handful of black faculty from school to school. For example, as of this writing there are about 10,700 philosophers teaching in the United States, of which 93 are black. In fields with somewhat more black Ph.D.s, when demand outstrips the supply of qualified candidates there will be a great temptation to hire unqualified ones (by the standards of the particular university and department). This pleases those who think one should just keep hiring (and, necessarily, creating more black Ph.D.s) until the proportion of African Americans equals their proportion of the general population. Even if this could be done, it would create a crisis as tenure time approaches. Black professors, appointed in a department that is several notches above their ability because of pressure within the university to hire African Americans, will be constantly on the defensive; they may become embittered and convinced they are victims of constant racism. They belong, say, in a community college and are hired by a good quality four-year college, or they belong in the good quality four-year college and are hired by a large state university with a Ph.D. program, and so on.

Is this justified anyway, if it puts an African American in front of classes and helps to create a more livable environment for black students? There are jobs begging for African Americans at major universities; will knowledge of this stimulate more and more black students to prepare for those jobs? Is it like sports and entertainment: blacks flock to wherever the obvious opportunities are? The analogy is weak because in high school, elementary school, and in the home, the cultural and educational prerequisites for academic careers are not often enough in place.

Attempting to hire African Americans to faculty positions proportionately to their percentage in the population would, at the present time, make demand wildly exceed supply. It is different in many other fields such as apprentice jobs in the skilled trades, where demand would not exceed supply. On the other hand, seeking to hire women and African Americans proportionately to the percentage of black and women Ph.D.s in the field does not make demand exceed supply and indeed would be a little less than what is already being done. Perhaps the best policy regarding African Americans is to keep demand slightly greater than supply and advertise that vigorously, so that the black community will know that opportunities are there. One must continually rebut charges that continuing racism in university hiring is the reason that so few blacks are on faculties, and many African Americans are not inclined to give universities the benefit of the doubt on the matter.

As we have seen, the situation of women academics is more complex. Large and increasing numbers of women Ph.D.s able to compete well with men are entering most academic fields. Women escape the social class and economic disadvantages, relative to white men, that handicap African Americans, since women are the siblings of men and do not differ from them in class or wealth. However, some disciplines have few women and some have many; where there are few, preferential hiring would not help since departments would merely recirculate a fixed number of, say, women chemists. It would be a zero-sum game, as in the similar practice with African Americans, with department A gaining only by department B losing.

When we turn from male-dominated disciplines to male-dominated departments the ethics and appropriate strategies are different. When a department of twenty in a discipline that nationally is 15 percent female has averaged between zero and one woman over the past ten years, the cause is less mysterious than in the case of male-dominated disciplines. In that department supply exceeds demand and some kind of affirmative action seems justified in order to bring the department in line with the national average. Preferential hiring and the creation of new positions both would do it, and the latter method would not do obvious injustice to male competitors. But even new positions, assuming universities would fund them, ought to be the last resort. Surely the university's administration can exert increasing pressure on a department that finds endless excuses for appointing almost no women in a discipline that is 15 percent women. Threats probably are more effective, and certainly more economical, than creating new positions.

Does it demand correction if women, by choice, are better represented in some fields than others? If today more women than men choose nursing, teacher training, and library science, in part because in the past they were discouraged from other careers, are these "choices" perhaps not real choices? Of course, all choice patterns have causes, and moreover, a pattern could be due partly to past coercion and partly to very different, noncoercive causes. If present career patterns are partly due to past coercion, universities have an obligation to do what they can to readjust them by loudly advertising equal opportunity for openings in traditionally male fields. Nonetheless, after a period of equal opportunity some of these gender-based preferences may persist, due to innocent cultural causes or to genetic predispositions. The idea that men and women, when raised correctly, will have the same ranges of interests, in the same proportions, expresses ethical and ideological views about what it is to be raised correctly that cannot simply be assumed to belong to a program of affirmative action. The idea is also very likely false. I suspect that more men than women will always like military history, and more women than men will always like nursing. Differences in the interests of men and women, to the extent that they are not caused by past discrimination, are not a matter of justice and not the business of universities to tamper with.

Today, perhaps the best policy is to enforce scrupulous fairness in recruitment and to exert administrative pressure on departments whose proportion of women persists in remaining below the national average for that discipline. The situation of women is further complicated by the fact that when both spouses have degrees, until recently they have tended to follow the man's job, leaving the woman to catch what job she can. I sense that this is changing. An interesting sidelight is the gradual demise of nepotism rules in universities because they conflict with affirmative action.

It surely would be best if there could be a system that did not mention race or gender, if only because our society will fare better when we think and talk less about race and gender and when people can cease to think so much about their sexual or racial identities in business and professional contexts. Basing attempts at justice on race and gender perpetuates a preoccupation with just those factors we know to be irrelevant and which we know we should not think about so much. Social and economic class are relevant, however, because a poor social/economic background can handicap people in the development of their potential. These are the categories—social and economic class—that we should focus on; unlike race and gender they are fortuitous and changeable, and they seldom play an important role in people's sense of who they are. If affirmative action, without preferential hiring, were in terms of enhanced opportunities for people from poor and culturally isolated backgrounds, we would help those African Americans, Appalachians, Native Americans, Hispanics, women, Asian Americans, and white males who most need help. African Americans, women, and Hispanics from privileged backgrounds would not be helped. We would be helping individual victims of circumstances; the very individuals who are disadvantaged would be helped, not "groups" or representatives or symbols of groups. Affirmative action by class and income makes sense because it cannot be accused of unfairness to people in virtue of being white males and it would not be monopolized by those in the target populations who have no need of it.

Most of the efforts on behalf of disadvantaged individuals need to take place in formative years, long before graduate program recruitment and faculty hiring. However, I certainly do not wish to leave the impression that nothing can be done at the university faculty level. The openness of graduate programs and faculty positions to African Americans and women certainly needs to be constantly publicized, and some departments have opportunities to create subspecialities attractive to black and women candidates.

Affirmative Action and the Multicultural Ideal

13

Philip L. Quinn

I suppose there is widespread agreement that faculty positions over the past couple of decades have been both much sought after and in short supply. And I think it would be hard to deny that members of the groups currently protected by affirmative action law have in the past, along with members of certain other groups, been unfairly excluded from such positions. It seems to me that the use of affirmative action to respond to this situation is morally problematic because it sets two intuitions at odds with one another. On the one hand, there is the intuition that it is right to take extraordinary steps in order to bring members of the heretofore excluded groups into faculty positions. On the other hand, there is the intuition that it is unfair to impose the whole burden of such policies as are adopted to achieve this goal on individual white male candidates for faculty positions who have worked hard to become qualified for such positions and are innocent of complicity in past discrimination.

I find that the two intuitions clash over some but not all affirmative action policies. In order to lay my own cards on the table, I shall begin by spelling out my own reactions to the several sorts of affirmative action delineated by Robert Simon. I consider procedural affirmative action, which requires special efforts to recruit members of under-represented groups into applicant pools for faculty positions, to be entirely unproblematic. No unfair burden is imposed on white male candidates by the mere fact that the result of such a policy is apt to be more competitors for positions they seek. I also believe that regulatory affirmative action, which treats as goals numerical projections of what the outcomes of proper selection procedures would be, is on balance a good thing. To be sure, there is a real risk that goals will be converted into quotas. But my own experience supports the view that this need not happen, and I judge that pressure to make it happen in the case of faculty appointments can in most instances be successfully resisted. Knowing how deep prejudice can run, we should regard it as no bad thing to be called upon to justify failure to achieve desirable goals that are by hypothesis the projected outcomes of proper procedures. If, as I believe, the likelihood that goals will turn into quotas is small, then the risk that white male candidates will be unfairly burdened by regulatory affirmative action will also be small and seems to me worth running.

Preferential selection is a different kettle of fish. Strong preferential affirmative action, which amounts to preferring the unqualified over the qualified, strikes me as obviously unconscionable. Weak preferential affirmative action, which involves preferring the less qualified, although presumably adequately qualified, over the more qualified, is in my opinion also wrong. And even minimal preferential affirmative action, which uses membership in the legally protected categories solely to break ties among equally qualified candidates, seems to me morally suspect. Genuine ties could be broken by some random procedure. If minimal preferential affirmative action is employed instead of such a procedure, white males will be automatically excluded from some positions it is highly probable they would have gotten under the random alternative. Because randomization is an ideally fair way of breaking ties, minimal preferential affirmative action does impose a special handicap on white males as a group, and this extra burden is arguably heavy enough to constitute unfair treatment.

Furthermore, I take it to be obvious that academic employers should tell prospective candidates for faculty positions just which affirmative action procedures, if any, they mean to follow in making appointments. As Steven Cahn has pointed out, those who adopt such procedures presumably consider them legitimate and so should have no objection to stating them publicly, without ambiguity or equivocation.

So I oppose both strong and weak forms of preferential hiring, and I am ambivalent but inclined to be suspicious of even the minimal form of preference involved in using membership in the legally protected categories to break ties. Of course these are controversial views. I recognize that there are people, whose rationality and good will I respect, who have no qualms at all about minimal preferential affirmative action and who support weak preferential affirmative action. Like Lawrence Becker, I have little hope that these disagreements will be resolved by means of further empirical discoveries or philosophical arguments bearing directly on the moral legitimacy of preferential selection. Yet I also fear that the goal of bringing members of certain heretofore excluded groups, particularly African Americans and Native Americans, into faculty positions simply will not be reached, or cannot be reached as quickly as it should, unless policies are adopted that have much the same effects as those anticipated from minimal and weak forms of preferential affirmative action by advocates of those policies. We could bypass the deadlocked debate about affirmative action if we were able to frame and justify on independent grounds policies that hold out real promise of having such effects. I think an opportunity to do precisely this is on the horizon in the form of the issue of multiculturalism in institutions of higher education. So I propose to sketch out an argument for the conclusion that we could achieve the goal of increased representation of heretofore excluded groups in faculty positions within a reasonable period of time and without resort to morally controversial policies of preferential selection.

The argument begins with a challenge to an assumption that is all too often taken for granted or held fixed in debates about faculty appointments. It is that we currently possess and employ in making faculty appointments criteria of excellence that are both relatively complete and fairly determinate. We operate as if we suppose that we can recognize all the kinds of academic excellence that now exist, can make fine-grained distinctions within each kind, and can straightforwardly aggregate and compare the several kinds. I doubt that our present criteria are that good. They are not, I think, radically subjective or wholly ideological. Appointing officers at their best are, to use current jargon, expert systems, but even the best expert systems have their limitations. One sort of limitation has to do with resolving power. Sometimes the criteria in use, good as they may be, simply do not suffice to pick out one among a small group of outstanding candidates for a position as the best. If there is only one position to be filled, a single candidate has to be given the nod. When discussion fails to produce consensus, closure is typically reached by voting. In retrospect, it is easy enough to construct a story according to which the top-ranked candidate is the best choice. But, of course, if the vote had produced a different result, an equally plausible story according to which that result was best could have been constructed. We deceive ourselves if we actually believe such comforting stories.

For present purposes, however, another sort of limitation is more salient. Our criteria are limited in scope because they are by design especially attuned to the excellence of traditional academic inquiries. They will surely need extension and may well need some revision if they are to be applied to the work of scholars who challenge familiar goals and methods. I do not mean to suggest that every novelty should be welcomed with open arms, for much that is new, in the academy as elsewhere, turns out in the long run to have been merely faddish. But there are success stories too. I would say that biomedical ethics is an example in philosophy. Two decades ago it struck me as long on promise but short on achievement; now it seems to me a fairly mature subfield of philosophy. In making these judgments, I rely in part on traditional criteria of philosophical excellence, but I also think I have learned to recognize a new kind of excellence in the course of reflecting on the recent literature in that field. There is in some of its best work a kind of discourse that manages to speak to both the concerns of academic philosophers and the problems of health care professionals, and this virtue, if it be a virtue as I suppose, is not often to be found in works of ethics addressed mainly to an audience of professional philosophers. Other philosophers will, I believe, have had similar learning experiences upon immersing themselves in the literature of feminist philosophy or Africana philosophy.

Academic specialization being what it is, none of us has the time and energy both to get on with his or her own work and to investigate in detail all the developments, disciplinary and interdisciplinary, that might reveal a new kind of excellence but, then again, might not. The temptation is to judge those with which we are not directly acquainted on the basis of some combination of hearsay, stereotyping, and the traditional criteria rather mechanically applied. To return to the example of biomedical ethics, it is still sometimes said, in a disapproving tone of voice, that this is merely applied ethics, as if it were obvious that applied ethics is inferior to some other kind, presumably theoretical or, if the analogy with mathematics is in view, pure ethics. And people who know no better are heard to say that those who specialize in biomedical ethics do so because they do not have what it takes to make real contributions to ethical theory. It is, of course, unlikely that such views would survive prolonged contact with leading figures in the field. But there is the rub. Opportunities for such contact will occur only to the extent that we are willing to make them by appointing, promoting, and supporting the work of specialists in the field. In some cases student demand for courses in biomedical ethics generates pressure in this direction. However, all too often the response to such pressure is merely to appoint the occasional visitor or adjunct, which leaves the field and its representatives in a distinctly marginal position with respect to the larger philosophical enterprise. I doubt that things will change very much unless those of us in positions of power are willing to accommodate the field by recognizing new forms of philosophical excellence and then appropriately adjusting our criteria to acknowledge them. And, again, I am convinced that there will have to be similar adjustments in our standards of excellence if such areas as feminist philosophy and Africana philosophy are to flourish in a timely fashion rather than after protracted and bitter struggles, if at all. In fact, I think this process of accommodation is already under way in each of the three philosophical cases I have used as examples, but the adjustments are being made at an uneven pace. As I see it, the process is well advanced in the cases of biomedical ethics and feminist philosophy but barely begun in the case of Africana philosophy.

Be that as it may, we shall have to make many such adjustments, not just in philosophy, but in most if not all disciplines if we choose to pursue the multicultural ideal with vigor in our colleges and universities. I take the term "multiculturalism" to be no more than a handy label for the pluralistic normative thesis that artifacts of all sorts from cultures hitherto excluded from or marginalized in our practices of teaching and research ought henceforth to be included and play an increasingly prominent role in those practices. The debate about multiculturalism is already upon us.[1] It has been rendered inescapable by such facts as these. Our country simply cannot afford the cultural parochialism that has characterized its past if it is to retain a leading role in the increasingly global economy of the future. Nor can we serve well a student population that will be increasingly nonmale and non-white if we persist in ignoring the very things that for many of our students shape their cultural identity and sense of self-worth. But to think of multiculturalism as no more than a response, and perhaps a rather grudging one at that, to such external pressures is to grant it only instrumental value. I speak deliberately of the multicultural ideal because I mean to attribute to multiculturalism intrinsic value as well. It is my view that not only our teaching but also our research would be, on balance, better if it were more deeply grounded than it is now in explicitly pluralistic and comparative approaches to most subject matter.

I hope that I do not appear naive in my enthusiasm for multiculturalism. Pursuit of this ideal is bound to be very difficult under the best of circumstances. Resource constraints being what they now are and are likely to be in the future, satisfying all the demands for inclusion that have acknowledged merit is not going to be feasible. Controversial priority judgments will have to be made, and there is often going to be a clear and present danger of politicizing the process of allocating scarce resources in counterproductive ways. But it seems to me that colleges and universities cannot avoid coming to grips with these issues, and I consider it better to grapple with them within the context of the active pursuit of an academic goal than to adopt the reactive posture of only responding to externally generated pressures and demands. Nor is the multicultural ideal apt to appeal equally to all segments of institutions of higher education. The humanities and social sciences stand to benefit most; mathematics and the natural sciences have little if anything to gain. The life sciences fall in between, although I think they have something to learn from feminist critics.[2] And institutions that conceive of their mission as the promotion of a particular religious agenda will be prone to thinking of multiculturalism as a distraction, if not a threat, rather than an ideal.

No doubt there are advocates of multiculturalism whose support for it rests on some variety of evaluative relativism. Mine does not. I think objective evaluations of cultural products are possible, although I concede that they are often hard to get right and so should usually be made with a certain amount of fear and trembling. Cross-cultural comparisons are especially problematic because the unfamiliar is not easy to appreciate at its true worth. Dismissive or even contemptuous attitudes toward other cultures characteristic of our past and not yet wholly eradicated have all too frequently led to comparative evaluations that are crude, superficial, and inaccurate. As I construe the multicultural ideal, it promises to help us improve our evaluations. Comparative evaluations informed by greater understanding of the objects being compared are, for normal humans, more likely to be on target. The better I understand Nazi practices, the less I am tempted to make excuses for those who engaged in them. Comparing Aquinas and Mencius on the virtues is illuminating because it increases my admiration for the ethical discernment of both thinkers.[3] And I take it that I speak truly in saying that Nazi behavior is inexcusable and that the moral thought of both Mencius and Aquinas is admirable.

The generosity of spirit involved in appreciating the excellence of diverse expressions of human culture is what I find most attractive about the multicultural ideal. It should therefore be plain that I oppose the lack of generosity and even self-indulgence displayed in some of the projects that mask themselves under the rhetoric of multiculturalism in current debate.[4]

To make the attractions of the multicultural ideal apparent more has to be done by way of fleshing it out. A benefit to be expected from moving toward it that deserves emphasis in the present context is that it holds out prospects of giving us reasons independent of affirmative action policies to bring members of heretofore excluded groups into faculty positions. This is because common sense tells us that there will be nonaccidental correlations between membership in such groups and possession of the kinds of qualifications that will promote the realization of the multicultural ideal. These correlations will, of course, not be as strong as exceptionless lawlike generalizations. But if one is seeking to fill a position in the area of feminist philosophy, one is very likely to find that the top candidate is a woman or even that all the outstanding candidates are women. Similarly, if one is looking to fill a slot in Africana philosophy, it is highly probable that one will discover that the best qualified candidate is an African American or an African looking to settle in North America. It is not that men cannot or should not do feminist philosophy or that women cannot or should not do other sorts of philosophy. That really should go without saying. It is, however, only to be expected that women will be disproportionately represented in the field because they are likely to be interested in the questions it addresses and so are apt to be motivated to acquire the qualifications needed to contribute to it. Similar things are the case with Africana philosophy and African Americans and, more generally, for other groups, both in philosophy and in other disciplines. Nor are correlations of this kind restricted to the particular groups covered by affirmative action law. Faculty positions in Jewish studies are, after all, typically filled by Jews, those in Roman Catholic theology by Roman Catholics.

So I see striving to achieve the multicultural ideal as bringing with it part of the solution to the problem affirmative action policies were designed to address. But we must not allow residual prejudice to trap us into thinking that members of previously underrepresented groups are valuable in colleges and universities only for their contributions to multiculturalism, important as these are. Pursuit of the multicultural ideal is no substitute for procedural and regulatory forms of affirmative action, applied quite generally in making faculty appointments.

What bringing members of such groups into faculty positions under the banner of multiculturalism can realistically be expected to achieve should therefore be regarded as a supplement to these forms of affirmative action and to other efforts to challenge such legacies of a discriminatory past as institutional racism and sexism.

By way of a conclusion, let me try to illustrate what I hope for from multiculturalism by telling a story meant to make an example of modest progress vivid. Imagine that you are a member of the philosophy faculty at a small midwestern university. There are a dozen philosophers on your campus, but none of them are African Americans. In recent years your institution's admissions and financial aid officers have been quite successful in increasing minority representation in the undergraduate student body. But minority students rarely have taken philosophy courses; indeed, quite a few of them have criticized the philosophy curriculum for being unresponsive to their concerns. This year a junior position in philosophy has become available. You and your colleagues decide to address the perceived curricular problem by specifying Africana philosophy as the area of specialization when you advertise the position. The applicant pool is small. The person who makes the best impression in his convention interview is an African American working on a dissertation on models of moral community in two African traditions. The philosophy faculty votes unanimously to invite this candidate for a campus visit. The sample class he teaches goes very well. He proves to be articulate and engaging, and the students report that he turned them on to some ideas they had not previously encountered. The paper the candidate reads produces mixed reactions. Some complain that it contains too much cultural anthropology and not enough philosophical argument. Others maintain that the discussion period made it clear that the candidate is in fact very skillful at extracting philosophical conclusions from the anthropological material he has studied. Someone argues that, while the candidate's philosophical views do seem to be original, they are still rather sketchy and will need considerable refinement before they could count as a solid contribution to the literature on communitarian ethics. Someone else observes that the candidate's views might have some immediate practical bearing on how black communities in the United States could respond to the destructive pressures of poverty and drugs. After lengthy discussion, an agreement is reached on the conclusion that the candidate is quite likely to be a productive scholar, but no consensus emerges on the question of just how promising the research is. By a vote of ten to two, the philosophy faculty decides to recommend to the administration that he be offered the position.

This little fable is meant to be a small success story. In it there is no question of preferring the less qualified to the more qualified. The leading candidate gets the job because he is the best qualified applicant in the area of specialization advertised, not because he happens also to be an African American. My tale also depicts the uncertainties involved in trying to give a fair shake to philosophical work that is a bit off the beaten track. The leading candidate gets the job because honest efforts are made to allow for the fact that his work does not look exactly like the kind of philosophical product the evaluators are accustomed to seeing. To be sure, it would at present take a good deal of optimism to advertise for a specialist in Africana philosophy since there are so very few of them. But, perhaps, if they were more in demand, it would be easier to persuade African American undergraduates to go to graduate school in philosophy and thus to increase the supply.[5]

NOTES

1. For some interesting contributions, see the articles by Arturo Madrid, William M. Chace, Eileen Stewart, Jean Ferguson Carr, and Daryl G. Smith in *Academe* 76 (November–December 1990): 15–33.

2. For examples, see Evelyn Fox Keller, *Reflections on Gender and Science* (New Haven: Yale University Press, 1985).

3. For details, see Lee H. Yearley, *Mencius and Aquinas* (Albany: SUNY Press, 1990).

4. For examples, see Fred Siegel, "The Cult of Multiculturalism," *The New Republic*, February 18, 1991, pp. 34–40.

5. I thank Alasdair MacIntyre for helpful comments.

"Affirmative Action" in the Cultural Wars

14

Frederick A. Olafson

The real issue in all of these essays is whether there is any adequate justification for a conception of "affirmative action" as compensation or redistribution rather than as an intensified requirement of fairness in the assessment of individual merit. As far as I can see, the arguments advanced by Robert Simon show, even more conclusively than he himself apparently thinks, how weak and sometimes incoherent the case for the former really is; and the endorsement offered by Leslie Francis for redistributive policies in certain circumstances is more a statement of personal inclination—itself not further explained or justified—than it is an argument. One could wish that the distinctions between these different versions of "affirmative action" were as clearly defined in practice as they are in these essays. As things stand, most people in the academic world agree that steps should be taken to see to it that our hiring procedures are really fair. (I would guess that this typically means that they should be as fair as the universities themselves can make them—not ideally fair as they might be in a wider society free of major injustice.) Typically, however, people who take this view do not clearly distinguish the kind of "affirmative action" they favor from other varieties in which the goal may be compensation or redistribution or both. Indeed, I have seen statements by academic officials in which it was tacitly assumed that all these goals were unproblematically compatible with one another. That is of course not the case; when "affirmative action" becomes a system of compensation or redistribution, it gives very different results than it does when fairness is the controlling standard. For the practice of preferential hiring that results, there would be little or no support if its character were clearly understood. In such a program quantitative considerations inevitably take precedence over the kinds of qualitative distinctions that are vital to the well-being of academic institutions but can be made to seem "subjective" and finicky by those who do not understand them. Predictably, too, the resulting dilution of the standards of excellence that have given our universities the standing they have in the world today will be largely invisible to advocates of such policies. The one thing that is certain in this confused situation is that someone who insists on pointing out these ambiguities in the conception of "affirmative action" is very likely to fall afoul of both groups of its supporters even though his aim may be to show how much they disagree with one another.

Although the three lead essays in this book lay out almost all the major arguments concerning "affirmative action," they have very little to say about certain aspects of the situation in our universities that quite significantly affect the implementation of such programs. It is to one feature in particular of this situation that I want to address my re-marks; and it has to do with the quite different levels of acceptance that these different ways of conceiving "affirmative action" have achieved in different parts of our universities. In the natural sciences, proce-dural fairness in the assessment of the qualifications of individual candidates for academic positions seems to be largely uncontested. As far as I can tell, no one has seriously argued that anyone should be hired to teach physics or mathematics in a university who is not at least as well qualified to do so by traditional standards of competence as any other candidate for the job. It is clear, moreover, that this means that progress toward almost any goal, however modest, that may be set for such programs will be slow and will not be reached until the Ph.D. pool comes to include many more people from groups that are now barely represented at all in these departments. Such progress will therefore depend heavily on improvements that are made in the science instruction offered in our elementary and secondary schools. Even so, I have heard no outcry against the recruitment practices of science departments in our universities; and the efforts they make to improve instruction in the schools and to attract undergraduates into science seem to be generally recognized as the appropriate way of trying to initiate a movement in the right direction and incidentally to tap a large unused reservoir of talent. In these quarters, then, the idea that as a form of compensation or in the interest of representa-tiveness a less qualified person might be preferred to a more qualified one as a teacher of these subjects is evidently not taken seriously by anyone. It is also worthy of note that when people from the groups in question do become chemists or mathematicians in a university, they do not try to transform that discipline in their own image even if they are active in other ways in promoting the interests of the group from which they come.

The situation in the social sciences and the humanities is quite different; and it is different in ways that tell us something about the self-understanding and the self-confidence of these disciplines. Here a sense of the integrity of the discipline and of the requirements it imposes is often not as strong as it is in the natural sciences, perhaps— at least in part—because the overwhelming intellectual prestige of the natural sciences in our day has left many academics outside the sciences quite unsure of the epistemic authority of their own disciplines. When there is added to this uncertainty a sense that universities are allied with the "haves" rather than the "have-nots" in the societies they serve, the fact that there have been so few people working in these disciplines who come from certain groups that have also been the victims of wider social disadvantages and injustices may even be interpreted as implying that there is something wrong with the practice of the discipline itself. Since these are disciplines like history or sociology or literature that also deal with themes that may impinge on the historical experience and interests of these groups, it is quite possible that the effective absence of the latter from the academy may have resulted in emphases and judgments that do indeed need review and perhaps revision. This is also the reason why these are more approachable fields of inquiry—more palpably relevant to other non-intellectual interests and less formidable because they do not require a mastery of mathematics. As a result, women or blacks who enter these disciplines may do so for the purpose of pursuing their own forms of group militancy and may declare the discipline itself in its traditional form to be corrupt and in dire need of reform by them. Such persons are often joined and encouraged by people of other backgrounds who share their political views and who are already sceptical about the authority of intellectual standards that are mainly perceived as a barrier to a more democratic or "representative" composition of university faculties. In these circumstances "affirmative action" can take on a wholly different aspect from what it has in the natural sciences.

Nor is this the whole story. In the humanities and social sciences there has been in the course of the past two or three decades a sizable secession from a prior consensus concerning the status of the ideals of truth and objectivity in the inquiries pursued by these disciplines. Although this movement began as a welcome critique of positivist methodology and of the superstitious veneration of "fact" that is so characteristic of the latter, its further development has proceeded under the auspices of a neo-Nietzschean conception of the imposition of meaning and value that leaves no room for intersubjective criteria of validity and truth that are not themselves simply the creatures of yet another "ideology." In these circumstances, it has come to be widely accepted that what drives inquiry of all kinds is an interest or desire that may masquerade as "truth" of some impersonal and universal kind but is at bottom always a modality of self-assertion, whether of an individual or a group. Since theses of this kind apply to the views of those who propound them just as they do to those of people who reject them, we have been treated to the incongruous spectacle of the former proclaiming their own "ideologies" with no apparent sense of how odd it is to propose to others views with which, *ex vi termini*, no truth claim can be associated. In any case, the main relevant implication of all this is that in the eyes of those who have moved with the times and accepted the extreme voluntaristic pragmatism of this view of language and thought, these disciplines can form no exception to these theses. They have, therefore, no sound tradition or valid core that has to be respected and maintained through even the most radical changes. Any appearance of such stability is merely an index of entrenched power and as such something to be challenged and resisted, especially by newcomers to a discipline who feel no natural affinity with its established icons.

By themselves, these conditions in the humanities and social sciences would be quite enough to make the introduction into these departments of the university of substantial numbers of people who have not shared in their more or less official culture a good deal more turbulent than it might otherwise have been. But there is still more. For some time now, American society and with it our universities and colleges have been swept by a wave of what can only be called populism. Originating in the political movements of the late 1960s and flourishing paradoxically in elite institutions, this set of attitudes has evolved into an explicit repudiation of the ideals of high humanistic culture that were the *raison d'être* of the study of—at least—literature, history, and philosophy. These ideas are disqualified, we are told, by reason of their "elitist" character—not everyone can share in them—as well as by the fraudulent pretense of universality that they inveterately make.

Departments of literature especially have eagerly embraced this doctrine and now seldom envisage their responsibility to their students as that of making them citizens of a potentially worldwide republic of letters along the lines that V. S. Naipaul has so eloquently described. Instead, their professors may find the most recent exploits of Madonna to be of at least as much interest and value as the traditional literary curriculum; and classic authors tend to be given an increasingly wide berth. More generally, the cause of the oppressed is uppermost in minds formed in this way; and anything that appears alien or inaccessible or perhaps just not very interesting to students from some group that the elite populist has taken under his wing can rather quickly find its place challenged even in the very flexible canon of works that has formed the basis for the curriculum of humane studies in American universities. The unhappy outcome of all these ritual acts of self-disqualification on the part of people who had been supposed to be most closely identified with the traditions of Western and world culture is that they are in no condition to represent anything to anyone, least of all their disciplines to those who are entering them from groups that have not been closely associated with them.

It seems quite evident that programs of "affirmative actions" that are administered by departments that stand in this negative relation to their own traditions and indeed to the mission with which they are generally understood to be entrusted will be quite different from such programs in departments like the sciences in which no such attitudes exist. In the former case, they become instruments in a political undertaking in which the reform of the university is a prelude to the reform of society generally. Recruitment for academic positions automatically becomes a matter of seeking out like-minded persons from groups that can be expected to support and participate actively in this great work. It is accordingly quite unimaginable that someone would be recruited from an "underrepresented" group who was not assumed to share these political attitudes, and this means that scholarly achievements as such cannot be judged independently from the political orientation of the individual in question. "Affirmative action" not only becomes preferential hiring in Simon's sense; the preferences that guide it are political. The persons who are chosen are chosen not because they are expected to identify themselves with the traditional goals of inquiry in these disciplines but because they promise to alter those goals out of all recognition. From the standpoint of the long-run interest of the university, "affirmative action" thus becomes a new way of giving away the store.

It would be quite false to suggest that the attitudes I have been describing are shared by even a majority of those working in the humanities and social sciences; but through confusion and not a little intimidation they exert a great and sometimes controlling influence nevertheless. It is only recently that the truth about this movement has begun to reach the general public or that part of it that cares about the state of our universities. What needs to be decided in the wider discussion of these matters that appears to be getting under way is whether our universities have generally sound traditions that they have a right to expect new recruits to their faculties to make their own or whether they are in a state of moral bankruptcy from which only great infusions of moral capital from those who have not formerly taken much part in the life of the universities can save them. If the former is the case, as I confidently believe, then the example of the sciences is the only one for our universities to follow in recruiting people from those groups to their faculties. The treatment that members of these groups received at the hands of their fellow human beings in the course of a long and cruel history cannot now be changed. The only response by the universities to that past that does not entail new injustice is a scrupulous fairness that is supplemented by appropriate forms of encouragement and assistance at the right points in the careers of prospective academics. If from now on no one who wishes to teach in our universities is prevented from doing so for reasons that are irrelevant to his or her merits, that and that alone will show that the lesson of the past has been learned.

Quotas by Any Name: Some Problems of Affirmative Action in Faculty Appointments

15

Tom L. Beauchamp

We have struggled with problems of justice and social utility in combating discrimination at least since President Lyndon Johnson's 1965 executive order announcing toughened federal requirements. My views on what have become the mainstream problems of affirmative action conform closely to the approach and the substantive moral views presented in this volume by Leslie Francis, who notes that I defended a version of one part of her strategy in the early 1970s. My convictions have not substantially changed since, and I cannot now improve on her arguments for these views. My intractability is typical of writers on the subject in the past two decades. As the essays by Robert Simon and Lawrence Becker rightly point out, the struggle over preferential treatment has led to competing camps, whose points of view are not likely to be altered by an increase of sophistication in the available arguments.

Nonetheless, writers about preferential treatment in academia have generally overlooked what seems to me today's most interesting moral problem about preferential appointments. This problem can be introduced through a story from a nonacademic setting told by Bob Woodward in his recent book, *The Commanders*. Woodward reports an encounter between White House Chief of Staff John Sununu and Secretary of Defense Richard Cheney. Sununu, an outspoken critic of all policies involving minority and gender quotas, is said to have told Cheney that he "wanted 30 percent of the remaining 42 top jobs in the Defense Department to be filled by women and minorities."[1] This certainly looks like a quota, and the White House chief of staff seems to be defending rival objectives that cannot be reconciled, although each is suited for a different political context. One can tone down the language of "quotas" by speaking of hopes, objectives, guidelines, and the like; but cosmetic changes of wording only thinly obscure any policy established to recruit minorities and women in which the goals are made explicit by numbers.

The moral vision that first gave prominence to the language of quotas has greater staying power in practice than in political rhetoric. So far as I can see, something like the Sununu approach is now widely used in the federal government, in private industry, and in more subtle ways in higher education. Many of my colleagues and acquaintances in academia seem much like Woodward's Sununu. They eschew talk of quotas and condemn reverse discrimination, many with the same rigid conviction and defense of principle expressed by President Bush in saying "I will not sign a quota bill." However, the behavior and stated goals of these same parties is considerably softer than their apparent outrage over the injustice of quotas.

This softening of otherwise severe principle occurs as soon as they glimpse an injustice close at home, that is, in their own departments. Here they readily support the vigorous recruitment of minorities and women; and if they believe there is some sort of statistical imbalance (e.g., "we only have one woman in a department of twenty-three), they often have no reservations about setting aside the next one, two, or three positions for targeted groups, perhaps even including a policy of one-year contracts for white males until the appropriate persons can be recruited.

In these attempts to redress a perceived imbalance, the word "quota" will likely not be heard. I do not believe I have ever heard the word or any surrogate ("goal," "percentage," etc.) used in departmental meetings or in other discussions I have had with colleagues, university administrators, and affirmative action committees in the last twenty years. The whole train of thought moves on a different plane. A few of the many reasons typically offered in defense of targeted affirmative action are the following: "We have many women and minority students who need and do not have an ample number of role models and mentors." "In the formalities of recruitment, typical male traits of aggressive argument are often overvalued and many female traits undervalued, so that women are downgraded unfairly." "The provost is very keen on bringing more minorities and women to the university." "More diversity is very much needed in this department."

"The goals and mission of this university strongly suggest a greater need for increased representation of women and minorities."

Such reasons make a strong appeal, leading departments, with little resistance from administrators, to set aside a position or a block of positions for women and minority candidates. These reasons, when articulated as arguments, incorporate a mixture of appeals to justice, utility, and tradition. They typically involve what Leslie Francis calls compensatory, corrective and redistributive arguments.

I will not attempt here to sort the good arguments from the poor ones. The present point does not rest on these arguments. The point is that departments commonly act, in setting out their goals, in ways that suggest department members willingly endorse what either is or has a strong family resemblance to a quota. In my experience only the rare department now insists that race and sex be considered irrelevant in making appointments. Moreover, university administrators, often more energetically than faculty, support particular percentages or numbers of faculty to be appointed from minority groups and women.

In the university we find the same forms of disagreement about the justifiability of reverse discrimination and quotas found elsewhere in society. Nonetheless, there is massive agreement regarding how the problem of preferential treatment should be handled in actual practice. The situation resembles contemporary casuists' reminders of the way decisions are often reached in forming public policy and making decisions in group meetings. We achieve a consensus about what should be done even when we who collectively make the decisions embrace rival ethical theories and have sharply different reasons supporting our convictions.

It would be difficult, I suspect, for many members of academic departments to articulate the full set of reasons underlying their beliefs about affirmative action. Many of us are more like the ambivalent Sununu than we imagine: We believe we know what is best for our departments, although we cannot articulate why it is best without at the same time admitting that deep problems of potential injustice (reverse discrimination, for example) haunt our favored guidelines.

Such ambivalence and uncertainty also spill over to another level, generating moral problems of truthfulness in advertising positions.[2] Once it has been determined that "almost certainly" a woman or a minority group member will be hired, departments place advertisements that include lines such as the following (which come at the end of a general, purely academic description of the position):

Women and minority-group candidates are especially encouraged to apply. The University of X is an equal opportunity, affirmative action employer.

Advertisements rarely if ever contain more information about affirmative action objectives than this, although often more information might be disclosed that would be of material relevance to applicants. The following are examples of facts or objectives that might be disclosed: A department may have reserved its position for a woman or minority; the chances may be overwhelming that only a minority group member will be hired; the interview team may have decided in advance that only women will be interviewed; the advertised position may be the result of a university policy that offers an explicit incentive (perhaps a new position) to a department if a minority representative is appointed, and so on.

In the full complexity of departmental deliberation, the reasoning involved is generally more arcane and the reasons never entirely shared across the group. Perhaps an interview team will have decided to allocate roughly three-quarters of its interview slots for women, contingent on the quality of the applicants. If so, there is a slender possibility that a white male will be hired, but it is remote. Such objectives are now widely adopted, but they are rarely advertised so as to reveal the true recruitment goals. This incompleteness in advertising sometimes stems from fear of legal liability but more often from fear of departmental embarrassment and harm either to reputation or to future recruiting efforts.

The greater moral embarrassment, however, is that we academics fear making public what we believe to be morally commendable and mandatory in our recruiting efforts. There is something deeply wrong in this circumstance, one that virtually every academic department now faces. The situation is reminiscent of the moral embarrassment of assisted suicide in medicine. There is mounting evidence in medical journals and commentary that many forms of assisted suicide have been going on for a long time in medicine, although no practitioner would advertise his or her practice in such terms, and, until recently, medical codes, judicial councils, and the like considered the topic taboo. The policy and practice of physician-assisted suicide is still condemned in every medical code of ethics that mentions the subject and in an abundance of state laws. As a consequence, some physicians routinely refer patients to the Hemlock Society rather than to the care of another physician.

It is an embarrassment to medicine that a practice so widespread is underground—little discussed, never publicly announced, and generally condemned in the profession. In academic appointments our recruitment embarrassment is even more difficult to explain. Our recruitment practices are rarely condemned, but they are also rarely acknowledged in a public form by even their most enthusiastic adherents. This situation is particularly striking, inasmuch as the justification for this special form of treatment, which makes recruitment far more difficult than it otherwise would be, is precisely that it is a morally praiseworthy endeavor.

I believe these endeavors often are morally praiseworthy. They are honest, open-in-the-department, fair attempts to shape the character of an institution for the better. Among the many problems, however, is that a loss of quality or some form of reverse discrimination does occasionally enter the appointment process. But there is also a need to distinguish between real and apparent reverse discrimination. Sometimes faculty are appointed through affirmative action who appear to be displacing better applicants, but the appearance is itself the result of discriminatory perceptions of the person's qualifications. Apparent reverse discrimination is then nullified by a deeper problem of discrimination. In these cases it would be unreasonable to expect faculty to agree over where to place the actual pattern of discrimination. As with so many problems in the moral life, we can only ask that faculty struggle conscientiously with the real problems.

NOTES

1. Bob Woodward, *The Commanders* (New York: Simon and Schuster, 1991), p. 72.

2. On this topic, see Steven M. Cahn, "Colleges Should Be Explicit about Who Will Be Considered for Jobs," *Chronicle of Higher Education*, April 5, 1989, p. B3 (reprinted in the Introduction to this volume).

16

Are Quotas Sometimes Justified?

James Rachels

Of the many kinds of policies that have been devised to combat discrimination, quotas are the most despised. Almost no one has a good word to say about them. Even those who defend other varieties of preferential treatment are eager, more often than not, to make it known that they do not approve of quotas. In an area in which there is little agreement about anything else, there is a remarkable consensus about this.

Why are quotas thought to be so objectionable? The key idea seems to be that justice is blind, or at least that it should be blind where race and gender are concerned. Jobs should go to the best qualified applicants, regardless of race or sex; anything else is unacceptably discriminatory. A race- or gender-based quota contradicts this fundamental principle. A hiring quota seems to involve—necessarily—the idea that a less qualified black or woman may be hired ahead of a better qualified white male. But if it is wrong to discriminate against blacks and women, how can it be right to discriminate against white men? This point seems to many people to be so obviously correct that quotas are ruled out peremptorily. It is no wonder that the very word has acquired a bad smell.

With so many other issues still unresolved, it may seem perverse to question the one thing about which there is agreement. Nevertheless, I believe that the prevailing consensus concerning quotas is misguided. There is nothing wrong with a quota used in the right circumstances and for the right reason. It needs to be emphasized, however, that there are significant differences in the ways that quotas may be used. They may be imposed in various sorts of circumstances and for various purposes. In what follows I describe a set of circumstances in which I believe the imposition of a quota is justified. I do not conclude from this that the imposition of quotas is in general a good thing or that they should be widely used. If only because they cause such resentment, they should be used sparingly. But I do conclude that the near-universal condemnation of quotas is misguided. It is wrong to think they should never be used.

Suppose you are the dean of a college—let us say that it is a good college, but not one of the most prestigious in the country—and you are concerned that only the best qualified scholars are hired for your faculty. Your college uses the standard procedure for selecting new faculty: The relevant department solicits applications, reviews them, and then recommends the best qualified to you. You then authorize the formal offer of employment. Your role is mainly that of an overseer; so long as everything seems to be in order, you go along with the departments' recommendations.

In your philosophy department, there are vacancies almost every year. You notice, however, that women are almost never hired to fill them. (One woman was hired years ago, so there is a token female. But that's as far as it has gone.) So you investigate. You discover that there are, indeed, lots of female philosophers looking for jobs each year. And you have no reason to think that these women are, on average, any less capable than their male counterparts. On the contrary, all available evidence suggests that they are equally as good. So you talk to the (male) chairperson of the philosophy department and you urge him to be careful to give full and fair consideration to the female applicants. Being a good liberal fellow, he finds this agreeable enough— although he may be a little offended by the suggestion that he is not already giving women due consideration. But your admonition has little apparent effect. Each time there is a vacancy in the philosophy faculty, and candidates are being considered, he continues to report, with evident sincerity, that in the particular group under review a male has turned out to be the best qualified. And so, he says each year, if we want to hire the best qualified applicant we have to hire the man, at least this time.

This is repeated annually, with minor variations. One of the variations is that the best female philosopher in the pool may be listed as the department's top choice. But when, predictably enough, she turns out to be unavailable (having been snapped up by a more prestigious university), no women in the second tier are considered to be good alternatives. Here you notice a peculiar asymmetry: namely, that although the very best males are also going to other universities, the males in the second tier are considered good alternatives. Momentarily, then, you consider whether the problem could be that philosophical talent is distributed in a funny way: While the very best women are equal to the very best men, at the next level down the men suddenly dominate. But that seems unlikely.

After further efforts have been made along these lines, without result, you might eventually conclude that there is an unconscious prejudice at work. Your department, despite its good intentions and its one female member, is biased. It isn't hard to understand why this could be so. In addition to the usual sources of prejudice against women—the stereotypes, the picture of women as less rational than men, and so forth—an all-male or mostly male group enjoys a kind of camaraderie that might seem impossible if females were significantly included. In choosing a new colleague the matter of how someone would "fit in" with the existing group will always have some influence. This will work against females, no matter what their talents as teachers and scholars.

Finally, then, you reach two conclusions. First, you are not getting the best qualified scholars for your faculty. Better qualified women are being passed over in favor of less qualified men. Second, this problem is unlikely to be corrected if the "standard" procedure of permitting the philosophy department to choose its own new members is continued.

Therefore, you issue a new instruction: You tell the philosophy department that it *must* hire some additional women, in numbers at least in proportion to the number of women in the applicant pool. (Why that number? Because, if talent is equally distributed among men and women, that is the number most likely to result in the best qualified individuals being hired.) The department's reaction is easily predictable. It will be objected that this policy could result in hiring a less qualified woman over a better qualified man. That would be unfair. Faculty should be hired, it will be said, according to their qualifications and not according to their gender.

But you agree that the best qualified should be hired. That is precisely what you are trying to achieve. You are not out to give women a special break. You are not trying to redress the injustices they have suffered in the past; nor are you trying to provide "role models" for female students. You may be pleased if your policy has these effects, but the purpose of your new instruction is not to achieve them. Your only purpose is to get the best qualified scholars for your faculty, regardless of gender. The question is simply what selection procedure will best serve that purpose. The fact of unconscious prejudice makes the usual system of simply allowing your experts—the philosophy department—to exercise their judgment an ineffective method. Allowing them to exercise their judgment within the limits of a quota, on the other hand, might be more effective because it reduces the influence of unconscious prejudice. The department's objection, along with all the other usual objections to quotas, misses the point.

That's the argument. It is worth emphasizing that this argument takes into account a feature of the selection process that is often ignored when "preferential treatment" is discussed. Often, the question is put like this: Assuming that X (a white man) is better qualified than Y (a black or a woman), is it justifiable to adopt a policy that would permit hiring or promoting Y rather than X? Then the debate begins, and various reasons are produced that might justify such a policy, such as that it redresses wrongs or that it helps to combat racism or sexism. The debate focuses on whether such reasons are sufficient, and the critical issue appears to be justice versus social utility: Justice argues for hiring X, while reasons of social utility weigh in on behalf of hiring Y.

When the issue is approached in this way, a crucial point is overlooked. People do not come prelabeled as better or worse qualified. Before we can say that X is better qualified than Y, someone has to have made that judgment. And this is where prejudice is most likely to enter the picture. A male philosopher, judging other philosophers, might very well rate women lower, without even realizing he is doing so. The argument we are considering is intended to address this problem, which arises before the terms of the conventional discussion are even set.

Of course, this argument does not purport to show that any system of quotas, applied in any circumstances, is fair. It implies nothing at all about whether schools should establish quotas for the admission of minority students, for example; nor does it imply anything about whether a certain number of government contracts should be set aside for minority businesses. Those remain separate issues. Moreover, the argument does not even say that hiring quotas should be used for all academic appointments. The argument is only a defense of quotas used in a certain way in certain particular circumstances.

But the type of circumstances I have described is not uncommon. Actual quota systems, of the sort that have been established and tested in the courts in recent years, often have just this character. They are instituted to counter the prejudice, conscious or otherwise, that corrupts judgments of merit. When Federal District Court Judge Frank Johnson ordered the Alabama State Police to hire black officers— an order that was widely condemned as just another objectionable "quota"—he was not attempting to redress past injustices or anything of the sort. He was, instead, attempting to curb present injustices against blacks whose qualifications were being systematically underrated by white officials. University people are likely to feel superior to the Alabama police officers: *They* may be guilty of bias, it will be said, but *we* are not. But of course it is almost always a mistake to think oneself an exception to tendencies that are well-nigh universal among human beings. Few of us are saints.

To summarize: Our argument envisions the imposition of a quota as a corrective to a "normal" decision-making process that has gone wrong. We may define a "normal" process as follows: (1) The goal of the process is to identify the best qualified individuals for the purpose at hand. (2) The nature of the qualifications is specified. (3) A pool of candidates is assembled. (4) The qualifications of the individuals in the pool are assessed, using the specified criteria, and the candidates are ranked from best to worst. (5) The jobs, promotions, or whatever are awarded to the best qualified individuals.

This process may go wrong in any number of ways, of course, some of them not involving prejudice. We are not concerned here with all the ways in which things can go wrong. We are concerned only with this possibility: First, we notice that, as the selection process is carried out, individuals from a certain group are regularly rated higher than members of another group. Second, we can find no reason to think that the members of the former group are in fact superior to the members of the latter group—on the contrary, there is reason to think the members of the two groups are, on average, equally well qualified. Moreover, the distribution of qualifications within the two groups seems normal, from top to bottom. And third, there is reason to think that the people performing the assessments are prejudiced against members of the latter group. These are the circumstances in which our argument says the imposition of a quota may be justified, if other corrective steps cannot do the job. The quota is justified as an effective method for making sure that the best qualified win out, despite the prejudices that inescapably operate against them. The quota does not introduce a new element of prejudice. It merely cancels out an old one.

In deciding what should be done, the policies that have the best reasons on their side should come out on top. In this area, however, emotions run so high that reason often takes second place, and arguments are adduced only to support views to which people are already viscerally committed. I cannot say for certain that the argument I have presented does not contain some flaw that has escaped my notice. But even if it is unassailable, I am pessimistic about whether it will make much difference in the public debate. The emotions that surround this whole subject are too powerful, and the lines that have been drawn are too firmly in place, to allow much optimism on behalf of reason. Nevertheless, if this argument is sound, it does show that the prevailing consensus against quotas does not have reason on its side, no matter how powerful are the emotions that sustain it.

17

Proportional Representation of Women and Minorities

Celia Wolf-Devine

I begin by asking a question, an affirmative answer to which seems presupposed by the current debate on affirmative action[1]: Is there necessarily something wrong if there is a low percentage of African Americans or women or Hispanics, et cetera, in the field of college teaching relative to their proportion in the population at large? Why is this a goal we should aim at? I do not mean to deny that women and racial and ethnic minorities have been victims of discrimination in academia (although this is by no means limited to blacks, Asians, Hispanics, and Native Americans—consider, for example, Polish, Lebanese, or Portuguese Americans) or that some discrimination still persists. Such discrimination is bad and should be eliminated; in fact, we ought to put more resources into enforcing antidiscrimination laws. My argument here is that there is no reason to believe that proportional representation of minorities and women among the professoriate is a requirement of justice or that a situation where such proportional representation obtained would necessarily be better than one in which it did not.[2]

Arguments that might be advanced in favor of the claim that something is wrong if women and minorities are not proportionally represented fall into two general categories: those that take the existence of such statistical disparities to be evidence of discrimination or injustice, and those based on the value of diversity. These two types of arguments differ in that those based on the need for diversity would not prove that universities are required as a matter of justice to appoint more women and minorities, but merely that it would be educationally desirable were they to do so. But if it could be shown that the lack of proportional representation of minority groups among the professoriate either itself constituted an injustice or provided adequate evidence of the existence of ongoing injustice, then the case for involvement of the federal government to correct this becomes stronger.[3]

Is Proportional Representation
a Requirement of Justice?

Does the lack of proportional representation of women and minorities among the professoriate constitute an injustice? Or is it necessarily evidence of discrimination or injustice of any sort? It would be evidence of injustice or discrimination only if it is reasonable to believe that, in the absence of discrimination and injustice, women and all racial and ethnic minorities would be proportionately represented in college teaching (and other professions). But *is* it reasonable to believe this?

The important issue here philosophically is where we place the burden of proof. Should we assume, as Becker does, that the statistics reflect some sort of discrimination or injustice unless we have evidence to the contrary?[4] But why put the burden of proof here? While it is legitimate to put the burden of proof on the employer in cases where the proportion of women and minorities hired is radically lower than their proportion *in the applicant pool*, the case is totally different when we are comparing the proportion of women and minorities in the professoriate with their proportion in the population as a whole.

Looking first at racial and ethnic groups, there is no prima facie reason to suppose that members of different racial and ethnic minorities would be equally likely to want to go into the professoriate and, on the contrary, many reasons to expect that they would not. To the extent that ethnic and racial groups form at least partially self-contained communities (and they do), members of one community will value different sorts of character traits, encourage the acquisition of different skills, and have different ideas about what sorts of jobs carry the most prestige.[5] Most arguments in favor of affirmative action in fact suppose that racial and ethnic groups differ in these sorts of ways; if they did not then bringing in a wider variety of such groups would not contribute to diversity.

In one culture, scientists might be particularly respected, while in another being a media personality might be viewed as the height of success. Sometimes traditional patterns in a culture predispose members toward certain professions, as the great respect for Torah scholars in Jewish culture fits very naturally with aspirations for careers as scholars or lawyers. Cultures that are highly verbal might be expected to produce more teachers than others. In addition, of course, as some members of a community go into a particular field, others aspire to go into it also since they already know something about it from their friends and relatives and have contacts in the field.[6]

So even if equal percentages of the members of all racial and ethnic groups might desire some sort of prestigious job, there is no reason to suppose that all of them would regard the same jobs as prestigious. Or to put the point more bluntly, not everyone would regard being a professor as prestigious. And there are special reasons why college teaching might be less attractive than other professions to those (for example, blacks and Hispanics) who are trying to struggle out of poverty. Due to its low salaries relative to the amount of training required, college teaching has long tended to attract people brought up in relatively secure financial conditions, plus a few other individuals who feel a strong calling to the intellectual life.

To put the dialogue about affirmative action in academia in the proper perspective, we need to keep in mind some background facts. Certainly there are some prestigious research institutions where professors make excellent salaries, and in business or technical fields professors can often make good money consulting and exercise some power in the larger society. But the salary of the average academic has not kept pace with salaries in other fields; non-academics I meet are universally shocked to learn how little professors are paid. An associate professor I know is forced to teach an extra night course each term, to teach both summer sessions, and on top of that to sell suits at a men's store during the Christmas season in order to be able to support a wife and two children and to meet mortgage payments on a house in an area that is adequate but by no means fancy.

In addition, the social status of professors (particularly in the humanities) has declined significantly from what it was in the 1950s and 1960s. (And if affirmative action is stronger in academia than elsewhere, this might lower the status of professors still more, since they would be perceived as being appointed because of their sex or race.) These problems, together with a widespread loss of a sense of purpose among academics, have led to a lot of demoralization among faculty. Ambitious young members of minority groups may quite reasonably prefer careers in law, politics, industry, or the media. Indeed, the problem of how to attract bright young people of *any* racial or ethnic group into college teaching is becoming increasingly severe. Even students who feel strongly drawn to the intellectual life are often deterred from pursuing academic careers by poor salaries and by what they hear about academic politics.

If I am right, then, one important reason why racial and ethnic minorities are not proportionately represented in the professoriate is because those who are in a position to acquire the credentials are going into other professions. Bright, ambitious members of such groups who have B.A.s often find careers in other areas more attractive than college teaching. This is partly a function of their cultures, which may not accord high prestige to professors relative to other professions, and partly a result of low salaries and demoralization among many (although certainly not all) professors. And in order to attract them into the professoriate, it is essential to begin by improving the situation of those already in the field in a number of ways (and not just salary, although that is important). We should then make it clear to minority members that they are genuinely welcome in academia and will receive fair consideration.

Another reason why racial and ethnic minorities are not proportionally represented in the professoriate is because large numbers of them have been deeply scarred by poverty (and often racism) and do not enter college. They are therefore not even in the running for becoming college teachers or for pursuing most careers with high status and pay. The difficulties involved in remedying this situation are massive, and the universities can play only a limited role. Universities could, for example, set up tutorial programs aimed at helping disadvantaged students (and staffed by faculty and student volunteers). Or they could offer scholarships for college and graduate school to talented disadvantaged students or have need-blind admissions if they can afford to do so. Since such programs are costly, government assistance would probably be necessary.

The big question that arises at this point is to what extent such remedial programs should be directed at racial and ethnic minorities. At this point I believe another background fact becomes relevant—one that is too often overlooked by supporters of affirmative action. During the Reagan years, American society underwent a marked polarization between rich and poor. We have, in fact, the most extreme polarization of any industralized country (measured by the gap between the wealth of the upper fifth of society and that of the lower fifth). And it is arguable that affirmative action has contributed to this polarization (at least it has done nothing to prevent it), since those women and blacks who were in a position to take advantage of it (i.e., those who had suffered less discrimination) did so, leaving the really poor no better off and simply displacing other groups and pushing them down into poverty.[7]

The problem of the widening gap of rich and poor should be confronted directly, rather than gearing remedial programs too closely to race and ethnic group (as affirmative action does). In addition to making people more rather than less race conscious and generating resentments along racial and ethnic lines, such programs are not radical enough, because they lead people to think that by appointing middle-class blacks, Hispanics, or Asians that they have thereby really helped the poor.

The poor need direct assistance, and it is not only minority members who are poor. There are enormous numbers of white poor, particularly in rural areas of the South. Many ethnic groups are impoverished and have suffered discrimination at least as severe as that against Hispanics and Asians. The children of single mothers of all races and ethnic groups have been pushed down into severe poverty, and many blue-collar workers have been impoverished (e.g., small farmers or residents of the Minnesota Iron Range). Programs targeted at the economically disadvantaged should perhaps be supplemented by special compensatory programs aimed at blacks and Native Americans (since most Hispanics and Asians are recent immigrants, compensatory arguments do not carry the same force in their case). I do not here take a position on this thorny issue, except to say that not all scholarships and special assistance programs should be earmarked for such groups, but a significant proportion should be awarded on the basis of merit and financial need alone.

The more poor people are brought up into the middle class, the more of them will obtain B.A.s and be in a position to consider college teaching as a career. We will still need to improve the situation of the professoriate if we are to be able to attract good Ph.D. candidates. But at least more people will have a chance to enter the profession, especially if graduate school scholarships are available to talented students who need them. The poor who are not upwardly mobile (e.g., the retired, the chronically ill, the mentally retarded, etc.) will still need direct financial and medical assistance.

The situation of women in academia is somewhat different from that of ethnic and racial minorities, in that they are closer to being proportionally represented, at least in the humanities, although they tend still to be absent from some scientific and technical fields and from the very most prestigious positions. Does this prove they are being discriminated against? Certainly in some cases they have been and still are discriminated against (especially in promotion and pay), and these abuses should be corrected. But here also the statistics alone do not establish discrimination. Their own choices to spend more time with their children may account for their failure to advance as far or as quickly as their male colleagues and for the fact that they hold part-time positions more frequently. Certainly not all women make these sorts of choices, but enough do to affect the statistics. (It could, of course, be argued to be unjust that women take on a larger share of child care, but we should beware of paternalistically telling people what choices they ought to make.)

In order to establish the presence of injustice or discrimination, we need to know more about the actual preferences of the women in question, and not just adopt a bureaucratic approach of trying to get the numbers to come out right. Suppose an academic couple who wish to combine career and family decide between themselves that he will work full time and she will work part time in order to spend time with the children. Then suppose that due to affirmative action he is unable to get a full-time job and she is forced to take full-time work to support the family. The statistics may look better, but both people are less happy than they would have been without affirmative action.

Proportional representation of women and of blacks, Hispanics, Native Americans, and Asians in the professoriate, then, is not a requirement of justice, and a situation where such proportional representation is present is not necessarily more just than one where it is not—for example, if it was obtained by overriding the preferences of those concerned without some reason other than a desire to get the statistics to come out right.[8] Furthermore, a society where such proportional representation was present along with a vast and un-bridgeable gap between rich and poor would be less just than one with a more equitable distribution of wealth and opportunities for advancement but which lacked proportional representation of women and minorities in some professions.

Promoting Diversity

Affirmative action is often defended as a means to greater diversity on college faculties, and a faculty that does not have proportional representation of women and minorities is regarded as not diverse enough. Diversity, unfortunately, has become something of a buzzword these days, and it is necessary to give thought to what sorts of diversity should be promoted and why. And this requires some reflection about what the purposes of the university are. Simon's article is an important contribution toward clarifying some of the issues, but considerably more work needs to be done. Diversity of opinion is not enough, but neither is diversity of methodology. Not all methodologies deserve representation. Consider, for example, astrology, or the systematic vilification of one's opponents.

If one agrees with Simon that encouraging intelligent dialogue about important issues is one of the purposes of the university (and I do), then this has at least some implications for the sort of diversity we want. If dialogue is of central importance, then it is desirable to have intellectual diversity. But limitless intellectual diversity is not good; the value of diversity must be weighed against the value of community. Certainly, there can be communities that are too ingrown and homogenous. If a psychology department appoints only behaviorists, then students are deprived of exposure to other quite legitimate traditions of thought within their discipline. And the same is true if an economics department appoints only followers of Milton Friedman, or a philosophy department appoints only Thomists or only phenomenologists. But on the other hand, too much diversity leads to the breakdown of communication between groups. If this occurs, faculty become unable to talk with each other and work within totally different conceptual frameworks, making no attempts to respond to positions other than their own. Students, then, tend to become hopelessly confused, give up even trying to develop coherent beliefs of their own, and retreat into just giving each professor what he or she wants. Maintaining community is, thus, just as important for education as introducing intellectual diversity.

Suppose, then, we are agreed that intellectual diversity, per se, is not simply a good to be maximized (and in real life, no one, not even the defenders of affirmative action, believe in the value of limitless diversity); we then must specify what sorts of diversity will contribute to stimulating intelligent dialogue and learning on college campuses.

And I see no reason why proportional representation of groups now officially recognized as protected minorities should be expected to produce the right sort of diversity. First of all, diversity of skin color is quite consistent with total ideological conformity and therefore need not conduce to dialogue at all.

Furthermore, as people like Stephen Carter have been pointing out lately, we ought not to suppose that because a person is black or Hispanic that he or she will have some particular set of beliefs or espouse a particular methodology.[9] This expectation is a form of racial stereotyping (as Simon also notes) and as such is demeaning to the person. Pressures toward ideological conformity among members of minority groups are increased by this sort of dishonest attempt to smuggle in one's ideological agendas under the guise of affirmative action. A Hispanic who is a Republican is no less a Hispanic, and a woman who is not a feminist is no less a woman.

There is, then, no good reason to suppose that proportional representation of the minority groups now officially recognized will yield the right sort of intellectual diversity. And the same sorts of arguments developed above could be applied to cultural diversity as well as to intellectual diversity. People from the same cultural background share common prereflective attitudes, patterns of feeling and imagination, ways of talking, and styles of behavior. But although it is educationally valuable for students to be exposed to people from different cultures, limitless cultural diversity is not a good thing (for the same reasons that limitless intellectual diversity is not), and skin color is not a reliable guide to culture. An enormous amount of cultural diversity exists, for example, among blacks and Hispanics. Poor rural Southern blacks, for example, may be culturally more similar to poor rural Southern whites than they are to Northern middle-class urban blacks.

In short, one cannot generate the right sort of diversity (intellectual or cultural) by simply pursuing neatly measurable goals like proportional representation of women, blacks, Hispanics, Asians, and Native Americans. In addition, the sort of diversity needed at a given school will itself be a function a number of factors, such as the character of the faculty already there, the student body, and the sorts of vocations for which students are preparing. A school preparing students for careers in international business or diplomacy might find that the sort of diversity introduced by appointing foreign nationals to their faculty was particularly valuable, for example. These sorts of judgments involve a great many complex considerations and cannot be made mechanically by trying to get statistics to meet some target percentages (comforting though it would be if things were so simple).[10]

Notes

1. By affirmative action, I mean preferential treatment and not just things like announcing openings and encouraging women and minorities to apply. And tie-breaking affirmative action might, I believe, be justified in some cases on the basis of the role model argument. The reason the role model argument does not support preferential appointments in order to attain proportional representation is that a minority member can only function as a model for excellence if he or she is perceived as having been appointed because of qualifications rather than race or sex. One really good minority faculty member is a more effective and inspiring role model than ten mediocre ones.

2. Note, again, that I am speaking of proportional representation relative to their percentage in the population at large.

3. I do not consider here compensatory arguments. That institutions should make compensation to individuals they have discriminated against is self-evident, but problems arise when those receiving compensation are not the persons who were wronged. For example, how are older women who have suffered discrimination in any way made whole from their injury by the appointment of younger women unrelated to them? In any case, there is no clear way compensatory arguments could tell us what proportion of minority groups should be on university faculties. How can we tell what proportion of Hispanics would have become professors in the absence of discrimination? And in the absence of slavery, the number of blacks teaching in American universities would be no higher than it is now. An additional problem with compensatory arguments is that, like redistributive arguments, they treat teaching appointments as plums to be distributed instead of as focusing on the responsibilities that such positions involve.

4. He holds that we should assume that members of all racial, ethnic, and gender groups are equally interested in the professoriate until we have evidence to the contrary—evidence he could only obtain by putting his plan into effect and seeing how many members of these groups choose to go into college teaching. But how can we tell when equal opportunity has been attained (i.e., the levers are within the reach of all)? Only, he says, when proportionate representation has been attained.

5. Perhaps instead of conceptualizing society as a pyramid with one top, we should think of it as a group of hills with many different peaks; people may choose different paths to wealth, power, and prestige.

6. This is called the "cousinhood advantage." While in academia it operates in favor of WASPs and Jews, this is not the case everywhere. Although

building contractors frequently make very good money, a WASP would be at a great disadvantage in this field in many parts of the country where the building trades are heavily dominated by certain ethnic groups.

7. See Kevin Phillips, *The Politics of Rich and Poor* (New York: Random House, 1990), pp. 18, 203, 207.

8. People should, I believe, be free to enter the occupation of their choice (subject, of course, to certain broad constraints based on the common good—such as that if everyone wanted to be lawyers and no one wanted to grow crops, some adjustments would be necessary) and make other career decisions as they see fit, even though we might think (rightly even) that it would be better for them to choose otherwise.

9. Stephen Carter, *Reflections of an Affirmative Action Baby* (New York: Basic Books, 1991).

10. I am indebted to my husband, Phil Devine, for many valuable discussions of the ideas in this article and for reading and commenting on the manuscript. I have also profited from discussions with Beth Soll, John McGrath, Joseph Ryshpan, and my colleagues Richard Capobianco, Soo Tan, and Richard Velkley.

18

An Ecological Concept of Diversity

La Verne Shelton

> Valuing gender and racial differences as well as differences in learning styles, encourages the range of human possibilities. . . . Methods for encouraging diversity are the focus of this college.
> —*Wisconsin Week*, 30 October, 1991

In his contribution to this volume, Lawrence Becker expresses exasperation about what he sees as a deadlock among intellectuals. He suggests that there is grave difficulty in arguing for anything beyond procedural and regulatory forms of affirmative action and, since thirty years of debate over affirmative action and twenty years of experience with it have given us no agreement in either principle or action as to how we can compensate for this country's brutal history of racism or even correct present racist ideas and practices, it is time to force a compromise. I question whether we have spent such a crushingly long time at this, given that attitudes are so deeply ingrained. We know who has received what educational degrees, but we have done little except speculate as to the causes of these statistics. We know little about ways in which attitudes have changed in response to affirmative procedures that have been typically quixotic or uneven, at best. Pertinent empirical data that may presuppose, for example, longitudinal studies over not just one but perhaps several generations of students are needed to assess the effectiveness of efforts to end discriminatory practices in academia.

In analogy, note that it ought to have been obvious in the 1950s that the markedly increasing affluence among large numbers of middle-class people would, since the rich never get poorer, result in the appearance in our midst of a large and increasing underclass. But well into the 1980s many otherwise astute individuals were still minimizing this problem.

So it is with affirmative action, which, in its slow and tentative way, also began in the 1950s when many public facilities were de-segregated. We may exaggerate the good effects of piecemeal efforts, minimize the importance of isolated successes with the label "token," and ignore the extent to which procedures intended to foster "equal opportunity" do nothing beyond increasing the phone and clerical bills of university search committees. But millions have been deeply affected by affirmative action in ways we have only begun to measure. Our impressions, even over a generation, about the effects of affirma-tive action efforts—even our impressions as to what these efforts have been—are not trustworthy. Hence the systematic collection of data must accompany our "observations."

The effects of racism and sexism are deeply enough entrenched in the entire U.S. population that the responses characteristic of them are unreflectingly taught by parents to their infants. A child born twenty years ago has been taught these racist and sexist responses and will not lose them just by virtue of the occurrence of affirmative action, ex-perienced either as an African American child given opportunities her parents did not have or as a white child who suddenly finds people of color among his peers. Among other things, chauvinistic responses cause such a child, now twenty years old, automatically to evaluate its female or nonwhite professors as inferior to its white male professors. And these female or nonwhite professors will see this as confirming their own racist or sexist opinions about themselves. Yet, the mere presence and influence of competent, "newtraditional"[1] professors in this child's life is likely to cause it to bring up its own children in such a way that they can see a person's abilities as less correlated with their race or sex. We'll detect these positive changes, which are effects of the affirmative action begun twenty years ago, only ten years from now. In contrast, such negative effects as backlash and the further vic-timization of oppressed peoples that are usually brought up in these discussions began almost with the advent of affirmative action.

We have a complete paper record of affirmative action programs and court decisions but have done little systematic and careful track-ing of the attitudes of ordinary people. We have difficulty in detecting differences between genuine attitude change and change in report-ing of attitudes. We do not know whether the sorts of programs that have been in effect have helped at all to correct the self-contempt and self-hatred every child of color in this country feels to some degree, whether its parent is a Supreme Court justice or an impoverished drug addict. Until self-reflexive racism is in the process of being at least reduced, affirmative action has not borne fruits that make it worth the trouble. The no-need/necessity debate is not deadlocked. Perhaps new questions need to be asked. Clearly, relevant empirical information is yet to come in.

I

An excellent argument for affirmative action as a corrective (as opposed to compensation) for the present discriminatory use of processes for appointing and promoting faculty is given in the paper in this volume by Leslie Francis. The main points I wish to make in my contribution support and, I believe, extend discussion of this issue.

I am against preferential treatment in the sense distinguished as strongest by Robert Simon according to which members of designated groups are favored for a job over members of other groups, even though all have roughly equal qualifications for the job. I do believe, however, that membership in groups whose members traditionally have been, and are still being, at least partially excluded from academia is part of one's credentials, part of the calculation of how "equal" one's qualifications are and, hence, is likely to be relevant in determining who is best suited for a given position. Group membership is not a moral, but an academic and, as I will argue, *ecological* qualification for academic positions today.

One of Simon's conclusions is that intellectual diversity in an academic community is a positive good and that there are some reasons for thinking that ethnic, sexual, and color diversity might contribute to intellectual diversity (and, hence, might also be a positive good, other things being equal). But he alleges that arguments about role models and unique perspectives and experience blur the distinction between qualifying criteria for a position and additional determinants, beyond qualifications. In the end he does not see diversity arguments as sufficient to sustain the strong form of affirmative action.

I believe that diversity arguments can be divorced from moral imperatives and can be made stronger purely by an appeal to academic qualifications. I claim that the sort of diversity ideally produced by affirmative action is, for all practical purposes and in the long run, necessary for optimal diversity. My central premiss is the following:

1. If an academic unit (see below) is going to survive as an academic unit into the next thirty years it must educate and educate well increasing proportions of newtraditional people.

I shall argue for this below. I take it, however, that the following conditional is true in any sort of society we could countenance.

2. If academic units are to educate well increasing proportions of newtraditional people, it must no longer be true that the unthinking or "visceral" response of anyone to a person of color or a woman or a member of any other economically and socially oppressed group (any newtraditional person) is that he or she is less likely to be academically competent or possess academic superiority than a white male ("oldtraditional") person in a similar position.

My final conclusion is to be

Being newtraditional is a positive qualification for an academic position.

"Qualification" is not to be understood as enhancement in the way that, say, a wealthy candidate's intention to donate all of his or her salary to a fund for graduate fellowships for students who were brought up in inner-city ghettos (for example) might be understood. Being of color or the female gender normally ought not to be a requirement for a particular position,[2] but it increases one's academic qualifications in the way that having received a university reward for teaching as a teaching assistant or having one's thesis published by a major academic press would do.

The natural bridge between (2) and my conclusion is controversial because the mentioned qualifications are not mere enhancements. The bridge is

3. If it is no longer to be part of the unthinking or "visceral" responses of anyone to any newtraditional person that they are less likely to be academically competent or possess academic superiority than an oldtraditional person, then being a newtraditional person increases one's academic qualifications for an academic position.

Provided that we add the assumption that we assume that it is true that our academic units are to survive into the next thirty years, the argument from this assumption, (1), (2), and (3) to my conclusion is valid.

My support for (3) is a likelihood argument. According to (3), in the climate of having a certain change of response to be taught, new-traditional academics have higher qualifications for their jobs. This is somewhat analogous to, in a climate of "publish or perish," candidates who take no more time with their thesis than it deserves having higher qualifications for their jobs.

A likelihood argument is not, by any means, too weak here; it is standard fare for judging an individual's qualifications. For example, we say that Ph.D.s who have written good theses are more likely to produce better publications when they become assistant professors than those who have not written good theses. There are plenty of examples of people who have written good theses who never publish anything good after that, and plenty of examples of people who have not written good theses who have a good publication record if they get a chance to become assistant professors.[3]

On the basis of such likelihood arguments, search committees consider having written a good dissertation to be a positive qualification for an academic position. With exactly the same force, being a new-traditional person is a positive qualification for an academic position. Part of what someone in that position needs to do, given the antecedent of (3), is to change the visceral response of the masses of people of the United States who have at least direct connections with the University. A newtraditional person will be in a better position to do that in virtue of her own excellence.

The central criteria for excellence as a professor are (a) success in artistic production, scholarship, or research, where this is measured by the "visibility" of one's writings and other products and (b) demonstrated teaching effectiveness, where this is "measured" by the degree to which the professor's students become and remain interested in the subject matter, are stimulated to learn, and, according to their abilities, attain competence within the subject matter.

There are plenty of cases where a competent assistant professor who is a woman or a person of color fails to make brilliant contributions to his or her field and fails to demonstrate excellence in teaching and some cases where oldtraditional males are able to foster or highlight the excellence of their newtraditional colleagues and students.

But the likelihood claim, which seems quite obvious once the relevant task that is currently part of being a professor is noted, is simply the following one.

> 3A. A newtraditional person is more likely than an oldtra-
> ditional one to demonstrate the way in which newtra-
> ditional people can be excellent both as researchers and
> as teachers.

If (3A) is accepted, (3) follows easily.

The qualifications argument for attempting to achieve diversity by appointing people because they are better qualified (partly) in virtue of being members of groups whose members have been discriminated against will be complete only when we have reasons for accepting (1). A clearer notion of "diversity" is required for this.

As Simon points out, "Diversity!" can be a hollow cry. The term is usually applied in a relative fashion (group A is more diverse than group B). And, furthermore, diversity is always diversity-in-certain-respects. (For any two groups, A and B, A is more diverse than B in some respects and less diverse than B in others.)

In spite of noting this, I do not think the most correct notion of diversity is going to be a careful list of spectra of variation together, perhaps, with weightings on these spectra according to how impor-tant it is for an academic department to have variety in each of them.[4] The most obvious reason is that the list and weightings would be dif-ferent across disciplines and even within disciplines across different types of institutions. The philosophy department at Haverford Col-lege might find a different profile healthy than would the philosophy department at the University of New Mexico. It is arguable that each academic unit would need its own hand-made profile.

It is readily apparent that the institution we call academia is not monolithic. It includes international conferences in various disciplines, sectors of the federal government such as the National Science Foun-dation, and the particular introductory logic class of a professor. As well as the sorts of profiles desirable, the need for any sort of diver-sity might vary among these various units. For the most part I will consider what diversity means for an academic unit construed mainly in terms of the faculty of a department, secondarily in terms of its graduate students (if any), and tertiarily in terms of undergraduate students who take a significant number of courses in that department. Even though this unit is homogeneous with respect to a field, it is apparent that it is an exceedingly artificial division of academia, given that most of the power, both economic and professional, lies outside it. The economic power lies with the administrators of the University,[5] the legislators and, more indirectly, the taxpayers in the state. The professional power lies with those individuals in the field most actively involved in book and journal editing and conference organization. (A few of these economic and professional power wielders may, of course, be in any department currently being discussed.) What this means is that the perceived need for a given degree of diversity in a unit evolves partly in response to these sources of power rather than entirely in accord with purely intellectual criteria (if there even are such).

In my home university, the word "diversity" and its verbal and adjectival forms are used by everyone (see the quote at the beginning of this essay). It is associated with the slogan "Let all the flowers bloom," and is intended to designate an ideal climate for most things academic. How do we apply this word and in what sense might it imply a good for an academic environment and, in particular, for an academic unit?

Let us start with a general sense and work our way forward to the sense propelled by the affirmative action debate.

A *Desirable Diversity Type* (DDT) is a profile of levels of variety over any number of significant spectra. The DDT in an average clothing store would have a high level of size variation, a lower level in color variation in a men's clothing store than in a woman's clothing store (traditionally), and a lower level of country-of-export variation in a bargain store in this country than in an exclusive shop in London. For our purposes, a DDT is restricted to variations in people types (at least the philosophical discussion has not yet gone beyond this) and will include variations among races, gender, learning style, age, physical and mental abilities, sexual persuasion, and other features that we currently consider to be significant means of distinguishing people socially.[6] We might specialize the name to socially desirable diversity type (SDDT.)

Any type of thing can have a DDT—a forest, for example. But only socially significant institutions can have an SDDT, which would codify the pattern of variation desired in people composing it. A broader DDT or SDDT is one that contains more variation in more spectra than another, narrower DDT or SDDT. For example, if we are looking at automobiles, the DDT of today is broader than that of 1930 in virtue of containing a greater variation in the spectrum size. To *positively (or nega-*

tively) target a spectrum in an SDDT is to question raising (or lowering) the variation in that particular spectrum.

In our affirmative action debate we are positively targeting race, color, and gender variation. Even in my simplified way of speaking it does not seem correct to say that we are positively targeting ethnic variation. I suspect that every white male in my department belongs to a different ethnic group from every other. The cry for diversity, therefore, does not express the goal of affirmative action with complete accuracy. If we were to push the metaphor on which my definitions are based, a morally targeted group would be a hue in a spectrum of ethnicity. A unit might have enough variation in a given spectrum but have the wrong hues. By our actions we attempt to have the spectrum more closely replicate in hues the spectrum in the general population.[7]

To advocate higher SDDT (HSDDT) for academia is to advocate a certain type of affirmative action: that of attempting to increase the representation of targeted groups in parts of academia in which they are underrepresented.

I believe that a very important source of the current use of "diversity" in academia is nonacademic and issues from the business world. In turn, a source of the business usage comes from biology, more specifically, in theories of evolution. In both business and biology, "Diversify for survival!" is an appropriate slogan. Within my lifetime, many large corporations in this country have entered entirely new areas of production, in addition to their original areas. Lawn seed companies began to produce candy; cereal companies began to manufacture airline machine tools, and so forth. Significantly, many Universities also diversified in exactly this way. In addition to standard M.A. and M.S. degrees, they began to offer professional degrees below the doctoral level in fields such as business and pharmacy. Institutions that were almost entirely liberal arts institutions, with perhaps a medical or law school added, became liberal arts and trade schools.[8] Both of these HDDTs were designed (certainly deliberately in the case of the businesses) to ensure survival in a changing market. Both Kellogg's and the University of Louisville wanted to ensure that they were the ones to provide goods or services to at least the same people to whom they had supplied these goods or services before.

In behaving this way, businesses (and Universities) mimic biological species: The broader the DDT of the gene pool—the more alternatives for a specific trait that are found among the reproducing members of the species—the greater the likelihood the species will survive in the long run. As the ecosystem changes, a means of coping with the change is required for survival. Only a species that incorporates among a significant number of its members some ability to cope with change will survive environmental upheavals.

A business that has a broader product DDT might survive better in a market that is changing than would a business that manufactures a small number of types of products. Today, Kellogg's might survive even if all of us stopped eating breakfast. That would have been less likely when the company produced only breakfast cereal.

The call for racial, ethnic, and sexual diversity in a University population can be seen as, in part, functioning in the same way that diversification within a species or within a business company functions. Only by depending fully on all available varieties of human intellectual ability is the University likely to survive in a changing environment. Changes the University is either already experiencing or looks forward to in the future include a reduction of funding for education for the sake of education, an even greater emphasis on the quality of the *product* the University is producing, where this quality is measured in some quantitative, socially insensitive way such as standardized testing, and an even greater need for technical, rather than artistic, rhetorical, scholarly, or scientific skills among individuals exiting the Universities.

An important, likely change for our purposes is demographic: In particular, there will be, through the next generation, a steadily increasing proportion of people of color in the college-age population. Perhaps we need to educate more than 50 percent of the college-age population to technical literacy by the year 2010. Universities that expect to survive well into the twenty-first century had better produce a technically literate majority. And this majority is likely to be largely or entirely nonwhite.

Today, a reasonable percentage of white males achieve technical literacy. It may even be argued that we have nearly reached saturation on this count with white males: There is little in the way of paralyzing negative group stereotyping internalized by a white male that must be corrected before he is encouraged to achieve a B.S. in computer science. If we can't expect much more from white males, the burden must be taken on by white women and by people of color of both sexes.

This is my first point then; although my path was roundabout, the conclusion is familiar: Currently, Universities are not doing as well, proportionately, at educating nonwhite, non-Asian peoples in technical skills as they are in educating the white majority in these skills. The difference is even more marked when standardized test scores are compared.[9]

Hence, Universities must admit and train well a much larger proportion of people of color and, in the relevant technical areas, of women, if this country is to maintain even its current secondary place as a technological power. This reason for significantly broadening the SDDT in academic units through the next generation is entirely "economic" in the broad sense—it is ecological in that it appeals only to our desire to make the most efficient use of scarce or dwindling resources or to replace lost resources.

This argument, which just covers technology, is easy to give, since good technology has been and probably will continue to be for some time a source of power for this country. For the humanities and the arts we have a parallel, but weaker, argument—weaker for two reasons: (1) "newtraditional" people are already much better represented in the arts and somewhat better represented in the humanities than in the basic sciences or in technology; (2) whatever my strong personal preferences, I do not have much of an *argument* that the arts and humanities ought to survive into the next generation. Still, since I suspect that most people would agree that they ought to survive, and since they will not survive unless proportionately more newtraditional people are educated in them, we need to broaden the finding that mandates the better education of newtraditional people to include basic sciences, humanities, and the arts.

If this is accepted, what I have said gives strong reasons for our earlier premiss that for an academic unit to survive into the next thirty years it must educate and educate well increasing proportions of new-traditional people.

However, we are not yet done. We have been considering academic units as ecological units. They might survive without "passing on the genes" we have come to know and love. Does increasing the proportions of newtraditional people help the survival of the academic unit as an *intellectual* unit? I think the answer is yes! If HSDDT is necessary for the survival of the ecological unit, it is trivial that it is also necessary for preserving the intellectual life of that unit; the unit will have *no* life without HSDDT. However, to show that HSDDT positively facilitates intellectual growth in the unit, we will borrow from and modify the "educational defense" of preferential treatment considered and deflated by Simon.

4. For all practical purposes, a HSDDT educational community is necessary for sharp intellectual debate.
5. Sharp intellectual debate is necessary for a community
to provide a good quality of education for anyone who
is a member of it.
6. Good quality of education for everyone in an educational community is a primary goal of such a community.
7. Therefore, educational communities must ensure diversity among their members.

The only weak point of this argument is its first premise. Simon has not attempted to show that diversity is *necessary* for sharpening intellectual dialogue. Rather, he gives considerations that show that diversity "helps" sharpen debate—and, hence, reaches only the weak conclusion that diversity arguments provide some but insufficient support for the need for affirmative action. For my stronger conclusion I will give reasons for accepting the first premiss given above.

Simon considers methodological and genetic and cultural ("g-c")[10] diversity. The former is clearly important for sharpening intellectual debate, but does the latter sort of diversity among faculty members contribute to intellectual debate? He points out that g-c diversity is more likely to lead to intellectual diversity than g-c homogeneity and cites the "special studies" areas, such as women's studies, as evidence.

Although this connection undoubtedly holds and supports the point I wish to make, it does so quite indirectly. If the special studies are what are sought in a department it will advertise for them and can appoint the best person they find in that field whether or not he or she belongs to the appropriate targeted group or even to any targeted group at all. There are two responses that must be made to this.

First, even if, as Simon indicates later, the recommended strategy would be the direct one of hiring those persons who are working in those fields, I would accept this provided that the oldtraditional search committee, as mandated by the oldtraditional unit, sees the need for these fields. If they are as narrow visioned as the bias in the hiring practices that is being corrected would indicate, it is not likely they see this need. A similar point might be made about the new perspective brought to an old field by a newtraditional person. If the people already in the unit appreciate the new perspective prior to the search for someone who can provide it, there is, indeed, no need for a search for a newtraditional person to provide the perspective. It is the narrowness and blindness of the oldtraditional people that force what I grant is a somewhat skewed search for a person likely to provide a new perspective; they don't know of the perspective's existence in a full enough sense to enable them to search for it directly.

Second, the scenario of a unit's introducing newtraditional studies into its scholarship and curriculum is just a special case of any important new areas of study arising in a discipline. Somewhere in the country there are a few academic units already in the forefront. They are likely to have appointed someone competent in such a new area already. Why are they innovators? Partly because they *are* the best, and part of what this means is having among their members those who make the changes in their discipline or who are likely to be aware of changes early enough to be leaders in facilitating them.

Perspectival diversity—that is, having high variation in the spectrum of intellectual points of view within a field—is necessary for sharp intellectual debate. Genetic and cultural diversity implies perspectival diversity. It is not necessary for it, but only among a very few highly gifted individuals—those usually found in "the best" departments—do we find persons who although they have but a single (their own) perspective, readily bring up, or carry as potential, alternative perspectives and are able to see the need to incorporate them into a departmental viewpoint. So, for practical purposes, in departments where there are no geniuses, g-c diversity is required to have a multiplicity of perspectives in readiness to be applied as a field shifts.

However, g-c diversity does not imply methodological diversity. As Simon argues, the expectation that it does is likely to promote conformity within a targeted group and, I would say, is, in itself, a racist or sexist expectation. A member of another race should be valued in a unit because he or she is a unique individual having special talents, not because he or she is a representative of that race.

Much of the discussion of what sort of diversity will promote intellectual and educational excellence has been skewed by our focus on immediate outcomes. However, our strongest suit is the ecological one of the potential that diversity engenders. Let us imagine a dilemma that might be faced by a unit committed to HSDDT for the sake of its healthy survival.

We consider a unit made up of (say) ten individuals. We ask, how we are to diversify this unit? We could choose an individual H from an important, but somewhat new subfield of the field for which the position has been advertised and who is excellent in her field. Or we could choose an individual J from a different (targeted) race, who is also excellent in her field. What should the department aim to do? There, is, of course, no presupposition that H ≠ J; nor is there the opposite presupposition. Is the need in the unit for immediately cashable methodological diversity or for g-c diversity? Clearly opting for the first, if the search is successful and H is appointed, will yield immediate intellectual diversity and will create, immediately, an improved climate for graduate students. If the unit opts for the second and J is hired, the immediate results are not at all predictable, even if J = H. The department might go into a mild state of shock, undermine J's efforts, and eventually, directly or indirectly, cause her to leave.

This is similar to what happens if a new sort of individual enters an ecosystem where there are distantly related individuals of its own species. The new individual may be thrown out. But, if the individual stays, not only does this mean that the community has changed in its actual features but, as well, in its ability to accommodate further changes. This potential is merely a result of its varied genotype, much of which initially may not be expressed phenotypically.

To take the analogy as far as it will go:[11] Individual J, assuming she remains in our previously homogenous unit, internalizes a different social history and, as a result, increases the unit's potential for constructive change as the field changes, the student body changes, and the power sources for the department change.

In sum, the considerations above strongly support (4) by supporting:

4A. Perspectival diversity is necessary for a good response to changes in the field, changes in the student body, and changes in the wielders of economic power.

4B. Genetic and cultural diversity is, for most practical purposes, necessary for perspectival diversity.

The less abstract the field, the better this argument. But even in mathematics it holds—witness the differences between French (emphasis on analysis and continuous structures) and British (more interest in algebra and other discrete systems) mathematics. In a field more closely tied to actual cultural patterns, such as history or sociology, the dependence is clear. Any discipline comes within a culture and is influenced by a culture. Even with two cultures that have evolved in such close proximity as the English and U.S. cultures, we find they are "quirky" at different points. And often one is unable to trace causal chains to determine the evolution of these features.

II

This completes the discussion of my initial argument that being a newtraditional person should be seen as a positive qualification for an academic position. It grows out of considering diversity ecologically and seeing a department as having requirements for survival as an ecological as well as an intellectual unit.

A footnote to the ecological account of diversity: One reason that has been given as a reason to add color or gender to the qualifications of some applicants for academic jobs is that a woman or person of color provides a "role model" for aspiring young women or people of color. Although I imply a limited version of this in my own argument for premiss (3), I think role models have been both under- and overplayed in the discussion. They are overplayed because in my experience (and the experience of others with whom I have spoken) knowing that there were people of my race [12] or gender in mathematics did not contribute at all to my decision to major in mathematics, nor to my decision, later on, to get a Ph.D. in philosophy. The first decision and my confidence in it were in place without any consideration of the small number of women mathematicians I had heard of. In the case of philosophy, if I had known, when I was deciding to study philosophy, some of the woman philosophers I later met and I had believed the traits in them I disliked were there *because* they were women, I might have been discouraged from my decision.

It is only in extraordinary cases that a "role model" *causes* a student to enter a course of study confidently and only in some cases when what we might call a "role countermodel" dissuades one from entering a course of study. In the first case, the model is likely to have many more important traits in common with the student than color or sex. And the countermodel is likely to be much more disparate in personality compared to the student than the similarity in race or gender might lead highly political individuals to believe. Given these considerations, the presence of individuals of similar color and sex in a field to which we aspire is not likely to help us make the decision to enter the field.

That is the sense in which role modeling has been much overplayed. It has been underplayed in the sense that when there are absolutely no people of one's color or sex in visible positions in a field, it may never occur to a student to enter the field. A young person may not realize the extent to which her kind of difference is politicized and may, without thinking, believe that the absence of women in the physics department just means that women are constitutionally less able to do physics.

Ecologically, there is a parallel. A mutation occurs and the first individual in the community to be able to hear differences in pitch is born. There is nothing to nurture this gift into something that can be perpetuated, for future generations. This is all-important—the negative influence of the vacuum. On the other side, once this trait is in a visible minority, new individuals are neither encouraged nor discouraged from developing their own gift by this instantiation.

CONCLUSION

My considerations have been, I believe, entirely amoral. Is there a moral argument for HSDDT? I think there is not. There are moral arguments for procedural and regulatory forms of affirmative action, since these are directed at ending discrimination. But I know of no sound moral arguments for considering membership in a morally targeted group as qualification for an academic position. Moral arguments may be required when deciding which, among various groups underrepresented in a spectrum of variation, to target for HSDDT. For example, is it appropriate to target Vietnamese Americans and not target white males who are veterans? These are by no means simple issues, for they involve a careful specification of the ways in which it is morally wrong for these people to be discriminated against (e.g., not being hired for certain kinds of positions) mainly, perhaps even just partly, by virtue of belonging to a particular social group. What we have been speaking of here is the following. Given that there is some morally targeted kind, there are sound reasons for increasing the representation of that kind in an academic unit by making membership in that kind one of the qualifications (or, even a necessary qualification) considered when seeking individuals to be part of an academic unit.

My discussion of the greater qualifications of the newtraditional for academic positions rests on the morally centered demonstration that they should be morally targeted and expresses the urgency of making our plans for affirmative action workable.

NOTES

1. Probably any expression referring to the multifarious class in academia consisting of most women, African-Americans, Latinos, Native Americans, Southeast Asians, and others, who are united only by their history of oppression in this country, becomes itself stigmatized. This is no less true of "women and minorities"—perhaps such expressions were stigmatized from the beginning, since minorities are not people but groups. Perhaps the expression "nontraditional" did not stay around long enough to become stigmatized; in any case, it wasn't quite correct. I choose the oxymoronic "newtraditional," which seems to me, at the moment, both correct and inoffensive.

2. The compromise offered by Becker in this volume would be an exception to this if understood in the following way. The extraordinary positions he envisions I would see as analogous to, although clearly not the same as, fostering areas of competence desired for particular positions. Newtraditional graduate students and faculty fill an academic need in their departments. It is secondary to their area of specialization, as my competence in teaching logic is secondary to my scholarly specialization in the philosophy of mathematics and philosophy of mind.

3. For another example, there is roughly a 30-percent correlation between GRE scores and achievement in the first year of graduate study. Yet GRE scores are typically a very important part of the qualifications for graduate school admissions.

4. *Nominalist . . . realist* might be such a spectrum. I occasionally deplore the fact that there are not more nominalists in this department of philosophy. But I do not want us to hire more of them (much less preferentially to hire more).

5. I use the word "University" (with upper-case U) to denote any institution of higher learning: colleges, junior colleges, business schools, professional schools, and universities in the usual sense ("university" with lower-case u will continue to denote only the last).

6. It follows that the various DDTs are time indexed. There may have been a time, for example, when those who were unable to walk could not go to an ordinary school. Today this is not the case, so our profile of physical ableness for students would now include the representation of such physical disabilities. Now our profile of mental ability for people attending University would not include people with certain mental disabilities. This would change if treatments enabled people with these disabilities to benefit from a University and to have the University benefit from their presence.

7. On some other appropriate standard. Obviously we would not wish the spectrum of I.Q. in the SDDT of Nobel Prize winners to even replicate that among physicists in general. For academic units, Becker takes the standard for each group to be that in the immediately preceding group: B.A.s for graduate

admissions and so on. It is partly a moral, not a purely ecological issue as to what the appropriate standard of comparison is.

8. This story for Universities is much more complex; and, to some degree, my simplification is a falsification. Part of what has happened, of course, is that the University has become a business. Much of the turmoil over undergraduate requirements (Why should students seeking a computer science degree learn to write papers in English?) results from this vision of the University as a business.

9. Of course, the problem is most severe when seen internationally. The U.S. white majority is currently lagging behind other industrialized nations as measured by test results. The University would like to correct this.

10. In most of the literature, "ethnic or religious" is used. The word "cultural" enables us to make finer distinctions—for example, between a Hispanic from Central America and one who was brought up in New Jersey by her Puerto Rican grandmother. No more and no less than in the case of ethnic groups do we need to distinguish politically relevant cultural differences.

11. Consider, also, the analogy that the author of this essay makes possible. As a philosopher, she is asked to make a contribution to a book on affirmative action in academe. Her specialty is not social philosophy or philosophy of law, or any one of a cluster of philosophical disciplines in which individuals might study the issue. Rather, her specialty is cognitive philosophy and the philosophy of mathematics. Her contribution may be irrelevant (the new individual is removed from the community), it may be an amateurish expression of what are already old ideas in the subfield, it may be bizarre and interesting. But the initial impact is much less important than the potential for stirring further debate. By her different perspective alone, the author increases the possibilities for discussion.

12. In fact, there were none of these that I knew of then.

19 Careers Open to Talent

Ellen Frankel Paul

Lawrence Becker is right about at least one thing when he expresses exasperation about the "normative literature" on affirmative action being stuck in a rut with the familiar arguments "repeated nearly verbatim year by year." The debate raged in the philosophical literature in the mid- to late 1970s, then exhausted itself for a decade, only to reemerge in the last few years. The old arguments have been resuscitated by a new generation of philosophers with a few new wrinkles added, such as the "diversity" rationale and the "counterfactual justice" criterion of selection. These second-wave justifications of affirmative action have involved ever more esoteric and strained theories, as Robert Simon demonstrates so delicately yet devastatingly in his dissections of "diversity" and "counterfactual justice" as an alternative theory of meritocratic selection.

To Simon's, and also Stephen Carter's,[1] critique of the "diversity" argument for affirmative action, I have little to add, except to emphasize that the assumption that all blacks, all women, all Hispanics, and all members of other "protected groups" share the same social philosophy is patronizing in the extreme and should be offensive to precisely those individuals it seeks to accommodate. No white male would tolerate such an ascription, and I fail to see why members of other groups ought to, either.

On the "counterfactual justice" criterion, however, I would like to suggest an example as an addendum to Simon's argument. The "counterfactual justice" argument is an attempt to surmount the strong pull of the "desert" critique of affirmative action (the argument that candidates for appointments or employment ought to be selected on the basis of merit). A "counterfactual justice" claim for advancement would contain a "but for" element: but for this candidate's disadvantages, he or she would have been the best. The conclusion, then, is that this candidate ought to be the one selected. Let us suppose that a position is advertised by the Boston Symphony for a violinist. Imagine what counterfactual vitae might look like. In drafting one's resume, instead of inventorying accomplishments, one would imagine what one might have been had not various misfortunes struck or had one been blessed with talents of various sorts. Candidate X might document his childhood in Watts, his unknown father, and his crack habit, and claim that but for these misfortunes, his indolence, and lack of musical talent, he would today have received an advanced degree from Juilliard and be a world-class violinist and, therefore, a prime candidate for the Boston Symphony. His competitor, Candidate Y, would reprise her disadvantages, including an incapacitating automobile accident that left her limbs paralyzed, and go on to list her counterfactual accomplishments, including her mastery of the violin, her successful solo tour of Europe, and, thus, her fitness for the position. How would the selection committee proceed when confronted with two such "counterfactually meritorious" applicants? How would they weigh the competing claims of disadvantage? How would they compare their competing "counterfactual accomplishments"?

This example, one might counter, is a bit far-fetched,[2] but what about a more realistic one. An opening for an associate professor of classics is advertised by an elite university. Candidate A holds a doctorate from a lowly ranked department, knows Latin but not Greek, and argues that but for her disadvantaged background as the daughter of impoverished sharecroppers she would have mastered Greek and produced a ream of first-class scholarship. Candidate B received her doctorate from an elite university, knows Greek and Latin, but has published little and even less of distinction, and has unenthusiastic letters of recommendation. Her counterfactual credentials, however, are impressive: but for being orphaned at a young age and subsequently bouncing between foster homes in which learning was not encouraged nor study habits instilled, she would now be much more industrious, and her publishing record stellar. How is a search committee to evaluate these two candidates, let alone another 150 with disparate claims of disadvantage and counterfactual accomplishments? Even leaving questions of race, gender, and ethnicity aside, and supposing that all candidates belong to the same group, I would suggest that these sorts of claims are impossible to mediate. Adding the complexities of race, gender, and ethnic differences back into the equation makes arriving at a metric even more inconceivable. Once we abandon standards of accomplishment and ask candidates to rehearse their disadvantages, we end up in an alternative universe of "but for's" and "might have been's." Even if we could come up with a lexical ordering of disadvantages, would this be desirable? Isn't it more salutary to encourage candidates to focus on their accomplishments rather than on their status as "victims of society"?

THE ORDINARY PERSON'S PERSPECTIVE ON PREFERENCES

My principal concern in this commentary, however, is not to augment Simon's finely wrought critique of the various arguments in support of affirmative action, but rather to contemplate why affirmative action, after nearly a quarter-century of application, still triggers such vehement and widespread opposition. I am not referring, here, primarily to opposition among philosophers but to opposition within the populace generally. While this opposition is often difficult to measure,[3] it is nonetheless real and seemingly growing not flagging in its vehemence. The recent proliferation on American campuses of ugly racist incidents and sophomoric lampoons of gender and racial preferences are harbingers of a much more widely felt but submerged discontent. My hunch is that the case for affirmative action made by philosophers and reflected by politicians and advocates in the public arena has failed to surmount the instincts about justice held by the average person, the man (or woman) in the street, the proverbial reasonable man (now person). I shall address two questions: What might this person in the street be thinking about affirmative action? Does his viewpoint have any merit?

The average man (or woman) holds no refined theory of justice, but an intuitive sense of what, for lack of a better term, I will call simply "fairness" or a "sense of fair play." There is nothing Rawlsian about this "sense," nothing that dictates egalitarianism unless departures benefit the least well-off. Rather, this "fairness" is what allows the average young man to accept the fact that he did not make the high school football team because Joe or Frank was more skillful than he; "fairness" is what convinces a young woman to acknowledge that she did not make the honor society because Sally and Tim had better grades and more distinguished records of extracurricular accomplishments.

It is this "sense of fair play" that is offended when our young man and woman see minority group members (or women) of less accomplishment than themselves win admission to prestigious universities, appointments to scarce faculty positions, or acceptance to highly competitive medical and law schools. Jane (ranked 30th in her high school class) can accept her rejection by an Ivy League university when she loses out to the class valedictorian. She can even come to realize that there may be reasons why that elite university selected the not terribly distinguished "legacy," or even the star quarterback rather than her. (Her acceptance of the legacy and the jock would, concededly, be more grudging than her acceptance of the valedictorian. She could be persuaded that a university depends on its alumni for considerable financial support, for tuition pays only a part of the costs of an elite college education, and that two ways of keeping alumni's pocketbooks open is by holding out the promise that scions will be favored for admission and competitive football and basketball teams fielded. While her meritocratic instinct might still be offended, she would see that there are pretty strong institutional reasons for preferring legacies and star athletes: they both bring the prospect of pecuniary benefits to the university.) However, her sense of fair play is violated when the university accepts an African American woman who is ranked 150th in her class.[4] Like herself, this black woman has no special connection to the university and can bring to it no special athletic skill. If this young black woman is, like her, a child of the middle class (as many beneficiaries of preferences are), the "diversity" argument, even if it holds some modicum of appeal, will seem inapplicable to a black woman who shared Jane's upbringing in nearly every way save the color of her skin and her ethnic identification.

In order to see why the ordinary person's sense of fairness is offended by preference on the basis of race or gender, let us ponder a hypothetical appointment to a prestigious law school faculty. The two finalists for a position teaching tax law are Candidate A, a white male, and Candidate B, a female or a minority-group member. Candidate A graduated at the top of his law school class from a law school ranked in the top five, served as the editor of the law review, and published three student notes in other law reviews. After graduation he spent a year clerking for a judge of the D.C. Circuit Court of Appeals. During that year, he published two articles in prestigious law reviews in his field of tax law. Candidate B graduated in the lower third of his (or her) class from a top-five ranked law school.[5] The faculty selection committee recommends to the faculty that Candidate B should be appointed because the law school suffers from a paucity of women and minority faculty, and an offer is made and accepted. When Faculty Member B comes up for tenure consideration six years later, his record of publications is meager, consisting of one short comment in a third-rate law review, his teaching receives mixed reviews in student and faculty evaluations, and the dean has often listened to complaints from disgruntled students about B's lack of organization and poor preparation for classes. Nevertheless, a majority of the tenured faculty argues that B ought to receive tenure because the law school has a distressing record of not tenuring women and minority faculty. A handful of faculty members grumble about the dilution of standards, the precedent such a decision would set for future tenure cases, and the likely effect of such a decision on the professional standing of the law school. Only two faculty members, however, speak out openly and forcefully against tenuring such a weak candidate: one, a black man, argues that by jettisoning the school's traditional tenure standards for the benefit of a minority (or woman) candidate, the effect will be to create in people's minds a presumption that all minorities (or women) need special dispensations to qualify for tenure; the other, a woman, speaks in defense of the preservation of the school's high standards of only tenuring faculty of the first rank, for doing anything less would deprive students of a legal education by the very best minds. The faculty votes, and B is granted tenure.

Most faculty members who have served on university hiring, promotion, and tenure committees over the last fifteen years will recognize some, if not all, parts of this "hypothetical" from their own experience. Decisions of this kind breach the ethical intuitions of the person in the street in several obvious ways. First, our person thinks that professional positions that require special expertise and training ought to go to the applicant who is the best. This may seem utterly uncomplicated to the average person but not all that simple to faculty who have served on selection committees. "The best" to teach philosophy of science at a college with about average students (mean SAT verbal score of 450) will not be "the best" to teach that subject at a highly selective university (mean score of 675). A high-powered philosopher of science with recondite research interests intelligible to only a half-dozen other philosophers and a convoluted lecture style may be judged "best" for the latter position but disastrous for the former. Yet a selection committee that engages in a discussion of this character—on which candidate is "the best for the position we have to fill" rather than the best in some abstract or absolute sense—is engaging in a debate over the merits of the candidates. In contrast, the faculty that hired Candidate B over A engaged in an entirely different enterprise, one that flouted considerations of "the best to teach tax law at our law school," and employed, instead, what the person in the street in his plain-spoken way would call a racist criterion: we don't have enough women, blacks, or Hispanics, so we will hire one, even if there are others more qualified for the job.

Second, our person in the street may be offended by racial origin or gender defining one's destiny, rather than factors that are within an individual's control. He recalls that back in the 1950s and 1960s the aspiration of those who fought for civil rights was the attainment of a color-blind society in which positions in universities, jobs in industry, and other opportunities would be open to anyone with ability, energy, and accomplishment—that, in short, gender and racial origin would not count. Our person scratches his head in bewilderment. How, he wonders, has the color-blind ideal resulted in a social policy in which each individual is labeled by sex and ethnic origin, universities send postcards to all applicants for faculty positions requesting this information, and appointment decisions are made on such immutable characteristics as skin color and gender.[6] Rather than becoming irrelevant, immutable factors have become the most relevant.

Do the Ordinary Person's Instincts Have Merit?

What can we make of the ordinary person's instincts about affirmative action? To some, the question might seem premature, because they might argue that I have misrepresented what the ordinary person's views are. Many people support affirmative action, for some of the same reasons that philosophers have articulated and Leslie Francis's article ably reprises, and their views are not represented in the picture that I painted above. Yet, even those who support affirmative action, both philosophers and others, sense the pull of the meritocratic argument, and that is why affirmative action has been accepted by our courts, and more generally, only as a temporary corrective, only if narrowly tailored, and only if its victims are widely diffused.[7] Even if one thinks that I have misrepresented the average person's sensibilities on this issue, the viewpoint needs to be taken seriously, for if such views are driven beyond respectable discourse they are likely to reemerge in very unpleasant forms: as racial incidents and as support for such figures as David Duke, the former Klan wizard who ran second in the 1991 Louisiana gubernatorial race.

Several points merit further scrutiny: (1) What effect does affirmative action have on the losers and those who exercise racial preferences? (2) Why are preferences carried out in the shadows, and what effects does this have in a democratic society? (3) Are there any good reasons for affirmative action that might surmount the ordinary person's instincts about the connection between merit and fairness?

(1) Black dissenters have spoken eloquently about the psychological effects of affirmative action, particularly the self-doubt that preferences trigger.[8] But what of others affected by affirmative action? How does Candidate A take his disappointment? At first, he faults himself, wondering whether an insufficiently polished answer to an interviewer's question ruined his chances of appointment, or thinking that perhaps he had lost out to someone even more accomplished than himself. When he later hears through the grapevine, maybe from a disgruntled faculty member at the law school who had supported him over Candidate B, that Candidate B was much less accomplished than he and was only hired because of his racial origin (or her gender), Candidate A is, at first, outraged, and then just cynical. Despite his best efforts over many years, his goal of teaching at a top-ranked law school will go unfulfilled simply because of his race and gender, factors that will forever remain beyond his control.

From the perspective of the victim of "reverse discrimination," the likely result is cynicism, but what of the mental state of those on the faculty who supported Candidate B over A? They tell themselves that on some better theory of justice or merit ("diversity" perhaps, or "counterfactual justice") than that held by the person in the street, they have done the right thing, they have chosen fairly, they have selected "the best for this position," they have not wronged Candidate A, or wronged him only slightly, inconsequentially, and inadvertently. Lurking beneath the surface, I suspect, is a nagging sense that Candidate A (and perhaps twenty-five other applicants who fell between the two) has been wronged, that professional standards have been eviscerated, and that they have participated in a selection process that they would loathe to see publicized.

(2) This last point deserves our consideration: Why is it that decisions to appoint faculty or select students on the basis of affirmative action criteria are kept from public scrutiny? Why is Candidate A not

told that he had no real chance to be appointed, that the successful candidate would be a minority group member or a woman? Why
is he left to question his own record and performance? Why aren't
candidates leveled with? A recent incident sheds some light on these
queries. When a Georgetown Law School student who worked in the
admissions office took it upon himself to publish a summary of the
grades and LSAT scores of accepted minority students compared to
nonminority students, the wrath of the administration fell upon him.
Their outrage was genuine, but their reasons for it are suspect. I doubt
that their rage resulted exclusively from this student's violation of the
confidentiality of admissions records. More likely, their outrage resulted from fear that their policies could not withstand public scrutiny,
that the gross disparities in the records of the two groups could not be
satisfactorily explained to alumni, financial supporters, disappointed
applicants, and the public.

If a social policy has to be conducted with a certain measure of
secretiveness, then that says something awfully damning about it,
especially in a democratic society. The confrontation over undergraduate admissions to the University of California at Berkeley suggests that
selection by race, when coupled with wide disparities in achievement
among various groups, results in just the kind of publicity that universities abhor.[9] Especially in public universities, supported substantially
by (involuntary) taxes, a policy of favoritism for some and barriers for
others is inevitably contentious. A democratic society should encourage in its tax-supported institutions a sense of fairness, and if it does
not, justified grievances will be created and social harmony thereby
diminished. The example of Malaysia is a telling one. For twenty years,
rigid preferences for Malays over Chinese, Indians, and other minorities have been enforced by the government in university admissions,
business activities, and government employment. Chinese and Indians, both economically more successful than the Malays, have been
systematically discriminated against in favor of the more socially and
economically backward Malays. The policies may differ in spirit (some
might call them "benign preferences") from the apartheid practiced
for over four decades in South Africa, but if you are a Chinese busi-
nessman in Malaysia who must employ 30 percent Malays, ensure
that 30 percent of your business is divested to Malays, and you are
unable to send your children to university because 55 percent of those
selected must be Malays, the difference may be indiscernible. This
does not seem to be a prescription for social harmony in a multiethnic

society, and it would be tragic if our society increasingly emulates the Malaysian example.

At least, Lawrence Becker's proposal has the advantage of explicitness over current practice. In a spirit of compromise between those who oppose and those who endorse affirmative action, Becker proposes to place a governmentally enforced standard of proportional representation by race and gender upon every department in every institution of higher education in the country. Becker aims at an Aristotelian mean, but his aim has badly misfired, for what he proposes seems more extreme, more rigid, indeed, more race and gender conscious than present affirmative action plans. Instead of careers open to talent, we would have careers open to one black, 3 women, 2.9 white men, .25 of an Hispanic, .02 of an Asian. This has been tried at the University of California at Berkeley for undergraduate admissions, and despite the administration's best efforts at keeping the admission criteria and results secret, they have become public with predictably controversial results. Asians discovered that they were denied admission not because there were better applicants but because there were too many talented, accomplished Asians. Whites discovered that standards were precipitously lowered for blacks and Hispanics. A firestorm of public criticism resulted, and the university was forced to back down somewhat, yet 50 percent (up from 40 percent formerly) of each freshman class will still be selected by nonmeritocratic standards, that is, by racial standards.[10] Becker's proposal for proportional representation, even though born of good intentions and frustration over the stalled affirmative action debate, would likewise ignite public indignation. It embraces rigid quotas based on immutable characteristics; it bases appointments on racial and gender qualities irrelevant to successful teaching and research; and it by implication labels its ostensible beneficiaries as incapable of competing in a fair game, as in effect charity cases. The last, as several successful black academics have recently lamented, is a stigma they neither deserve nor appreciate. Becker's proposal suffers from other conspicuous defects: it ignores costs, as though university budgets were inexhaustible or government largess limitless; and public choice theory aside, its claim that a large government bureaucracy would not develop to enforce the scheme lacks credibility. Likewise, his claim that if minority candidates of sufficient merit were not available the designated slots for them would go unfilled seems fine in theory, but unlikely to withstand the pressure of measuring success by actual hires rather than mere good intentions. Pressure from government overseers and activist groups would surely push universities to fill their minority slots, at some diminution of standards.

(3) Are there arguments that might surmount the intuitions of the person in the street? Most persuasive of all the arguments in support of affirmative action to the average person would likely be an argument based on compensatory justice, that is, an argument that affirmative action is in some sense a reparation owed to blacks for their ancestors' enslavement (and for whom, in consequence, the argument is much stronger than it is for other groups). If the argument for affirmative action hinges only on present discrimination or on the lingering effects of past discrimination, it is much weaker for three reasons: (1) discrimination has diminished appreciably since the passage of the Civil Rights Act of 1964, certainly in its outward displays and, most commentators agree, in its inward dimensions; (2) if present discrimination is the problem, then a solution that does not create a fresh set of victims (namely, young white males) seems preferable—one that insists on fair selection procedures, a candidate pool open to all, and the encouragement of applications by members of groups formerly discriminated against; and (3) overcoming lingering effects need not entail preferences, but exerting extra effort and availing oneself of the numerous opportunities provided by universities to disadvantaged students of all racial backgrounds, as the success of recent Asian immigrants attests. Thus, Leslie Francis, by jettisoning the compensatory argument leaves affirmative action, I think, without its moorings. But, as I have argued extensively elsewhere,[11] the compensatory argument is problematical, for unlike reparations designed to compensate actual victims or their immediate heirs (e.g., the belated and nugatory U.S. plan to compensate the Japanese internees from World War II or the German reparations to surviving Jews, the children of victims, and Jewish social agencies helping them), compensation of the descendants of black slaves would go to great- or great-great grandchildren, and those preferences would come at the expense of the descendants of those who came to America to flee oppression elsewhere, most of whom are the progeny of immigrants who came after emancipation. History is ugly; its wrongs cannot be redressed by "reverse discrimination" without committing fresh wrongs, especially when over a century has passed since the wrong ended. Even more recent wrongs are

difficult to address, as the Baltic governments are discovering as they try to return property to those plundered by the Bolsheviks a mere fifty years ago.

Perhaps what is most discouraging about affirmative action is the message that it sends to young blacks, women, Hispanics, and other "beneficiaries." That message tells these young people to see themselves as victims: victims of a racist society, victims of patriarchal capitalism, but above all, victims. A far more constructive message, and one that might be more appealing to youthful energies, is the one that Stephen Carter has so eloquently articulated: You can do it if you try; you can beat the system by working hard; strive to be so good that no one can ignore you or disparge your accomplishments. This message gives hope, and it is realizable, especially when we recognize that our society since the 1950s has manifested good will, has tried to encourage those formerly excluded by law or custom. If affirmative action ended tomorrow, I doubt that this good will would evaporate with it, as it did not during the Reagan administration's hostility to affirmative action; quite the opposite: the good will intensified when government pressure lapsed. While I would argue that some of this good will was misdirected into racial and gender preferences, as a society we have a genuine belief in equality of opportunity and careers open to talent that the early civil rights movement reinvigorated. That movement cast aside government-imposed segregation. Affirmative action, imposed by courts and furthered by presidential orders and administrative rule-making, has reimposed government policies on the basis of race, policies that are difficult to reconcile with the civil rights movement's original quest for equality of opportunity. It is this difficulty in reconciling preferences by race with the original goal of a color-blind society that is at the heart of the ordinary person's objection to affirmative action. Intuitively, the ordinary person senses that there are no short-cuts in effecting equality of opportunity and that questionable means may undercut and alter this desirable end.

NOTES

1. See Stephen L. Carter, *Reflections of an Affirmative Action Baby* (New York: Basic Books, 1991), especially chap. 5.

2. Although this is not as outrageous as it might appear on first impression. Recently, Michigan legislators pressured the Detroit Symphony Orches-

tra into hiring more black musicians, under the twin threats of withholding state funds and a boycott. These legislators wanted the orchestra to reflect the 60 percent black composition of the city and bemoaned the fact that only two members of the ninety-eight-piece orchestra were black. Black symphonic musicians were among the most vociferous critics of this pressure. Michael Morgan, assistant conductor of the Chicago Symphony Orchestra, and himself black, stated, "Now even when a black player is hired on the merits of his playing, he will always have the stigma that it was to appease some state legislator." For over a decade, musicians have been selected by blind auditions, in which the performer plays behind a screen, to prevent favoritism of any sort. Another black conductor, James DePriest of the Oregon Symphony Orchestra, turned down an overture from the Detroit Symphony because "It's impossible for me to go to Detroit because of the atmosphere. People mean well, but you fight for years to make race irrelevant, and now they are making race an issue." Isabel Wilkerson, "Discordant Notes in Detroit: Music and Affirmative Action," *New York Times*, March 5, 1989, pp. 1, 18.

While the extreme of counterfactual justice was not imposed on the Detroit Symphony, the orchestra does hold auditions now only if a black musician is among the candidates.

3. As Carter notes, polls show varying degrees of opposition to affirmative action, with a great deal of the disparity attributable to the way in which the poll questions are couched. Nevertheless, majorities or at least pluralities of both the white and black populations display reservations about racial and gender preferences. Carter, *Reflections*, p. 266 n. 25.

4. This is precisely the point that the "diversity" argument is supposed to surmount, with the claim that blacks or women or other preferred groups bring something unique to the university that just another very bright white student could not. But the persuasiveness of this tack, again, depends on the assumption that all members of preferred groups share the same social, political, and cultural viewpoints, which they manifestly do not. As Carter argues, such an assumption carries the implicit warning that all those blacks, women, and others who do not share the supposed group viewpoint are not authentic representatives of the group and therefore ought to be ostracized. (Carter, *Reflections*, especially chap. 7).

5. The disparities between the two candidates could, concededly, be much smaller but I have modeled this hypothetical scenario on an actual hiring decision at a top-ten law school. Affirmative action in university hiring, I suspect, comes closer to this paradigm than to one where disparities are nearly indiscernible. The following factors lead me to this hypothesis, a hypothesis that is I grant difficult to prove, given the nature of university hiring decisions and their confidentiality, especially when preferences might be involved:

(1) The paucity of the yearly production of black Ph.D.s overall and their

complete absence in many disciplines. This makes the quest for black faculty by elite and less august universities a difficult or impossible one for every institution, or indeed many institutions, to satisfy. If only three or four mathematics Ph.D.s are produced each year, then it is obvious that the "pool problem" renders good intentions unrealizable. (For an interesting discussion of the "pool problem" see Randall Kennedy, "Racial Critiques of Legal Academia," *Harvard Law Review* 102 (1989): 745. On the production of black mathematics Ph.D.s see Carolyn J. Mooney, "Only Four Black Americans Said to Have Earned Math Ph.D.s in 1987–88," *Chronicle of Higher Education*, August 2, 1989, p. A11. On the paucity of black Ph.D.s in other disciplines, see Abigail M. Thernstron, "On the Scarcity of Black Professors," *Commentary* 90 (July 1990): 23.

(2) Black scholars in many fields have experienced bidding wars for their services; they continue to receive many unsolicited overtures, and when offers are made they often involve lucrative salaries and perquisites beyond what an ordinary faculty member commands. This fertile market for black scholars is perceived by many, although not all, of its targets as motivated by their race and little more. See Denise K. Magner, "The Courting of Black and Ethnic Scholars: Bidding War or Just a Few New Entrants in the Academic Star System?" *Chronicle of Higher Education*, October 3, 1990, pp. A19–A21.

6. An excellent history of affirmative action that traces the factors that contributed to this metamorphosis is Herman Belz, *Equality Transformed* (New Brunswick, N.J.: Social Philosophy and Policy Center and Transaction Publishers, 1991).

7. This may explain why the Supreme Court is harsher on layoff plans that upset expectations arising from seniority systems: the victims are readily identifiable.

8. Shelby Steele, *The Content of Our Character* (New York: St. Martin's Press, 1990), especially chap. 8.

9. While white and Asian applicants to University of California at Berkeley are seldom admitted with a GPA below 3.7, minority students are admitted who meet the minimum requirements. On admission policy at Berkeley, see John H. Bunzel, "Choosing Freshmen: Who Deserves an Edge?" *Wall Street Journal*, February 1, 1988, p. 26. (Bunzel notes that graduation disparities between groups are substantial; within five years of entry, 66 percent of white students and 61 percent of Asian students graduate, while only 41 percent of Hispanics and 27 percent of blacks do so.) James S. Gibney, "The Berkeley Squeeze: The Future of Affirmative Action," *New Republic*, April 11, 1988, pp. 15–17. Deidre Carmody, "Berkeley Announces Plan to Overhaul Its Admissions Policy," *New York Times*, May 25, 1989.

10. Support for proportional representation in the California legislature extends even beyond admissions policy. In 1990, the legislature passed, but the governor eventually vetoed, a measure that would have required universities to graduate students in proportion to their racial representation in the state.

See "College in California: The Numbers Game," *Fortune*, February 11, 1991, p. 6.

11. "Set-Asides and Reparations as Compensatory Justice," in John Chapman, ed., *Compensatory Justice, NOMOS*, vol. 33 (New York: New York University Press, 1991).

20 — Some Sceptical Doubts

Alasdair MacIntyre

What is most remarkable about the articles by Leslie Francis and Robert Simon is the uniform level of abstract generality at which their arguments move. Both articles could have been written by people who had heard and read about universities and colleges but had never actually been in one. And both authors share certain large assumptions that need to be put in question. Here I can raise sceptical doubts about only a few of them.

A first assumption seems to be that in academia we already possess an adequate and generally agreed conception of what it is to be either the best qualified candidate for a particular academic appointment or at least a candidate as well qualified as any other. But for prejudice it would always and rightly be such a candidate who would be appointed. So that what we have to secure, without violating norms of justice in so doing, is a state of affairs in which it is always a candidate at least as well qualified as any other who is appointed. But what if it were the case that the concept of such a candidate is itself all too often a mask worn by prejudice? Consider the following three examples of types of appointment or tenure decision.

A and B are candidates for the same position in a history department. Both are women. A is at work on a historical problem that requires skills in Latin, Old Slavonic, and the quantitative analysis of archaeological data. She has an excellent supporting letter from the only scholar competent to evaluate her work. She is aggressive and intolerant of pretentious questions about her work that exhibit the questioner's ignorance of that area. Only such questions are asked at her interview. B has what is called an interesting new feminist approach to the psychohistory of twentieth-century male politicians.

She has enthusiastic supporting letters from several leading figures in her field. She is witty, well-mannered, and a subtle flatterer of aging, narcissistic, academic white males. Who gets the job?

M and N are candidates for a position in a humanities department that has over a long period developed strength in a particular area. M is an excellent scholar in that area whose addition to the department would finally put it in the first rank. M is a man. N is a woman, also an excellent scholar, but in an area that the department had decided some years ago not to develop. An ambitious dean lets the department know that it will retain positions left vacant by approaching retirements only if a woman is appointed. Who gets the job?

V and W are candidates for tenure in the same humanities department. Both are men. W is a mediocre teacher, whose friendly, joking ways with his students secure him excellent teaching evaluations. W has published a dull book with a university press. V is an excellent, devoted, and demanding teacher, who antagonizes many of his students by requiring more of them than they enjoy giving. He therefore receives mixed teaching evaluations, including many negative ones. V has published one brilliant, path-breaking article. When asked how long it will be before he next publishes, he explains that his follow-up of his article involves a long-term project and that no publications can be expected for quite some time. Who gets tenure?

Experience has taught me both that these kinds of cases are not at all untypical and that the answers would almost always have been B, N, and W. Notice that, by the standards by which candidates for appointment and tenure are conventionally evaluated, there are available excellent arguments to show that in each such case it would have been by the received standards a candidate at least as well qualified as any other who got the job or received tenure. Yet it would in each case have been the wrong decision, and an appeal to the best standards that are currently shared in academia would have done nothing to prevent it.

Why do I judge that it would have been the wrong decision? An adequate answer would require appeal to a highly controversial account of the proper ends and functions of universities and colleges. But this is the controversy that we need to have. And on all the issues that concern it both Francis and Simon are silent. They seem to agree in presupposing, like almost all proponents and critics of affirmative action in general and of academic affirmative action in particular, a picture of the American social order and of the place of a college education within it that obstructs discussion of just those issues. It is a picture in which individuals compete for the rewards attached to privileged positions and status, privilege being defined in terms of the conventional hierarchies of the relevant institutions. Both contending parties agree that, where individuals have an equal opportunity both to acquire the resources to compete and to compete, they could and should be rank-ordered in terms of what are taken to be objective standards of meritorious achievement and that positions and status in the conventional hierarchies should be allocated in accordance with that rank order. Both parties agree in condemning violations of such equality and in attempting to find remedies for such violations that are not themselves further violations of what equality requires. Their disagreements about affirmative action are over whether or not it provides such a remedy.

By contrast I want to suggest that it is the prevalence of this same ideological picture that has in significant ways distorted the self-understanding of the academic community, so that it has made the discussion of affirmative action too often a red herring. For this picture persuasively conveys to those enchanted by it the thought that what is morally at stake both in faculty appointments and in student admissions is primarily and perhaps only a matter of the rights of individuals to equal opportunity and to be judged by the standards of meritorious achievement. But we ought rather to begin with duties—this of course needs to be argued, but cannot be argued here—and more particularly with the duties of universities and colleges not only to individuals *qua* individuals, but also to individuals as members of and representative of a variety of social groups and to the society as a whole. What those duties are can be discerned only when we have raised and adequately answered questions about the purpose and point of universities and colleges. Consider, for example, the implications of one particular answer to the question: What are the proper ends of a college education?—namely, that they are twofold: first, to educate students into valuing and enjoying high intellectual achievement, both for its own sake and for what such achievement can contribute to enriching human community and, second, to enable students from each of the constituent groups of our society to participate in and to value the argumentative and deliberative discourse of an educated public, in which the voices of each group as well as the voices of individuals contribute to the conversation of the whole society. Each of those ends imposes constraints upon what are acceptable policies for recruitment to and admission into student bodies, graduate schools, and faculty positions. The second is at first sight more obviously relevant to affirmative action issues, for it requires that there be a substantial presence in the better ranks of the college population of every group whose voice needs to be heard in the conversation of an educated public, just because if each such voice is not heard the whole will be diminished and we shall all be impoverished—as we are indeed now and will be, so long as we treat America exclusively as a society of individuals rather than also as a society of societies. So we need to do whatever will ensure that substantial numbers of women and men who are African American, Navaho, Sioux, Latino, or whatever are educated in the disciplines that will enable them to do their duty by speaking *for* both themselves and their own and *to* each other and the rest of us. Such an education would have to be a good deal more demanding than what it takes nowadays to get through college. And to provide students for it there would have to be a massive shift of economic and intellectual resources to selected and favored community colleges, high schools, and indeed kindergartens in particular areas. Solve the problems at this level and two generations later a good many of the problems about recruitment of women and minority students to graduate schools and to faculty positions will turn out also to have been solved; fail to solve them at this level and the problems will remain to some large degree insoluble at other levels too, even if enlightened proposals, such as that advanced by Professor Becker, were to be adopted.

If this strategy is to be successful, however, we need also to respect the constraints imposed by the first of the two ends which, so I suggested, are the proper ends of a college education, notably that students should learn both before and in college how to respect intellectual excellence by learning how to respond to what is most intellectually demanding. If women or minority students are denied this type of learning, then the effect of promoting their academic cause, whether by affirmative action of by any other means, will be to admit them only to the study of those courses and those disciplines where it is the exception rather than the rule for first-rate work to be done. And, were this to be so, it would not be a significant gain for women or minority students. What matters, then, much more than the overall proportion of women or minorities among undergraduate students or graduate students or faculty in universities, is their proportions at each of these levels in such demanding disciplines as mathematics, physics, classics, philosophy, Chinese, or Slavonic studies and of course a number of others rather than . . . "How absurd!" someone—perhaps Francis— will say. "Who are *you* to rank-order the academic disciplines?" To which the answer is that *I* did not rank-order them. They have been rank-ordered by the choices of those who have gone to work in them. Consider the telling evidence provided by the average GRE scores of those who enter graduate school in each discipline and subdiscipline, and the very large differences in such scores between one discipline or subdiscipline and another, and it becomes plain that, although there are certainly some very able people in almost every discipline, the disparities in the abilities of those who research and teach are quite remarkable. It is this compelling evidence, rather than I, which sug- gests that there are some disciplines and subdisciplines which, as they are taught in many places, are just not worth studying. It would be alarming if these turned out to be the disciplines and subdisciplines most hospitable to women and to minority students.

I therefore hold that an increase in academic positions held by women or by members of minority groups by itself may represent much less of a significant change than Francis supposes. And I hold that the opposition to preferential appointment articulated by Simon is only morally tolerable if it is accompanied by forceful advocacy of a very large redistribution of resources in favor of women and minori- ties at other educational levels from kindergarten onward. Lawrence Becker's proposal is admirable in many respects, not least that even those of us in the most radical disagreement with present-day ortho- doxies can join with our colleagues in urging its implementation.

21

Affirmative Action and Tenure Decisions

Richard T. De George

Three years ago my department had its first tenure track opening in fifteen years. We were a department of thirteen members—all white males. The university's affirmative action office told us we had a target of 2.4 women and 1 minority member. Although we disliked being told what our target is, the members of the department agreed it would be desirable, all things considered, to have women and minority members on our faculty, and we agreed with the aims of affirmative action. We were also unanimous in rejecting any notion of quotas and agreed not to hire anyone the members feel does not come up to the standards we have set for ourselves. We considered over two hundred candidates—men and women—for our position and finally hired a woman who was a new Ph.D. Two years ago we made another appointment, a man. This year we made our third appointment, a woman who was on a tenure track at another university. But the first woman we hired is leaving for a position at yet another university.

The story of my department's hiring is not unusual. In our hiring we behave egoistically, considering only our own goals and needs, and our affirmative action office encourages us in this approach. Most other departments act similarly. We are interested in achieving our targets, even if it means hiring members of the targeted groups away from other universities, which also have targets. And we suffer from that attitude when our faculty members are hired away.

If morally justifiable, the practice is certainly inefficient.

Affirmative action is applied to each institution. Each has a certain goal with respect to the mix of men and women, whites and blacks, or other designated minorities. These goals are usually further broken down to apply to each department within the university. There can be no justifiable timetable to reach those goals if there are not enough of the given kind of applicants in the job pool. When the number of persons available is less than the number of departments of a certain type seeking such persons, the situation becomes one of musical chairs. There are fewer blacks in philosophy than there are departments seeking black philosophy teachers because of goals that have been set for them by affirmative action offices of their respective universities. As a result, University X may be successful in hiring a black philosopher. The next year University Y may hire that person away. The philosopher has probably increased his or her compensation. But overall, we still have one department with a black philosopher and the other without one. University Y approached its goal and in doing so set University X back in its attempt to achieve its goal. This is a common occurrence. Yet it makes little sense from the broad perspective of our society's affirmative action aims.

There is a remedy to this situation. It consists in each university's affirmative action office agreeing that in the initial hiring process it will not count those persons who already have tenure-track positions elsewhere as coming under affirmative action guidelines. Those persons may of course be considered for a position, just as a white male may. But those persons will not be considered as members of the target group for affirmative action purposes. This means that there is no justification for preferring such persons over any others for affirmative action purposes. It also means that if such persons are chosen for a position, the hiring department must show that the chosen person was appropriately chosen over all other candidates from targeted groups in the same way that a white male must be shown to have been appropriately chosen.

This procedure might help slow down the game of musical chairs and the zero-sum game that departments engage in with respect to members of targeted groups.

Two objections might be made against this proposal. One is that not only does a department benefit if it has its targeted number of minorities or women in it, but it also may profit from having had such persons even for only a short period, say for a year or two before they are hired away. That person leaves a trace, such that it is better to have had such a person for a short period than not to have had such a person at all. Hence musical chairs does serve some purpose, even if it is not ideal for the departments involved.

The argument has some merit. But the merit it has must be weighed against the cost to the various departments and the tokenism that it promotes.

The second objection says that the proposal fails adequately to consider a number of relevant factors. For instance, suppose Department A has more than its targeted number of women and Department B has none. From a societal affirmative action perspective, if Department B hires away a woman faculty member from Department A, B gains without any affirmative action damage to A. If that is the case, why should not that faculty member be considered an affirmative action candidate, just as those who are just finishing their graduate work are? The answer is that although they can be (and currently are), departments and affirmative action offices are not usually in a position to know how hiring a person away from another university will affect that university from an affirmative action perspective. There are too many other variables—for example, how many of the women in that department are being considered for positions elsewhere—for any easy determination of that impact.

Since I am proposing a procedure that will help promote efficiency, my claim is that adopting it will not adversely affect overall societal affirmative action purposes, that it is consistent with the spirit of affirmative action, and that it does no one an injustice. By introducing some efficiency into the implementation of affirmative action hiring it might well save many institutions considerable time and expense. By making the process somewhat more efficient, it may render the process somewhat more rational and perhaps more acceptable than it currently is to those who see affirmative action as it is actually implemented as an imposed, unjustified expense that produces little in the way of long-term change.

Affirmative action in hiring is an established fact in most universities. Does affirmative action end with the initial appointment? I hope that in my own department we shall tenure any women or minority members we hire and are able to keep. But I hope the same thing about any white males we may hire. The caveat in all cases is that I hope those we hire will produce and work as we expect they will, and that they will thus earn tenure.

With respect to tenure, affirmative action requires that departments and schools pay attention to possible existing discriminatory barriers or biases, and it demands they take corrective action where necessary. Beyond that, it can justifiably require no special consideration because of the targets or goals affirmative action offices set. My department's goal of hiring 2.4 women and 1 minority member is acceptable as long as it remains a goal and not a quota. If such goals are acceptable in hiring, why not in tenuring? It is not acceptable in tenuring, I suggest, on the condition that tenure-track positions are actually that. This means that if a person on that track fulfills the criteria for tenure, tenure will be granted, no matter how many people are being considered for tenure at the same time, and no matter what percentage of the faculty is already tenured. This is what a tenure-track position should mean. Each decision should be made independently. Hence there will be no place for preferential treatment or for choosing a woman or minority member over a white male if both are being considered for tenure at the same time.

In this way tenure and promotion within academic ranks differ from promotion within firms. In firms the number of upper-level managerial positions is limited, and affirmative action can legitimately come into play at each step on the hierarchy in a way comparable to the way it does in initial hiring. This is not true of tenure, if the process is as I have described it.

Fairness requires that every faculty member, regardless of gender or race, be given tenure if that faculty member measures up to whatever criteria the institution appropriately determines and publicly announces for granting tenure. In some institutions this may be excellence or some other designated level of performance in teaching and/or in the quantity and quality of research; in other institutions a balance of a certain level of teaching, research, and service may be required. In still others the criteria may simply be competent performance of assigned duties. Institutions vary, and the criteria for tenure vary accordingly.

This does not mean it is inappropriate for an institution to grant tenure on the basis of the institution's desire for role models of certain types, a mix of genders and races, or whatever else is determined to suit the institution and is publicly announced. Such norms could justifiably be criteria for granting tenure, since they do no injustice to any other faculty member. They cannot justifiably be a basis for denying tenure. It would be unfair to deny someone tenure because granting it to that individual would worsen a desired gender mix or racial balance, and any such condition added to a tenure-track position would in fact not make that a tenure track for the person holding it.

Non-competence-based criteria are not morally mandatory. Institutions that ignore such considerations may be charged with elitism, but academic elitism is not necessarily racist or morally inappropriate. Elitism consists in discriminating on the basis of competence and accomplishment, regardless of gender or race. Such elitism in itself favors neither men nor women, neither whites nor blacks. Such elitist institutions should be as open to tenuring women and minority faculty as to tenuring white male faculty members. No one should assume that women or minority members cannot meet the criteria for tenure that white males can. If an institution in fact denies tenure to a larger proportion of women and minority members than to its white male faculty members on the tenure track, then a hard look at the criteria and the way they are applied is in order. But one cannot assume bias on the basis of failure to grant tenure to any given individual faculty member, male or female, white or black.

As long as entrance into tenure-track positions is in accordance with the spirit of affirmative action, neither goals nor quotas should be mandated for granting tenure. This means that consideration of the number of women or minority members with tenure can be justifiably ignored in granting tenure, even though the total number of them on the faculty is pertinent in setting hiring goals.

To hold otherwise is to mandate changes in tenure requirements on the basis of the percentage of women or minority members in a department or institution. This is to dilute the standards, or to apply a dual standard—one for white males and another for all others. Each person's case should stand or fall on the record of accomplishment. There is no injustice done by giving final notice to those who fail to achieve the publicly stated requirements. But there might well be damage done to the institution and to the quality that it wishes to maintain if it is forced by whatever means to award tenure to those who do not meet the announced standards. Justice does not require the dilution of institutional standards of scholarship or teaching for affirmative action purposes. To hold otherwise is to subordinate academic excellence—and perhaps even competence—to some preordained level based on proportional goals of gender or race. These may be justifiable in selecting at the entrance level between candidates who meet the stated qualifications for a position. They are not morally mandatory beyond that.

Some may object to this position as a defense of the status quo, as a means of effectively keeping members of targeted groups from achieving tenure, and as an indication of blindness to the fact that criteria for tenure—which often include publication in certain prestigious journals or with certain prestigious presses—are subtly discriminatory. The reply is that the criteria for tenure can and should be fairly evaluated by the department, and complaints about the criteria considered, perhaps by those competent outside the department. But if the criteria are known to those hired for a tenure-track position, concerns about the criteria should be voiced and handled before tenure decisions are forced, not only when they are to be applied or after tenure has been denied.

Affirmative action will probably be required for a long time. There is good reason to make it as efficient as possible and to keep it from either eroding or being perceived as eroding the academic quality that an institution wishes to preserve or meet. Both my proposal with respect to hiring and my defense of making affirmative action considerations operable only on the tenure criteria to be used and not in the individual decision for tenure are compatible with the spirit of affirmative action. My aim in proposing them is to make affirmative action within morally defensible limits more generally acceptable to some of its critics than it currently is.

Affirmative Action and the Awarding of Tenure

22

Peter J. Markie

The three main essays in this collection concentrate on affirmative action in the appointment of university faculty; I shall concentrate on a closely related but separate topic: affirmative action in the awarding of tenure. After I make some initial distinctions to organize my discussion, I shall argue that, at least in the awarding of tenure, one particular kind of affirmative action—what I call the primary form of preferential treatment—is unethical. My argument has important implications for the related case of affirmative action in faculty promotions, but I shall not draw them out here.

A university can practice affirmative action both directly and indirectly in awarding tenure. It practices affirmative action directly when it adopts an affirmative action program with regard to the award of tenure itself. It practices affirmative action indirectly when it adopts an affirmative action program with regard to some other decision that has an impact on the number of target group members likely to receive tenure. If a university practices affirmative action in distributing grants intended to help tenure-track assistant professors establish a research program, it is indirectly practicing affirmative action with regard to awarding tenure. I am concerned only with the direct practice of affirmative action in tenure decisions.

A university can directly practice affirmative action in tenure decisions in each of the usual three ways.[1] Procedural affirmative action consists of positive procedural steps to increase the extent to which an applicant pool represents a larger body in its percentage of target group members. A university might, for example, adjust its procedures to allow for early tenure and encourage early applications from target faculty. Regulatory affirmative action is the specifying of goals representing the number of members of a target group who would be appointed under a proper selection procedure. A university might specify what percentage of its tenured faculty should be drawn from each target group. Preferential affirmative action consists of giving special treatment to some candidates on the basis of their membership in a target group. A university might give credit for target group membership in the tenure evaluation, just as it does for research, teaching, and service accomplishments. Some of these forms of affirmative action are more interesting and important than others. The mere specification of goals in regulatory affirmative action is empty without the adoption of specific forms of procedural and preferential affirmative action to meet them. Since tenure candidates are not recruited from the faculty at large, a university cannot use procedural affirmative action in awarding tenure to the extent it can in initially appointing faculty. This leaves preferential affirmative action as perhaps the most interesting and important of a university's options when it comes to awarding tenure. I shall concentrate on it.

What form can preferential affirmative action take in tenure decisions? In the initial appointment of faculty, preferential affirmative action takes the form of preferring members of a designated group over nongroup members in the competition for faculty positions, and it comes in different strengths: a qualified target candidate can be preferred over an otherwise equally qualified nontarget candidate, a qualified target candidate can be preferred over a more qualified nontarget candidate, or an unqualified target candidate can be preferred over a qualified nontarget candidate. If a university has a tenure quota so that faculty compete for a limited number of tenured professorships, preferential affirmative action in awarding tenure can take any of these forms. Yet, most universities have no tenure quota, and candidates for tenure do not compete against each other in the ordinary way.[2] Preferential affirmative action must generally be limited, then, to another form: counting target group membership as a positive factor along with academic achievements. Affirmative action candidates are given "extra credit" for belonging to a target group, in addition to the credit they earn on the basis of their research, teaching, and service. I will call this the primary form of preferential treatment in awarding tenure; it is the form, I shall argue, that is unethical.

The primary form of preferential treatment in awarding tenure obviously comes in different strengths, depending on how much extra credit is given for target group membership, yet it is important to note that, even in its weakest form, the practice must involve giving enough extra credit to make it possible for a target candidate to gain tenure when he or she would not obtain it solely on the basis of overall accomplishments in research, teaching, and service. If the amount of extra credit is never enough to gain tenure for a candidate who would not otherwise gain it on the regular criteria, it is effectively zero and we really do not have a preferential treatment program. Target group members don't receive any preferential treatment if they are required to have the same overall accomplishments in research, teaching, and service as other candidates.[3] This is a simple point but easily missed. Faculty and administrators sometimes claim to practice affirmative action by taking race and sex into account in tenure decisions while also claiming that their practice would never allow the award of tenure to someone who did not already deserve it on the basis of overall academic achievement. This is a case of conceptual confusion, at best.

It may seem that the primary form of preferential treatment in awarding tenure is always ethically permissible. After all, the main worry about preferential treatment in the case of appointing faculty is that it involves doing an injustice to qualified candidates who are not appointed in order to make way for an affirmative action candidate of equal or lesser qualifications, and in the case at hand no such injustice occurs. The university gives target faculty extra credit in the tenure review without ever having to deny tenure to a nontarget professor. No one is harmed, so no ethical justification is required. Things are not this simple, however. The primary form of preferential treatment needs an ethical justification for at least three reasons.

First, whenever we treat people differently, and especially when we hold some to a higher standard than others, there must be some difference between them to justify the difference in treatment. In the primary form of preferential treatment, some non-affirmative action candidates who do not have a certain level of combined achievement in teaching, research, and service may be denied tenure, while affirmative action candidates with comparable combined achievements in these areas may gain tenure on the basis of the extra credit awarded them. Thus, when it comes to teaching, research, and service, the non-affirmative action candidates must meet a higher standard to gain tenure. It is the same as when I give my class three exams and then award extra points to a proper subset of the class. Those who do not receive the extra points are held to a higher standard in that they have to do better on the exams to pass the course. Clearly, my grading system requires an ethical justification; so, too, does the primary form of preferential treatment.

Second, university faculty and administrators have an obligation to their university and to their disciplines to maintain high academic standards for tenure appointments. The general quality of a university is largely determined by the quality of its tenured faculty. The future of each discipline is determined by those who practice it, and this, too, is largely determined by who gains tenure. The primary form of preferential treatment involves awarding tenure on the basis of considerations that include, but also go beyond, academic achievement; it thus has the potential for leading faculty and administrators to violate their obligation to maintain high academic standards. It needs to be shown that it will not lead them to do so or that, insofar as it does, the violation is justified by other considerations.

Third, in its simplest version, the primary form of preferential treatment denies successful affirmative action candidates a benefit it provides to successful non-affirmative action candidates. In the simplest form of the practice, affirmative action faculty do not get to choose whether they will be evaluated without regard to their membership in a target group, and when they are granted tenure no indication is given of whether or not extra points for group membership played a crucial role in the decision. As a result, while successful non-affirmative action candidates have the quality of their achievements unequivocally and publicly acknowledged by the award of tenure, successful affirmative action candidates do not. The acknowledgement of their accomplishments through the award of tenure is rendered equivocal by the open question of whether group membership was a determining factor.

Given that the primary form of preferential treatment needs to be ethically justified, one way to argue against it is to argue against every alternative justification one can find. I shall take a more direct route. We can see that the primary form of preferential treatment is unethical without finding the flaws in all of its potential justifications; the place to start is with a point widely accepted by both proponents and opponents of affirmative action.

Put the case of tenure aside for a moment and consider the initial appointment of faculty. It is generally agreed by parties on all sides that a preferential treatment program with regard to faculty appointments must apply only to job candidates who are qualified. What is it for a target candidate to be qualified? Certainly, to be qualified, the target candidate must meet the same standard of ability and achievement that nontarget candidates must meet to be qualified. If a target candidate for a faculty appointment has a level of ability and achievement that would make a nontarget candidate unqualified, then the target candidate is unqualified. To put the point another way, the target candidate is qualified only if he or she has a level of ability and achievement beyond that of a nontarget candidate who would be appropriately rejected even if the budget expanded to allow the university to hire every applicant. In all, then, a preferential treatment program for the appointment of faculty is unethical if it sanctions the appointment of target candidates who are not otherwise qualified, and a target candidate is otherwise qualified only if his or her abilities and achievements are above the level at which a nontarget candidate would be appropriately judged unqualified.

The awarding of tenure is a special case of the appointment of faculty in general. Instead of just being appointed to the faculty, the successful tenure candidate is appointed with tenure. It's a special case because it brings certain rights, privileges, and responsibilities with it, and as a result it requires a higher level of qualification, but since the appointment of faculty with tenure is a special case of the appointment of faculty in general, we should adopt the same limitation on when a preferential treatment program is justified: when it comes to the appointment of faculty with tenure, a preferential treatment program is unethical if it sanctions the appointment of affirmative action candidates who are not qualified for tenure, and an affirmative action candidate is qualified for tenure only if his or her level of combined achievement in teaching, research, and service is above the level at which a non-affirmative action candidate would appropriately be judged unqualified. To put the point another way, an affirmative action candidate is qualified for tenure only if his or her combined achievements in teaching, research, and service are beyond the level at which a non-affirmative action candidate would be appropriately denied tenure, even though the university had a tenured position available for every candidate. Primary preferential treatment programs all fail to meet this standard by their very nature. They all sanction granting tenure to affirmative action candidates who do not merit tenure on the basis of their combined achievements in research, teaching, and service alone and so whose combined achievements in these areas are not above the level at which a non-affirmative action candidate would be judged unqualified. Hence, all primary preferential treatment programs are unethical.

I now want to consider four possible replies to my argument. One reply is that I have misunderstood the purpose and nature of primary preferential treatment programs with regard to tenure. The problem is not that if a university adopts a primary preferential treatment program it will sanction the award of tenure to unqualified candidates. The problem is that if a university does not adopt a primary preferential treatment program, it will deny tenure to qualified candidates through acts of discrimination. Target group candidates for tenure are discriminated against in the tenure process, and it is necessary to grant them extra points for group membership to counter-balance this discrimination. The extra points don't make unqualified candidates appear qualified to otherwise objective reviewers; they prevent qualified candidates from appearing unqualified to reviewers whose judgment is directly or indirectly clouded by prejudice.[4]

Indeed, the critic might suggest that we consider an analogous case. A university that is very strong in the sciences has a reputation for seldom giving tenure to humanities faculty. Eighty percent of the science candidates for tenure have been successful, but only 30 percent of the humanities candidates. Moreover, the faculty and administrators involved in the tenure reviews beyond the department level have largely been scientists, and their remarks at meetings clearly indicate a prejudice against the humanities. Humanities candidates are also held to standards that are appropriate only for science candidates, such as having gained substantial grant funding. In short, qualified humanists are not receiving tenure because the review process is unfair. How can the university rectify this situation? For the long run, ways must be found to eliminate the prejudice against the humanities in the minds of faculty and administrators in the sciences. In the short run, the criteria for tenure have to be changed so that humanities candidates are no longer held to inappropriate expectations, and, just as importantly, some way must be found to neutralize the bias present in the judgment of the reviewers. The best way to do this is to grant each humanities candidate extra points. This is a primary preferential treatment program, but the extra points granted to target candidates don't cause unqualified humanists to gain tenure; they prevent qualified humanists from being denied tenure. Isn't this program justified? Yet, some science faculty would criticize it nonetheless through arguments remarkably similar to mine: science candidates are now held to a higher standard than humanities candidates, the university risks violating its obligation to maintain a high quality faculty, successful humanities candidates are deprived of an unequivocal recognition of their achievement, and the preferential treatment program sanctions awarding tenure to unqualified humanities candidates.

This reply rests on two main premises: first, that target group candidates are currently treated unfairly; second, that a primary preferential treatment program is the best response to this injustice. Let's start with the first. Target faculty can be denied equal opportunity in two ways. A structural bias against target candidates or their work may exist in the university's procedures or standards. A personal bias against target candidates or their work may exist in the minds of those charged with the tenure evaluation and decision. I am willing to grant for the sake of the argument that we are concerned with the case of a university at which there is both structural and personal bias against target candidates. Note in passing, however, that this premise is not an easy one for proponents of primary preferential treatment to establish, particularly with regard to the existence of personal bias. Statistical evidence about the number of target candidates denied tenure at universities in general and even at the particular university at hand is not sufficient to show the present existence of personal bias at the university, without additional information to link the statistics to the attitudes of those currently involved in tenure reviews there.

Is a primary preferential treatment program the best response to the lack of equality of opportunity? The answer is clearly no, when the bias is simply structural. There is no need for a preferential treatment program, since the university need only change the offending procedures or standards.[5] Better ways to respond to personal bias are also available. The preferential treatment response has all the drawbacks I've already noted, including the fact that even when instituted as a remedy to personal bias it is likely to at least sometimes sanction granting tenure to the unqualified. No matter who is charged with giving the extra points, it is unlikely that they will always give just enough points to cancel out the effects of personal bias against qualified target candidates without ever giving enough to gain tenure for unqualified ones. At least one superior option is to counteract the personal bias by either removing from the review process those whom the university is justified in believing to be biased or ensuring that their judgment of target candidates' qualifications is subject to review by some person or persons known to be without bias. This option is not a preferential treatment program; indeed, the review program can be made available to any candidate denied tenure, and a charge of personal bias can be just one possible basis for reconsideration. Since it does not involve holding target candidates to a different standard than nontarget candidates with regard to the basic academic criteria for tenure, it does not have the drawbacks of a preferential treatment program.[6]

A second reply is that my argument overlooks an alternative form of primary preferential treatment in awarding tenure. Suppose target group membership is only taken into account when those doing the tenure review are unsure of whether the basic standard for overall academic accomplishment has been met. It's not that the basic standard is not met and tenure is granted on the basis of extra credit for group membership; it's that the faculty and administrators evaluating the candidate are not sure whether the basic standard has been met, and they eliminate their indecision by taking group membership into account. When a case is unclear, the issue cannot be decided just by considering whether the basic academic standard has been met, for that is what is unclear. Those conducting the tenure review must find some additional consideration to settle the issue; membership in a target group may be used as an additional positive consideration.

Close examination reveals that this practice is not an alternative to the one I have already shown to be unethical. A tenure decision is warranted, not simply when the candidate has made significant overall achievements in research, teaching, and service, but when the existence of those achievements has been convincingly established through peer research reviews, teaching evaluations, and so on. The standard qualifications for tenure include not only significant academic achievements but also that the fact of those achievements be demonstrated beyond a certain degree of reasonable doubt. The criteria for tenure include a standard of evidence. The practice at hand sanctions the award of tenure to an affirmative action candidate when the evidential strength of his or her case is at a level at which tenure would be denied to a non-affirmative action candidate, for whom the additional factor of target group membership does not exist. The practice thus involves preferential treatment by holding non-affirmative action candidates to a higher evidential standard. It sanctions granting tenure to affirmative action candidates whose cases lack the evidential strength to qualify a non-affirmative action candidate for tenure. It sanctions granting tenure to unqualified candidates.

A third reply is that preferential treatment in the award of tenure is ethically justified even when the affirmative action candidate is not qualified for tenure, so long as he or she is at least qualified for a faculty appointment. This reply fails to appreciate the importance of tenure. Given the additional rights, privileges, and responsibilities that accompany tenure, the justification standards for preferential treatment in faculty appointments with tenure should be at least as stringent as those for preferential treatment in faculty appointments without tenure. Yet, we would rightly reject a preferential treatment program that would allow us to appoint as a nontenured professor someone only qualified to be a graduate teaching assistant. We should not, then, accept an affirmative action program that would allow us to appoint as a tenured professor someone who is qualified to be only a nontenured professor.

A final reply is that while my argument shows that primary preferential treatment programs for awarding tenure are unjustified, it does not show that it is always unethical for faculty tenure committees and university administrators to take membership in a target group into account in tenure decisions. Membership in a target group is often a reliable indicator of ability to serve as a role model for some students and to contribute to the intellectual diversity of the university. Target group membership is, thus, evidence in support of the candidate's qualifications in the areas of teaching and research.

This reply misses a very simple point. A tenure decision is supposed to be based, not on the candidate's abilities in teaching and research, but on the candidate's accomplishments in those areas and the extent to which those accomplishments indicate the likelihood of similar accomplishments in the future. Let's assume just for argument's sake that membership in a target group is a reliable indication of a special teaching ability (as a role model) and a special research ability (as someone working in a new and very different area). Nonetheless, a candidate's mere possession of a special ability in teaching and research is not an important qualification for tenure. The important qualification for tenure is the candidate's level of accomplishment in these areas. Has the candidate actually been an effective and appropriate role model for students? Has the candidate actually developed new and very different areas of research? The mere fact of target group membership is not relevant to these questions. What is relevant is the same type of evidence concerning quality of teaching and research that is expected of non-affirmative action candidates. Note too that it won't do to suggest that target group candidates should be judged more on ability than accomplishment, for that is to fall back into a form of primary preferential treatment by adopting a weaker standard for target group members.

I submit, then, that no matter what we may be justified in doing by way of affirmative action in the initial appointment of faculty and in providing junior faculty with opportunities to prepare for their tenure review, we should not adopt the primary form of preferential treatment in awarding tenure. Here is one point at which one form of affirmative action should end.

NOTES

1. I have adopted the classification used by Robert L. Simon in Chapter 2.

2. Candidates may still "compete" in another way, since the level of achievement an evaluation committee expects of one candidate is likely to be influenced by the level of achievement demonstrated by the others.

3. The practice of giving extra credit but never enough to gain tenure for someone who would not otherwise gain it is like the practice of giving extra credit when initially appointing faculty but never giving enough to gain an appointment for someone who would not otherwise gain it anyway. Neither is a form of preferential treatment.

4. This objection was suggested to me by Steven M. Cahn.

5. Consider some structural elements that are suggested by remarks by Leslie P. Francis in Chapter 1. Female candidates may not have the same full six years of candidacy as male candidates, since they may have to sacrifice research time in order to have children. If we believe this results in an unfair structural bias against female candidates, we can simply revise the guidelines to allow candidates to request an extension to their probationary period and count demands associated with parenthood as a justifying reason for an extension. This will not be preferential treatment in disguise, as long as we are fair and make extensions available to any similarly situated male candidates. Francis also mentions excessive committee service demands placed on target faculty. This can be dealt with by adjusting the amount of credit given for service accomplishments relative to teaching and research. Again, this will not be a case of preferential treatment, as long as similar provisions are made for nontarget candidates who have been expected or required to perform extra service duties.

6. Some may object to my assumption that the university can establish some review board that is without personal bias. Besides needing some argument, this objection has the potential to undercut even the preferential treatment position. If personal bias is so pervasive, what basis do we have for believ-

ing that even a preferential treatment program will be successful? Those in charge of the program will be infected with personal bias and will be led by their bias to give target candidates evaluations just low enough to ensure that they remain unqualified even after receiving extra points for target group membership.

The Case for Preferential Treatment

23

James P. Sterba

In their interesting and thoughtful contributions to this volume, Lawrence Becker, Leslie Francis, and Robert Simon all favor the use of affirmative action programs by institutions of higher education. Affirmative action for them encompasses various procedural and regulatory policies designed to remove forms of discrimination and prejudice that keep women and minority candidates, when they are most qualified, from being selected, appointed, or retained within institutions of higher education. However, none of the three favor preferential treatment, that is, the policy of preferring women or minority candidates who have been disadvantaged by discrimination or prejudice over equally or more qualified white male candidates who have not been similarly disadvantaged. In these comments, what I propose to argue is that a strong case can be made for preferential treatment so defined and that in fact elements of Becker's, Francis's, and Simon's analyses can be seen to support this case for preferential treatment.

As I indicated, preferential treatment is a policy of preferring qualified women and minority candidates who have been disadvantaged by discrimination and prejudice over equally or more qualified white male candidates who have not been similarly disadvantaged. In fact, it is generally the case that the white male candidates who are passed over by a policy of preferential treatment have themselves benefited in the past from the discrimination and prejudice that were shown to women and minority candidates (e.g., through unequal educational opportunities). To be justified, however, such a policy of preferential treatment must favor only candidates whose qualifications are such that when their selection or appointment is combined with a suitably designed educational enhancement program, they will normally turn out within a reasonably short time to be as qualified or even more qualified than their peers. Such candidates have the potential to be as qualified or more qualified than their peers, but that potential has not yet been actualized because of past discrimination and prejudice. Preferential treatment with its suitably designed educational enhancement program purports to actualize just that potential. In this way, persons who receive preferential treatment are like runners in a race who for a time are forced to compete at a disadvantage with other runners, e.g., by having weights tied to their legs, but then later are allowed to transfer those weights to the runners in the race who had previously benefited from the unfair competitive advantage so that the results of the race will now be fair. Preferential treatment, therefore, is a policy that is directed at only those women and minority candidates who are highly qualified, yet because of past discrimination and prejudice, are less qualified than they would otherwise be; it seeks to provide such candidates with a benefit that will nullify the effects of the past discrimination and prejudice by enabling them to become as qualified or more qualified than their peers.

In his essay, Becker rejects all forms of preferential treatment while favoring a two-pronged affirmative action program that incorporates procedural safeguards with a set-aside of a certain number of positions for fully qualified women and minority candidates. Becker concedes that women and minority candidates have been disadvantaged by past discrimination and prejudice, but the only remedy he proposes is his two-pronged affirmative action program. Thus, when past discrimination and prejudice have in fact kept women and minority candidates from becoming fully qualified, Becker proposes no remedy. It is just here that Becker's analysis points to a need for some form of preferential treatment to remedy this injustice.

Becker might respond to my contention that his view needs to incorporate preferential treatment by claiming that he was attempting to defend a form of affirmative action that preceded from what is common ground between critics and advocates of affirmative action. But since the common ground he appeals to in order to support his two-pronged affirmative action program includes the principle that we "must be active and vigilant in eliminating . . . discrimination," it would seem that if we are to eliminate all the effects of discrimination, some form of preferential treatment is also required.

In her contribution to this volume, Francis argues in favor of what she calls process-directed and outcome-directed affirmative action programs to correct for current discrimination in selection, appointment, and retention policies at institutions of higher education. She focuses her attention on forms of discrimination and prejudice that keep women and minorities when they happen to be the most qualified candidates from being selected, appointed, or retained at institutions of higher education. Accordingly, she has little or nothing to say about what should be done for less qualified women or minority candidates when their lesser qualifications are traceable to past discrimination and prejudice.[1]

In her defense, Francis might contend that the reason for her disregard of preferential treatment is that Supreme Court cases have limited the possibility for implementing such programs. Thus, institutions of higher education are legally prohibited from seeking "to remedy the effects of societal discrimination"[2] and are, in fact, generally limited to correcting for discrimination and prejudice within their own institutional structures. But Francis does not confine her own analysis to the limits of the law. She herself criticizes the *Wards Cove* decision (1989) for making "it nearly impossible for plaintiffs to identify and prove some kinds of process-based discrimination when there is a moral argument for correction." She also disapproves of the *Croson* decision (1989) because it makes "it very difficult for state universities to defend any kind of redistributive affirmative action." Moreover, it would seem to be morally indefensible to prohibit institutions of higher education from correcting for the effects of societal discrimination or, more specifically, from correcting for the forms of discrimination and prejudice found in our institutions of elementary or secondary education, when they are in a good position to do so.

In contrast to Becker or Francis, who never explicitly argue against a policy of preferential treatment, Simon directs most of the argument of his paper against just such a policy. In these brief comments, I obviously can't address all of the aspects of his argument, but I will focus on the two main contentions of his argument against preferential treatment: (1) that preferential treatment may turn out to help the wrong people and (2) that preferential treatment fails to help many of the right people, that is, the people that should be helped by such a policy.

According to Simon, preferential treatment may turn out to help the wrong people because it assumes that we are able to determine who would be most qualified in an ideally just society. But how can we tell who would be most qualified in a perfectly just society? Simon is right in thinking that we cannot. Fortunately, we do not need to know who are the most qualified in a perfectly just society to carry out a policy of preferential treatment. All we need to know or reasonably believe is that if we appoint certain candidates for preferential treatment and put them through a suitably designed educational enhancement program, they would be as qualified or more qualified than the available white male candidates who have in fact benefited from past discrimination and prejudice. Surely, there are many instances where we are reasonably justified in making this hypothetical judgment.

But even if we assume that the people who would be helped by preferential treatment are the right people, that is, that they are people who should be helped by such a policy, Simon contends that they are at best only some of the right people. This is because candidates besides women and minorities have suffered from discrimination and prejudice or from simply being economically disadvantaged. Why should we not seek to correct for these disadvantages as well as the disadvantages suffered by women and minorities?

Why not indeed! Surely if other individuals have suffered comparable hardships from discrimination and prejudice or from simply being economically disadvantaged some remedy would be appropriate. So Simon's objection is not an objection to preferential treatment per se, but rather an objection to preferential treatment as a narrowly conceived rather than as a broadly conceived program. So, in fact, Simon's analysis points to the need for a more broadly conceived preferential treatment program.

It should be noted, however, that if preferential treatment is to be extended in this way to deal with other injustices in society, it must become a larger program. The few positions that have been targeted for preferential treatment candidates have been created with the idea of simply remedying injustices suffered by women and minorities. If we now wish to remedy other comparable injustices in society as well, we will need to create many more positions to deal with the increased scope of preferential treatment. Consequently, Simon's analysis seems to point to the need for just such an expansion of preferential treatment.

In sum, I have argued that there is a strong case to be made for a preferential treatment program to go along with the affirmative action programs favored by Becker, Francis and Simon, and that elements of Becker's, Francis's and Simon's own analyses point to the need for just such a program. Of course, the exact shape such a program should take in our society is a topic for further inquiry.

NOTES

1. Francis only remarks, "Discussion of whether preferential selection is justified . . . [is] in my view not the most important issue in the current situation of American higher education."

2. *Regents of the University of California v. Bakke*, 438 U.S. 254 (1978).

24

Saying What We Think

Fred Sommers

A quarter-century of affirmative action law (AAL) has been accompanied by as many years of moral scrutiny. By now Lawrence Becker's conclusion that the philosophical debate over AAL has for some time been stalled seems uncontestable. Philosophers on either side of the issue appear to have found no common ground from which to form decisive arguments to convince the opposition. But that may be due to an insistence on a standard of proof that is not appropriate to the subject. In any event discussion has become more muted. Articles on affirmative action are now more valedictory than groundbreaking, more reflective than argumentative, more judicious than importunate. Lawrence Becker does not believe that the debate can be usefully restarted. ("The probability of finding new evidence or a new theory or principle that will break the deadlock is remote.") Under the circumstances Becker feels the best one can do is offer reasonable compromises that will palliate the opponent of preferential treatment (PT) while satisfying some of its proponents. Even Leslie Francis, who argues traditionally for AAL as a corrective for actual bias, is concessive, suggesting that Becker's compromise proposal is thoughtful and acceptable.

All three articles would have been more authoritative had they paid more attention to the social and economic effects of a policy that regulates the distribution of intellectual resources. Even if one confines oneself to the campus, affirmative action policies must now be viewed in the wider context of controversial policies for promoting diversity and multiculturalism, two ideals that are so badly defined as to be seriously misleading. Moral philosophers are neither economists nor journalists; it is perhaps unfair to demand of them that they be alert and sensitive to a swiftly changing contemporary scene. But where the facts are available evaluation of policy is made easier, not harder, by bringing them to bear. In the present instance, where we are concerned about the effects of AAL, we have good reason to believe that what is happening is far from what was intended or expected to happen by proponents of preferential policies. Recent critics have persuasively argued that preferential policies are often responsible for racially "balkanizing" the campus. Alan Charles Kors, an intellectual historian at the University of Pennsylvania, has said that preferential attitudes are disintegrative, breeding on many a campus "the cultural diversity of Beirut." If these unhappy effects can indeed be attributed to preferential policies they will not be easy to dismiss. This is the sort of thing that bids fair to get the debates on affirmative action restarted and perhaps redirected. So while acknowledging that debate has been stalled, one may disagree with Becker's assessment that no new relevant evidence is in the offing.

I believe that empirical considerations will soon be seen to support a clear negative judgment on preferential treatment. But the moral assumptions we bring to bear in assigning significance to the empirical facts remain primary. Here we may rely on Simon's paper, which seems to me to be a fine example of careful and persuasive critical analysis. Simon's verdict on preferential policy is largely negative. He quite properly begins his critique by attempting to undermine the Nagel-Dworkin defenses against the charge that PT is reverse discrimination. In this he succeeds and the effect is to leave the burden of proof where it always was and always will be: on the PT proponent.

The proof that the favoring of a less qualified candidate over a more qualified candidate is morally unjustified lies first of all in the fact that no one has succeeded in justifying it. Strong arguments that PT is in principle unjustifiable have also been presented. Such arguments do not have the tight structure that yields formally ineluctable conclusions. But, the demand for that kind of closure must always defeat the urgent point of practical reasoning. Thus Simon is aware that a strong empirical case could in principle still be offered on behalf of PT as an extraordinary tactic instituted in a critical time to right past and potentially future wrongs. But nothing short of such a case would do. "At the very least preferential treatment would be justified only if there is strong reason to think it produces benefits of unusually great significance which cannot be obtained through less obstructive policy options." Simon makes it reasonably clear that no such strong reasons are forthcoming.

Yet in another way Simon ironically illustrates Becker's contention that the philosophical debate is stalled. For while his reasoning points unerringly to the unequivocal conclusion that preferential treatment is wrong and should be terminated, he nowhere says so in as many words. Instead, he avoids a straightforward final verdict by submitting some very lame assessments of the weight of his own arguments. In the end he says only that his article "suggests that the policy of preferential appointment is not obviously morally correct and that in fact it faces serious moral objections." As for the objections to PT, Simon says they "may or may not be decisive" without indicating what it would take to decide. We get the impression that all further argument on PT would be evaluated by him in the same diffident manner.

Philosophers often err on the side of claiming too much for their arguments. Simon claims too little. "While my discussion suggests that preferential treatment by race or sex is ethically problematic, it suggests even more the value of the kind of sustained rational enquiry on ethically controversial social policies to which this volume contributes." It also suggests that Simon is like a chess player who, having got his opponent in a hopeless position, exasperates admiring spectators by offering a draw.

Like Becker, Simon goes on to propose an affirmative action alternative that avoids some of the pitfalls of PT. Few moral philosophers object to moderate affirmative action practices such as special enrichment programs and college preparatory programs for disadvantaged minority students or to admission and hiring policies of preferring women and minorities in pools of equally qualified candidates. But such programs and policies have never been the problem. The live issue is what to do about ramified preferential policies.

On many a campus, the implementation of preferential policy extends far beyond hiring and admissions. One extreme is the practice at Pennsylvania State University of presenting $580 to black students who maintain a C to C+ grade average and $1,160 to those who do better. Non-black students get nothing. Norms of "sensitivity" are another case in point. Women and minority students and faculty are often allowed a latitude and style of expression that has been effectively interdicted to all others on campus. It is, for example, acceptable for women and minorities to accuse (with uninhibited impunity) white males of sexism or racism but the reverse is unacceptable and, in many colleges, subject to official reproof and chastisement.

On some campuses preferential policies have had the effect of segregating minority groups from the rest of the student body. Having been selected in a way that inevitably puts them at a competitive academic disadvantage, minority students are immediately set apart and many turn inward to their own group. Many drop out, but those who stay the course may do so in their own segregated dorms and with their own yearbooks and finally with their own graduation ceremony. Many are happy to join the new sophists who attack "objective" academic standards as instruments deployed by those in power to ensure continued dominance. Unfortunately, the moderate proposals of Simon and Becker along with their reasonable arguments for adopting morally defensible alternatives to PT have diminished force in the highly charged and increasingly polarized arena of the contemporary academy where preferential policies fit in very well with the drive for "inclusiveness" and "diversity."

The concrete situation calls for moral clarity and staunchness. Since the 1960s, moral philosophers have been increasingly invited to offer their wisdom on important questions of social policy. That is as it should be. But excessive diffidence can leave legislators and policymakers without the clear guidance they are requesting and that they urgently need. And it may leave the campus without a defense to some very real threats to its academic integrity and social cohesiveness. There are principled reformers who do not blink at measures that have the effect of vitiating academic and liberal standards and of polarizing the campus along racial and sexual lines. It is a mistake to think of such threats to the life of the academy as unrelated to the impact of affirmative action.

Moral evaluation of preferential treatment will not be stalled for much longer. But it seems likely that the coming discussion will consider it within the context of the wider debate over the future of an academy that has increasingly become the locus of sexual and racial politics. In that debate moral philosophers have a historic and indispensable role to play. How well they play it depends on how clearly they say what they think.

25

Comments on Compromise and Affirmative Action

Alan H. Goldman

The authors of the three main essays in this volume all advocate a similar methodological approach to the issue of affirmative action at this point in the history of the debate on the policy. After so many years of philosophical and political argument, after so many interested parties have made up their minds on the issue, after so much flip-flopping by judges, members of Congress, and executive administrations, it is time, they suggest, to seek intelligent compromises that might be acceptable to all sides. Unfortunately, their well-intentioned and well-argued essays only illustrate again just how difficult compromise is to accept in this area. This will be the somewhat depressing message of my brief comments here.

Lawrence Becker proposes the most detailed practical compromise. His idea is to add positions to university units in areas in which target group members are underrepresented, so that the costs of bringing such groups up to proportionate representation are not borne by members of nontargeted groups that would obtain positions in the absence of preferential policies. As I interpret his description of the proposed policy, whenever a new position opens in a unit with underrepresentation and that position is not filled by a target group member, another position is to be created that will be filled by a qualified target group member. This extra line will then convert to an ordinary position when the next line opens. The process will continue until proportionate representation is achieved.

One minor objection to this policy is that concentrating exclusively on units with underrepresentation while ignoring those in which target groups are "overrepresented" will result in an overall greater-than-proportionate share of positions being reserved for target groups. This is minor, because I assume that adjustments can be made, because we are not close to a time in which overrepresentation is perceived as a problem by anyone, and because Becker is sensitive to real problems regarding the size of units to be measured against ratios of target group members in availability pools.

The more serious question is whether under the proposed policy individuals who are not members of target groups will lose positions they would have acquired in the absence of any preference. Is it true that they will not bear the costs? Let us say that the first entry-level position that opens in a department is filled by a white male judged to be most qualified and that a woman applicant who is somewhat less qualified but still acceptable is appointed to a second, added position according to the policy's requirement. (I assume here no problem in judging qualifications in a nondiscriminatory way; more on that below.) When a second ordinary position opens several years later, it is considered filled by her (her extraordinary position is converted as the policy requires to keep costs manageable). Suppose also that were the new position to be advertised, it would be filled by a new graduate most qualified for it. Then that new graduate will not be acquiring a position she or he would have acquired in the absence of preference (in fact, the strongest kind of set-aside preference). If the policy is widespread, then that new potential applicant will have sharply reduced opportunities. It should make no difference to opponents of preference whether the later graduate is male or female. They see it as unfair that those who have worked to achieve the highest qualifications for positions do not obtain those positions to which they would have been appointed under nondiscriminatory and nonpreferential criteria.

Given the economic realities of the past twenty years and the very limited resources available to university administrations, Becker's proposal to convert added positions to ordinary ones seems far more feasible than simply adding however many positions are required to achieve proportionate representation quickly. But without such permanent additions, the costs of achieving such representation faster than the market would will still be borne in the form of reduced opportunities for individuals, some men and some women, who had no part in earlier discrimination. This will not be acceptable as a compromise by present opponents of preference who understand the effects of the policy. We still need to wrestle with the question of whether proportionate representation of different groups is a legitimate goal in itself or one we need to achieve before we can achieve nondiscrimination in new appointments.

Robert Simon, by contrast, after an excellent review of the issues, suggests as a compromise that we concentrate on nonpreferential requirements of affirmative action. If we limit ourselves to what is demonstrably nonpreferential, this certainly will not satisfy advocates of present affirmative action programs or those who defend preference. But there is also the old question of which policies are preferential. Simon seems to think that target goals need not be—perhaps not in the logical sense of "need," but many of us have first-hand knowledge that departments eager to please administrations by meeting target goals do so, when necessary, with preferential appointments (or at least with appointments that count race or gender as a factor). Simon's other proposal, that graduate school scholarships be created for disadvantaged applicants, might be acceptable to all, but its sufficiency in the present context certainly will not be acceptable to all. And if, as he suggests, these scholarships are not reserved for present target group members, proponents of strong affirmative action and preferential treatment will take them to be irrelevant to the issue of injustice that they are addressing.

The article by Leslie Francis, while thorough in its review of the legal status of current policies, illustrates again how much disagreement there is about when practices are preferential and when they involve matters of justice. On the one hand, she seems to think that initially preferring candidates from more prestigious graduate programs and seeking recommendations from those known to the appointing officers are discriminatory practices. On the other hand, many advocates of affirmative action seem to accept another practice that she mentions, namely, placing target group members in their tenure-earning years on many university committees, while basing tenure decisions on scholarship. In my view, this is discrimination in the name of affirmative action against its supposed beneficiaries.

Francis argues that it is difficult to know whether discrimination against target group members occurs in the absence of target goals or outcome-based policies. The appointment process involves too many subjective factors. But this can be taken equally as an argument to minimize such factors, by downplaying the importance of interviews, for example. If more objective criteria are predictive of future performance and can be enforced, then opponents of preference would certainly prefer that strategy, given that goals are known to encourage preference. She also questions traditional criteria of academic merit on the grounds that they do not take into consideration such factors as ability to teach minority students or new fields and subject matter. But suggesting that minority faculty teach minority students better strikes me as just as dangerous and misguided as suggesting that nonminority faculty teach nonminority students better. Expertise in new areas, if that is desired, can be measured directly rather than relying on correlations with gender or race. We should be very cautious, I believe, in abandoning the quest for objective, nondiscriminatory criteria for appointments just when we have begun to make moral progress in this area. Criteria are fair only when they are publicly announced and when potential applicants can aim their efforts toward meeting them.

We find illustrated here not only disputes about when discrimination occurs, but more broadly about when justice and injustice are involved in appointment practices. Francis holds that concern for non-target group members who may be most qualified (according to traditional criteria) for positions that are awarded on the basis of preference is a matter of sympathy and not justice. But if individuals have a right to equal opportunity, and if this right entails a right to have credentials judged according to fair criteria for awarding positions, then this certainly is a matter of justice. (It is a separate question whether preference in the present context is fair.)

The short editorial by Steven M. Cahn concerns this issue of fair criteria for appointment and suggests one criterion for fairness not emphasized before in the literature on this subject. The criterion is that of publicity. Proponents of strong affirmative action, involving what others perceive as preference, often seem unwilling to admit that preferential policies are being employed. Their reticence may have to do with avoiding legal problems, but, as Cahn points out, it raises independent moral problems of unfairness to applicants who are encouraged to make the effort to apply but are kept in the dark about how they are to be judged. Perhaps the most common way to deny preference is to view gender or race as itself a qualification capable of outweighing others. But it is never explained how these could be qualifications in themselves. Instead, proponents of this view rely on correlations between race and gender and other factors such as diversity in academic viewpoints or expertise in such areas as feminism or African American studies. But when these other factors are easily measurable in themselves, as they are for potential faculty with written work to submit, then such statistical correlations should be irrelevant.

I shall not debate these substantive issues further. My point here has been only to illustrate the depth of disagreement that makes compromise to which all well-intentioned parties could agree so difficult to achieve. Interested persons coming to this literature for the first time may have no choice but to review its now extensive history and make an informed choice to come down on one side or the other. Having injected this cynical note, however, perhaps these comments should conclude by pointing to the best hope and the one on which politicians and judges seem to have been relying for some time: namely, that the passage of time and continued attempts to prevent discrimination against members of target groups will make the issue of preference, at least in university appointments, moot.

About the Authors

RICHARD J. ARNESON is a professor of philosophy at the University of California at San Diego. He has held visiting appointments at California Institute of Technology and the University of California at Davis. He has written papers on philosophical ideas in literature, on the interpretation of the works of John Stuart Mill and Karl Marx, and on contemporary theories of justice, where his current research interests lie. He is an associate editor of the journal *Ethics* and a member of the board of editorial consultants for *NOMOS*, the annual yearbook of the American Society for Political and Legal Philosophy.

TOM L. BEAUCHAMP is a professor of philosophy at Georgetown University. He is the author of *Philosophical Ethics* (2nd ed., 1991), and co-author of *A History and Theory of Informed Consent* (1986), *Principles of Biomedical Ethics* (3rd ed., 1989), and *Hume and the Problem of Causation* (1981). He is general editor of the critical edition of the literary, political, and philosophical works of Hume.

LAWRENCE C. BECKER is a professor of philosophy and Kenan Professor of Humanities at the College of William and Mary. He is the editor, with Charlotte Becker, of the *Encyclopedia of Ethics* (1992) and the author of several books, including *Property Rights* (1977, 1980) and *Reciprocity* (1986, 1990).

STEVEN M. CAHN is a professor of philosophy and former provost and vice-president for academic affairs at the Graduate School of the City University of New York. Previously he taught at Vassar College, New York University, and the University of Vermont, where he chaired the Department of Philosophy. He is the author of *Fate, Logic, and Time* (1967), *A New Introduction to Philosophy* (1971), *The Eclipse of Excellence* (1973), *Education and the Democratic Ideal* (1979), *Saints and Scamps: Ethics in Academia* (1986), and *Philosophical Explorations: Freedom, God and Goodness* (1989). He has edited eight other volumes, including *The Philosophical Foundations of Education* (1970), *Scholars Who Teach: The Art of College Teaching* (1978), *Classics of Western Philosophy* (3rd ed., 1990), and *Morality, Responsibility, and the University: Studies in Academic Ethics* (1990).

RICHARD T. DE GEORGE is University Distinguished Professor at the University of Kansas. He is the author or editor of sixteen books, including *Business Ethics* (3rd ed., 1990) and *The Nature and Limits of Authority* (1985), and the author of over a hundred scholarly articles on ethical theory, applied ethics, and social and political philosophy. He is a past president of the American Philosophical Association and of the Metaphysical Society of America, and a past vice president of the International Federation of Philosophical Societies.

LESLIE PICKERING FRANCIS is a professor of law and an associate professor of philosophy at the University of Utah. She is the author of a number of papers on the philosophy of law and bioethics and is currently at work on a book titled *Legitimate Expectations*. In 1990–91, she served as the first elected faculty chair of the academic senate at the University of Utah.

ALAN H. GOLDMAN is a professor of philosophy and chairman of the Department of Philosophy at the University of Miami. He is author of *Moral Knowledge* (1988), *Empirical Knowledge* (1988), *The Moral Foundations of Professional Ethics* (1980), and *Justice and Reverse Discrimination* (1979) and has contributed to many philosophical journals.

KAREN HANSON is a professor of philosophy and an adjunct professor of both American studies and women's studies at Indiana University. She served as secretary treasurer of the central division of the American Philosophical Association. She is the author of *The Self Imagined: Philosophical Reflections on the Social Character of Psyche* (1986) and co-editor of *Romantic Revolutions—Theory and Practice* (1990), and she has published journal articles on a variety of topics in philosophy of mind, ethics, and aesthetics.

ANN HARTLE is an associate professor of philosophy at Emory University. She is the author of *The Modern Self in Rousseau's Confessions* (1983) and *Death and the Disinterested Spectator: An Inquiry into the Nature of Philosophy* (1986).

JOHN KEKES is a professor of philosophy and public policy at the State University of New York at Albany. He is the author of *A Justification of Rationality* (1976), *The Nature of Philosophy* (1980), *The Examined Life* (1987), *Moral Tradition and Individuality* (1989), and *Facing Evil* (1990). He is a frequent contributor to scholarly journals on moral, political, and epistemological topics.

JOEL J. KUPPERMAN is a professor at the University of Connecticut and has held visiting fellowships at Corpus Christi College, Oxford, Clare Hall, Cambridge, and the Rockefeller Foundation Study Center at Bellagio. He is the author of *Ethical Knowledge* (1970), *The Foundations of Morality* (1983), and *Character* (1991) and of articles in the areas of ethics, metaphysics, and Asian and comparative philosophy.

ALASDAIR MACINTYRE is the McMahon/Hank Professor of Philosophy at the University of Notre Dame. He has taught at a number of institutions in England and the United States, including Oxford University, Princeton University, Wellesley College, Boston University, and Vanderbilt University. He is a past president of the Eastern Division of the American Philosophical Association. His books include *A Short History of Ethics* (1966) and *After Virtue* (1981).

PETER J. MARKIE is a professor of philosophy and chairman of the Department of Philosophy at the University of Missouri, Columbia. He is the author of *Descartes's Gambit* (1986) and has contributed articles on ethics, intentionality, and Descartes to various philosophical journals.

JEFFRIE G. MURPHY is a professor of law and philosophy at Arizona State University. He is the author of numerous articles and several books, including *Retribution, Justice and Therapy: Essays in the Philosophy of Law* (1979), *The Philosophy of Law: An Introduction to Jurisprudence* (co-authored with Jules Coleman, Revised Edition, 1990), and *Forgiveness and Mercy* (co-authored with Jean Hampton, 1988). He writes chiefly in the areas of legal and moral philosophy (particularly on philosophical problems in the criminal law), and a second collection of his essays, *Retribution Reconsidered*, appeared in 1992.

FREDERICK A. OLAFSON has just retired as professor of philosophy at the University of California, San Diego, where he also served as chairman of the Department of Philosophy and associate dean of graduate studies and research. He was previously a professor of education and philosophy at Harvard University and has taught at Johns Hopkins University and Vassar College. Among the books he has published are *Principles and Persons* (1967), *The Dialectic of Action* (1979), and *Heidegger and the Philosophy of Mind* (1987).

ANDREW OLDENQUIST is a professor emeritus of philosophy at Ohio State University. He is the author of *Normative Behavior* (1983) and *The Non-Suicidal Society* (1986). He has edited *Readings in Moral Philosophy* (1965), *Moral Philosophy, Text and Readings* (1978), and co-edited *Society and the Individual: Readings in Political and Social Philosophy* (1989) and *Alienation, Community, and Work* (1991). He has published articles on the theory of action, ethics, social philosophy, political philosophy, philosophy of education, and other topics.

ELLEN FRANKEL PAUL is the editor of *Social Philosophy & Policy* and deputy director of the Social Philosophy and Policy Center at Bowling Green State University, where she is a professor of political science. She is the author of numerous scholarly articles and books, including *Moral Revolution and Economic Science* (1979), *Property Rights and Eminent Domain* (1987), and *Equity and Gender: The Comparable Worth Debate* (1989).

PHILIP L. QUINN is John A. O'Brien Professor of Philosophy at the University of Notre Dame and was former William Herbert Perry Faunce Professor of Philosophy at Brown University. He has also taught at the University of Michigan, the University of Illinois at Chicago, Ohio State University, and Princeton University. He is the author of *Divine Commands and Moral Requirements* (1978). He writes chiefly on the areas of philosophy of religion and philosophy of science but has also published papers in theoretical physics and religious studies. He has served the American Philosophical Association both as chair of its Committee on Career Opportunities and as secretary treasurer of its Eastern Division. He is currently the editor of *Faith and Philosophy*.

JAMES RACHELS is University Professor of Philosophy at the University of Alabama at Birmingham and the author of *The Elements of Moral Philosophy* (1986), *The End of Life: Euthanasia and Morality* (1986), and *Created from Animals: The Moral Implications of Darwinism* (1990). He has previously taught at the University of Richmond, New York University, Duke University, and the University of Miami.

LA VERNE SHELTON is an assistant professor of philosophy at the University of Wisconsin, Madison. She has also taught at Rutgers/New Brunswick, Haverford College, and the College of Charleston (South Carolina). She has published papers on the philosophy of language, metaphysics, and the philosophy of mathematics.

ROBERT L. SIMON is a professor of philosophy at Hamilton College. He is the co-author of *The Individual and the Political Order* (1985) and author of *Fair Play: Sports and Social Values* (1991). He also has written articles on a wide variety of topics in ethical theory and social philosophy and has served as associate editor of *Ethics: An International Journal of Social, Political, and Legal Philosophy* and of *The Encyclopedia of Ethics*. He currently is at work on a book about whether colleges and universities should be politically neutral.

FRED SOMMERS is Harry Austryn Wolfson Professor of Philosophy at Brandeis University. He has also taught at Columbia University, City College of New York, and the Hebrew University at Jerusalem. He is author of *The Logic of Natural Language* (1982) and co-author of *Vice and Virtue in Everyday Life* (1987). He writes primarily on logic, ontology, and the philosophy of language.

JAMES P. STERBA is a professor of philosophy and a faculty fellow of the Institute for International Peace Studies at the University of Notre Dame. In addition to over a hundred articles, his publications include *Justice: Alternative Political Perspectives* (2nd ed., 1991), *The Demands of Justice* (1980), *Morality in Practice* (3rd ed., 1990), *The Ethics of War and Nuclear Deterrence* (1984), *Contemporary Ethics* (1988), *How to Make People Just* (1988), and *Feminist Philosophies* (1991). He is president of the North American Society for Social Philosophy, president of Concerned Philosophers for Peace, and a past president of the International Association for Philosophy of Law and Social Philosophy, American section. He is also general editor of the *Political Philosophy* series for Rowman and Littlefield and of the *Basic Issues in Philosophy* series for Wadsworth Publishing Co. During 1989 under the Fulbright program, he lectured in the Soviet Union on topics of peace and justice.

LAURENCE THOMAS teaches at Syracuse University in the Departments of Philosophy, Political Science, and Judaic Studies. He is the author of *Living Morally: A Psychology of Moral Character* (Temple University Press, 1989) and the forthcoming *Vessels of Evil* (also to be published by Temple University Press). In 1992, he was awarded an honorary doctorate of laws by New England College.

ROBERT G. TURNBULL is a professor emeritus of philosophy and former department chair at The Ohio State University. He has taught at the University of Minnesota, the University of Iowa (where he was department chair for twelve years), Northwestern University, and Oberlin College. He has held several offices in the American Philosophical Association including secretary treasurer of the Board of Officers and president (Central Division) and is currently chair of the Board of Officers. He directed the Council for Philosophical Studies' 1970 Institute in Greek Philosophy and Science (Colorado College) and its 1971 encore at Bennington College. With Peter K. Machamer he edited and co-authored *Motion and Time, Space and Matter* (1976) and *Studies in Perception* (1978). For eight years he was editor of *Philosophy Research Archives*. His articles, reviews, and book chapters are largely in the history of philosophy, especially early Greek philosophy.

CELIA WOLF-DEVINE is an assistant professor of philosophy at Stonehill College. She is the author of "An Inequity in Affirmative Action" (*Journal of Applied Philosophy*, March 1988) and "Abortion and the Feminine Voice" (*Public Affairs Quarterly*, July 1989). She is also the author of a monograph, *Descartes on Seeing: Epistemology and Visual Perception*, which is forthcoming in the *Journal of the History of Philosophy* monograph series. Her current research interests are in early modern philosophy, philosophy of perception, and philosophy of sex and gender.

Index